Restructuring
High Schools for All Students

Restructuring High Schools for All Students

Taking Inclusion to the Next Level

by

Cheryl M. Jorgensen, Ph.D.
Institute on Disability
University Affiliated Program
University of New Hampshire
Durham

with invited contributors

·P·A·U·L·H·
BROOKES
PUBLISHING Co.

Baltimore • London • Toronto • Sydney

Paul H. Brookes Publishing Co.
Post Office Box 10624
Baltimore, Maryland 21285-0624

Typeset by PRO-Image Corp., Techna-Type Division, York, Pennsylvania.
Manufactured in the United States of America by
Versa Press, East Peoria, Illinois.

Photographs appearing on pages 15, 49, 71, 107, and 145 and on the front
cover were taken and provided by Gary Samson.

Most of the case studies described in this book represent actual people and
circumstances. Some names have been changed to protect identities. Selected
case studies are composites based on the authors' experiences; these case studies do not represent the lives or experiences of specific individuals, and no
implications should be inferred. Case studies based on real people or circumstances are presented herein with the individuals' written consent.

Library of Congress Cataloging-in-Publication Data

Restructuring high schools for all students: taking inclusion to the
  next level/by Cheryl M. Jorgensen with invited contributions.
     p. cm.
  Includes bibliographical references and index.
  ISBN 1-55766-313-0
  1. Inclusive education—United States.   2. Mainstreaming in
education—United States.   3. High schools—United States—
Administration.   4. Handicapped youth—Education (Secondary)—
United States.   I. Jorgensen, Cheryl M.
LC1201.R67   1998
371.9'046'0973—DC21   97-20065
                                                             CIP

British Cataloguing in Publication data are available from the British Library.

Contents

About the Author

Cheryl M. Jorgensen, Ph.D., Research Associate Professor and Project Coordinator, Institute on Disability, University Affiliated Program, University of New Hampshire, 312 Morrill Hall, 62 College Road, Durham, New Hampshire 03824. Cheryl M. Jorgensen is Research Associate Professor and Project Coordinator with the Institute on Disability, a University Affiliated Program at the University of New Hampshire, Durham. Since 1985, she has worked with New Hampshire schools to help them increase their commitment and capacity to include students with disabilities within the mainstream of general education. More recently, her research and systems change efforts have focused on the inclusion of students with disabilities within school reform efforts, especially at the high school level. She was Editor of the *Equity and Excellence* newsletter and is a coauthor of *Including Students with Severe Disabilities in Schools* (Singular Publishing Group, 1994) and author of numerous chapters on inclusive curriculum design.

About the Contributors

Myong-Ye Bang, Ph.D., Research Associate, Holt Public Schools, 1784 Aurelius Road, Holt, Michigan 48842. Dr. Bang is a research associate at Holt Public Schools in Holt, Michigan. She received her doctoral degree from Michigan State University, Lansing, in 1992, specializing in the inclusion of students with severe disabilities in general education classes. She has contributed to various model demonstration projects relating to postschool adjustment and transition of students with disabilities and research projects relating to inclusive education and the future of special education in Michigan. Her work on this book was part of the federally funded Education Plus grant awarded to Holt High School by the Office of Special Education and Rehabilitative Services, U.S. Department of Education.

Douglas Fisher, Ph.D., Project Coordinator, Interwork Institute, San Diego State University, 5850 Hardy Avenue #112, San Diego, California 92182. Dr. Fisher is a project coordinator at the Interwork Institute and a faculty member in the Department of Special Education at San Diego State University. He has provided technical assistance to a number of schools and families in southern California and New Mexico. He is a coordinator of the National Consortium on Inclusive Schooling Practices and a policy fellow at the National Association of State Boards of Education. His current interests are the impact of standards-based reform on students with disabilities, teacher-generated research, and the coordination of systems change efforts.

Robert L. Fried, Ed.D., Associate Professor of Educational Leadership, University of Hartford, 200 Bloomfield Avenue, West Hartford, Connecticut 06117. Dr. Fried works as a school reform consultant and is the author of *The Passionate Teacher* (Beacon Press, 1995). He is the parent of two children and is a former public school principal and school board member. In 1996, he provided testimony in the landmark lawsuit brought by five New Hampshire school districts challenging the funding of public education through property tax revenues.

Thomas Michael Holub, Ph.D., Professor, Department of Education, Edgewood College, 855 Woodrow Street, Madison, Wisconsin 53711. Dr. Holub is a transition facilitator for the Madison, Wisconsin, Metropolitan School District and an instructor in the teacher education program at Edgewood College. A sibling of two brothers with disabilities, Dr. Holub has dedicated his career to improving the quality of life for all. His self-determination curriculum is in use in many school districts, and the transition model he developed received exemplary status certification by the U.S. Department of Education. He provides technical assistance to a number of school districts and parent groups.

Jay Klein, M.S.W., Director, National Home of Your Own Alliance, Institute on Disability, University Affiliated Program, University of New Hampshire, 7 Leavitt Lane, Durham, New Hampshire 03825. Mr. Klein is the director of the National Home of Your Own Alliance, a technical assistance center at the Institute on Disability, which is a University Affiliated Program at the University of New Hampshire. The alliance is funded by the Administration on Developmental Disabilities to advance the opportunities of people to own and control their homes by providing technical assistance to state coalitions consisting of members of the housing and finance industry, service providers, and individuals. As an educator, community organizer, and author, he has worked on policy and practice related to the economic and social participation of people with disabilities in order to foster more and higher-quality inclusion in their communities.

Peg Lamb, Ph.D., Project Director, Education Plus, Holt High School, 1784 Aurelius Road, Holt, Michigan 48842. Dr. Lamb serves as the project director of Education Plus, a project funded by a grant awarded to Holt High School, Holt, Michigan, by the Office of Special Education and Rehabilitative Services, U.S. Department of Education. She received her doctoral degree from Michigan State University in teacher education and staff development. Her research interests include the merger of general and special education, curriculum development through teacher collaboration, and self-determination skills for all students, especially those with disabilities. At Holt High School, she has played a major role in developing linkages among parents, human services agencies, and the community at large through a transition coalition.

Stephen J. Lichtenstein, Ph.D., Research Assistant Professor, Department of Education, University of New Hampshire, 312 Morrill Hall, 62 College Road, Durham, New Hampshire 03824. While this book was in press, Dr. Lichtenstein was a program coordinator at Winnacunnet High School in Hampton, New Hampshire. From 1988 until 1996, he was a project coordinator with the University of New Hampshire's Institute on Disability, working primarily on grants related to the transition of students with disabilities from school to adult life. He conducted the first comprehensive follow-along study of New Hampshire students graduating from special education programs during the late 1980s. His research interests focus on the role of mentorships in reducing dropout rates and on factors related to students with disabilities leaving school with a general education diploma.

Joanne M. Malloy, M.S.W., Project Director, Institute on Emotional Disabilities, University Affiliated Program, Keene State College, 229 Main Street, Keene, New Hampshire 03435-2903. Ms. Malloy is the project director of the Comprehensive Career and Employment Project for Youth with Severe Emotional Disturbance or Mental Illness, funded by the Rehabilitative Services Administration of the U.S. Department of Education. She has a broad range of career experience in the areas of natural supports, benefits planning, public policy, and supported employment and is the author of *Benefits for Adults with Disabilities* (N.H. Department of Health and Human Services, 1994), *Benefits for Children and Youth with Disabilities* (N.H. Department of Health and Human Services, 1995), and *Career Planning Manual* (University of New Hampshire, 1996).

Jill Martin, B.A., Graduate Student, Department of Social Work, School of Health and Human Services, University of New Hampshire, Hewitt Hall, Durham, New Hampshire 03824. After doing a yearlong internship at Souhegan High School in 1994, Ms. Martin worked for 2 years as a program educator for the University of New Hampshire Institute on Disability's Partnerships for Educational Innovations project. She traveled all around the state of New Hampshire, talking with students about friendships for students with disabilities. She is a coeditor, with Carol Tashie, of the videotape *Voices of Friendships* (Institute on Disability, 1996).

Joseph J. Onosko, Ph.D., Associate Professor, Department of Education, University of New Hampshire, Morrill Hall, Durham, New Hampshire 03824. Dr. Onosko supervises social studies and English interns and teaches social studies methods, educational psychology, and an introduction to education course for the 5-year master's degree program in the Department of Education at the University of New Hampshire. He also teaches a curriculum theory course for the department's doctoral program and advises doctoral candidates. While a doctoral student at the University of Wisconsin, he worked as a researcher for the National Center on Effective Secondary Schools. He serves as Assistant Chair for the National Board for Professional Teaching Standards' Adolescence and Young Adult Social Studies/ History Committee.

Caren Sax, M.S.Ed., Project Coordinator/Adjunct Faculty, Interwork Institute, San Diego State University, 5850 Hardy Avenue #112, San Diego, California 92182. Ms. Sax is a project coordinator at the Interwork Institute, a faculty member, and a doctoral candidate in educational leadership at San Diego State University. After teaching in public schools, she now coordinates projects in the areas of assistive technology and continuing education for professionals in education and rehabilitation. She is actively involved in inclusive education efforts in southern California and provides training and technical assistance to schools, families, and organizations that provide support to individuals with disabilities.

Mary C. Schuh, M.Ed., Project Director, Institute on Disability, University Affiliated Program, University of New Hampshire, 10 Ferry Street, Unit 14, Concord, New Hampshire 03301-5019. Ms. Schuh has coordinated projects in the areas of systems change, in-service training, family leadership, and activities within New Hampshire's University Affiliated Program related to improvement of knowledge, policy, and practice regarding the economic and social participation of people with disabilities in New Hampshire. She is the editor of the institute's newest publication on leadership, *From Vision to Reality: A Manual to Replicate the New Hampshire Leadership Series* (Institute on Disability, 1996).

Susan Shapiro-Barnard, M.Ed., Research Associate, Institute on Disability, University Affiliated Program, University of New Hampshire, 10 Ferry Street, Unit 14, Concord, New Hampshire 03301-5019. Ms. Shapiro-Barnard is a coauthor of the Institute on Disability's publications *Petroglyphs: The Writing on the Wall* (Institute on Disability, 1996) and *From Special to Regular, From Ordinary to Extraordinary* (Institute on Disability, 1993). She is an educational consultant focusing on assisting schools to fully include students with disabilities in their neighborhood schools. As a teacher with both general and special education training and certification, she has firsthand experience in creating a classroom environment in which all students belong and learn.

Kathryn L. Skoglund, M.Ed., Director of Special Instructional Services, Amherst and Souhegan School Districts, c/o Souhegan High School, Post Office Box 1152, Boston Post Road, Amherst, New Hampshire 03031. Ms. Skoglund received her undergraduate degree from Boston University in speech, hearing, and language pathology and her master's degree in school administration from Plymouth State College, Plymouth, New Hampshire. As a special education administrator for more than 20 years, she has been an innovator in service delivery. During her 1995–1996 sabbatical year, she served as Interim Director of the Center for Professional Educational Partnerships at Plymouth State College and helped design their Certificate of Advanced Graduate Study program, in which she is a part-time student. She also serves as president of the New Hampshire Association of Special Education Administrators.

Carol Tashie, M.Ed., Project Coordinator, Institute on Disability, University Affiliated Program, University of New Hampshire, 10 Ferry Street, Unit 14, Concord, New Hampshire 03301-5019. Ms. Tashie is the coordinator of both New Hampshire's Statewide Systems Change Project and the Postsecondary Education Consortium of New Hampshire, administered by the Institute on Disability. She has conducted a 4-year systems change project in transition called Turning Points and is a coauthor of *From Special to Regular, From Ordinary to Extraordinary* (Institute on Disability, 1993), *Petroglyphs: The Writing on the Wall* (Institute on Disability, 1996), and *Planning Your Future: A Manual for Career and Life Planning* (Institute on Disability, 1996). Prior to coming to the Institute on Disability in 1989, Ms. Tashie was one of the first inclusion facilitators in the state of New Hampshire responsible for returning all of her districts' students to their neighborhood schools.

Foreword

Historically, students who could not meet the goals of public education in the United States simply dropped out of school and assumed different stations in an economy and society able to absorb a wide range of worker competence. However, throughout the 20th century, the need to complete school (more precisely, to earn a high school diploma) became an increasingly important economic imperative that necessitated widening the band of accomplishment acceptable for high school graduation (Orfield, 1988). Widening the band, in turn, led to diversifying the high school curriculum to the point where students have become tracked according to predictions of future economic success, often based on race, class, or perceived disability (Oakes, 1985; Wheelock, 1992).

In the early 1980s, policy makers, business leaders, and educators all sounded an alarm at what this trend had created—higher levels of high school graduation but lower overall levels of student achievement as measured against earlier U.S. performance and international comparison (National Commission on Excellence in Education, 1983). Educators began to chronicle the malaise in U.S. high schools and proposed new approaches to organizing their structure, culture, and curricula (Goodlad, 1984; Hirsch, 1987; Sizer, 1985). From these efforts emerged two important facets of present-day educational reform: standards-based reform and school restructuring.

STANDARDS-BASED REFORM

Standards-based reform, adopted by a majority of states and many local districts, posits that educational systems, like their business counterparts, need to set clear, high standards that provide succinct targets for students and teachers alike, as well as providing a vehicle for communicating to the public the goals of the system (Massell, Kirst, & Hoppe, 1997; Smith & O'Day, 1991). Tenets of standards-based reform include setting high, rigorous standards for student achievement while providing greater flexibility at the local school and classroom levels for how educators help students achieve those standards. With the increased "front line" flexibility, however, policy makers also seek greater accountability on the part of schools and districts for student performance. As a result, what students know and are able to do by the time they graduate from high school has taken on a new importance throughout the 1990s.

From an instructional standpoint, standards-based reform represents a dramatic departure from traditional practices in education (Dewey notwithstanding!). In the past, public education was seen as time driven, with student expectations—and achievement—varying. That is, at the end of 12 years of schooling, students with a wide range of skills and knowledge all graduate with the same diploma. In standards-based reform, the theory posits, the expectations (i.e., standards) remain fixed and the amount of time and support needed to ensure that every student reaches those standards are variable.

SCHOOL RESTRUCTURING

Coupled with standards-based reform are new restructuring paradigms created by educators such as Goodlad (1984), Hirsch (1987), and Sizer (1985) that propose a reform of the high school culture, its structure and organization, and its curriculum. These reforms attempt to

- Create a school culture of unhurried expectation in which each individual student's talents and needs are accommodated and valued
- Organize the school day and academic year so that students study and master fewer topics in greater depth (Canady & Rettig, 1995; Newman, 1988; Tyson-Bernstein, 1988; Wiggins, 1987)
- Change the role of the teacher from content deliverer to facilitator or coach of student learning (Sizer, 1985)
- Eliminate the stratification of students into perceived-ability tracks (Oakes, 1985; Wheelock, 1992)
- Involve teachers and students in school governance (Glasser, 1984, 1990)
- Introduce new instructional techniques and curricular approaches so that diverse learning styles are accommodated and students have more control over their learning (Gardner, 1993; Glasser, 1984, 1990; Slavin, 1990)

INCLUSIVE EDUCATION

As is eloquently pointed out in this book, many of the principles that underlie school reform and restructuring are also the principles that underlie inclusive education. Like standards-based reform, inclusion is based on the premise that all students present themselves with varying characteristics and that, rather than relegating students with different characteristics into different curricular tracks, all students should be provided the supports and services necessary for them to learn together within a heterogeneous classroom (Lipsky & Gartner, 1997).

Inclusive schools seek to

- Create a school culture in which differences are celebrated, not merely tolerated or accommodated, and in which every student is seen as talented and as having a contribution to make
- Foster interactive teacher–student partnerships to assist students in constructing new knowledge and skills (Vygotsky, 1978)
- Provide students with enough time to have well-grounded, meaningful learning opportunities
- Design curriculum and teaching so that all students study within a common thematic unit while pursuing individualized learning objectives and performance criteria

Given the similarities between the goals and practices of educational reform and those of inclusion, it is ironic that students with disabilities are included less once they reach secondary school (U.S. Department of Education, 1995). Where does the breakdown occur? Why has educational reform pressed forward but left students with disabilities behind?

FACTORS RELATED TO SEPARATE HIGH SCHOOL PROGRAMS FOR STUDENTS WITH DISABILITIES

There are four interrelated factors that explain the exclusion of students with disabilities from the progress of educational reform. First, the culture of most high schools is impersonal, hurried, hierarchical, and competitive. Students who are "the best" at something when judged competitively against the performance of their classmates are the most valued. Teachers generally are responsible for teaching upwards of 150 students, and guidance counselors have caseloads in the hundreds. Curricular and instructional decisions are often prescribed by district or state guidelines, and teacher collaboration occurs in the hallways and "on the fly" between class periods.

Second, most people envision that students with disabilities (particularly those with significant disabilities) will have an adult life that is very different from those of students without disabilities. Therefore, parents and educators alike believe that these two groups of students need different knowledge and skills to prepare them for the future. From this belief emerges a continuum of courses and educational tracks designed to prepare some students for work and some for college. In a traditional high school, high-achieving students with mild disabilities have access to the college preparatory curriculum; but those who struggle with learning (and who many predict will be relegated to low-paying, low-status jobs) are placed in vocational courses or lower-level academic tracks. Students who have been labeled as having cognitive disabilities are members of "functional skill" classes that focus on life skills, independent living, and, in some cases, menial job skills.

The third factor that is related to the greater segregation of students with disabilities in high school is the mistaken belief that the most important learning goal for students is subject-specific knowledge. This belief influences teaching practices, course content, and student placement. Teachers lecture, believing that this is the best way for students to learn large amounts of content. The ability to apply knowledge to real-life problems and the inculcation of habits of learning and working characterize vocational programs and lower-level academic classes (e.g., consumer math), in which students with disabilities are overrepresented (U.S. Department of Labor, 1991).

Finally, the structure of the school day (and other organizational factors) impedes the inclusion of students with disabilities in the mainstream of general education. When the school day is organized into 50-minute periods, teachers do not have time to use instructional methods that are effective for diverse learners. Once again, the lecture predominates and the focus is on facts and memorization. Even when students with disabilities elect a college preparatory class, support from special education teachers is difficult to arrange because they are busy teaching their own classes and have no time to collaborate with general education teachers to plan curriculum or to share teaching in the classroom. In summary, the barriers to high school inclusion—a competitive school culture in which only "the best and the brightest" are valued, a belief in a different future for students with disabilities, a single-minded focus on content, and the way schools are organized—stand in the way of higher achievement for all students.

MERGING REFORM AND INCLUSION

Through numerous stories of real students, teachers, and schools, this book proposes how high schools can be restructured *and* be inclusive, and it explains why they should be: to benefit students with and without disabilities. Jorgensen and her colleagues address the thorny question, "What does it mean to meet high educational standards?" rather than suggest that the standards may not be for each and every student (see Chapter 2). The importance of school culture as a factor in student learning and a sense of belonging is discussed in Chapters 3 and 7. In Chapter 4, organizational barriers to inclusion and achievement of high standards are addressed by suggesting innovative scheduling models, describing new roles for general and special education teachers, and documenting the benefits of untracking. Curriculum design—the link between high standards and student performance—takes on a new look in Chapters 5 and 6. The indifference to learning that characterizes far too many students is related in part to their lack of control over their education. In Chapter 8, the authors take the traditional special education construct of self-determination and show how it can be used to engage all students in school. The final two chapters address community-based learning and graduation planning and bring the book full circle to a unified view of the goals of schooling for all students—the acquisition of skills, knowledge, and dispositions necessary to be productive workers and responsible citizens.

This book makes the case for including students in the restructured high school. It provides specific examples to demonstrate how high schools can change to restructure and be inclusive and how schools can accommodate the needs of an ever-diversifying student population, not just students with individualized education programs. Yet the book also asks the reader to carefully consider what it means to meet standards. In the 1990s, policy makers, educators, and families have focused on developing new content and performance standards on which to base curricular reform and measure student progress toward meeting those standards.

These same stakeholders are beginning to consider the critical implementation questions that will drive curricular reform, such as "When students, schools and districts are held accountable for standards, does that mean each and every student must meet each and every standard? Or does it mean that students must prove competency in a percentage of the standards? Or a degree of competency in each standard?" If we look at state assessment and accountability policy in states such as Kentucky, Maryland, and Missouri, meeting the standards means continually striving for more students to obtain a greater degree of competency in a greater number of standards, but by no means all students, all standards, or complete competency. In this context, absolutely every student, regardless of label, color, or status, should be included—continually included—in reform. By bringing the reader to these questions and using specific classroom and school examples, this book is a must read for those interested in including all high school students in reform efforts, such as policy makers, educators, and families who are beginning to contemplate how to implement standards-based reform.

Virginia Roach, Ed.D.
National Association of State Boards of Education
Alexandria, Virginia

REFERENCES

Canady, R., & Rettig, M. (1995). The power of innovative scheduling. *Educational Leadership, 53*(3), 4–10.

Gardner, H. (1993). Educating for understanding. *American School Board Journal, 180*(7), 20–24.

Glasser, W. (1984). *Control theory.* New York: HarperCollins.

Glasser, W. (1990). *The quality school.* New York: HarperCollins.

Goodlad, J.I. (1984). *A place called school: Prospects for the future.* New York: McGraw-Hill.

Hirsch, E.D. (1987). *Cultural literacy: What every American needs to know.* Boston: Houghton Mifflin.

Lipsky, D.K., & Gartner, A. (1997). *Inclusion and school reform: Transforming America's classrooms.* Baltimore: Paul H. Brookes Publishing Co.

Massell, D., Kirst, M., & Hoppe, M. (1997, March). *Persistence and change: Standards-based systemic reform in nine states* (CPRE Policy Brief). Philadelphia: University of Pennsylvania.

National Commission on Excellence in Education. (1983). *A nation at risk: The imperative for educational reform.* Washington, DC: U.S. Department of Education.

Newman, F.M. (1988, January). Can depth replace coverage in the high school curriculum? *Phi Delta Kappan, 69,* 345–348.

Oakes, J. (1985). *Keeping track: How schools structure inequality.* New Haven, CT: Yale University Press.

Orfield, G. (1988). Race, income, and educational inequality. In *School success for students at risk* (pp. 45–71). Washington, DC: Council of Chief State School Officers.

Sizer, T.R. (1985). *Horace's compromise: The dilemma of the American high school.* Boston: Houghton Mifflin.

Slavin, R. (1990). *Cooperative learning: Theory, research and practice.* Englewood Cliffs, NJ: Prentice Hall.

Smith, M., & O'Day, J. (1991). Systemic school reform. In S.H. Fuhrman & B. Malen (Eds.), *The politics of curriculum and testing* (pp. 223–267). New York: Falmer Press.

Tyson-Bernstein, H. (1988, April). A conspiracy of good intentions: America's textbook fiasco. *Basic Education, 32,* 2–14.

U.S. Department of Education. (1995). *Seventeenth annual report to Congress on the implementation of the Individuals with Disabilities Education Act.* Washington, DC: Author.

U.S. Department of Labor. (1991). *What work requires of schools: A SCANS report for America 2000.* Washington, DC: U.S. Government Printing Office.

Vygotsky, L. (1978). *Mind in society: The development of higher psychological processes.* Cambridge, MA: Harvard University Press.

Wheelock, A. (1992). *Crossing the tracks: How "untracking" can save America's schools.* New York: New Press.

Wiggins, G. (1987, Winter). Creating a thought-provoking curriculum. *American Educator, 11,* 10–17.

Preface

In 1990, I heard that a new high school, Souhegan High School, was being built to serve the towns of Amherst and Mont Vernon, New Hampshire. The word was that the school was going to be a laboratory for the latest educational philosophies and practices. Because I had provided technical assistance to folks from those towns regarding the inclusion of students with significant disabilities who attend their elementary schools, I thought that this district might be willing to make the new school fully inclusive right from the start. It seemed like a natural extension of their elementary and middle school philosophies, and the timing was right for a somewhat radical new model.

After a series of meetings with various committees regarding issues of curriculum and recommended practices for students with disabilities, members of the planning team and I wrote a grant proposal to support a 4-year research project to investigate how students with disabilities might be included in systemic efforts to restructure high schools. The grant was funded, and it signaled the beginning of a 4-year journey of discovery for all of us.

This book represents some of the lessons that I learned through my involvement with Souhegan High School, broadened with similar experiences of my colleagues from other high schools around the United States. You will notice the heavy reliance on stories throughout the book—stories about students, teachers, and schools. I believe that unless people see how educational policies and practices affect the lives of students and teachers, they will not be moved to making the fundamental changes that both inclusion and school reform require. When people's hearts change, their heads usually follow. As you read about the students and schools described, think about the young people who you know and reflect on how what you are reading might affect their lives. Throughout the book, suggestions for "next steps" for both teachers and administrators provide guidance for how they might be catalysts for change. At the end of most chapters, implementation suggestions are given for teachers and administrators who are moved to action but need help in figuring out where to start.

In Chapter 1, Susan Shapiro-Barnard of the Institute on Disability at the University of New Hampshire (UNH) explains the benefits of inclusion for high school students and for whole school communities in a style that is provocative and a welcome departure from the usual dry literature review. Chapter 2, by Robert L. Fried, of the educational leadership faculty at the University of Hartford, and me, describes the tension that exists between the ideas and principles underlying the inclusive education movement and the school reform movement.

In Chapters 3 and 4, Interwork Institute Project Coordinators Douglas Fisher and Caren Sax of San Diego State University, Souhegan administrator Kathryn L. Skoglund, and I share our observations about the philosophical foundations and nuts-and-bolts practices that are common to schools doing a respectable job of addressing both inclusion and school reform.

Joseph J. Onosko, a UNH Department of Education faculty member, and I describe in Chapter 5 a process of designing curriculum units that naturally addresses student diversity. Examples of creative, inclusive curriculum are presented in Chapter 6.

Life is not worth living without friends, and Institute on Disability staff Jill Martin, Jay Klein, and I describe in Chapter 7 how to make the promise of friendship a reality for students with disabilities.

In Chapter 8, Thomas Michael Holub of the Madison, Wisconsin, School District, and Peg Lamb and Myong-Ye Bang of Holt High School, Holt, Michigan, share examples from schools across the United States that are discovering that self-determination principles—traditionally taught just to students with disabilities—can benefit all students.

A new view of community-based learning that includes all students is presented in Chapter 9, authored by Institute on Disability Coordinators Mary C. Schuh and Carol Tashie, as well as Peg Lamb, Myong-Ye Bang, and me.

In Chapter 10, Carol Tashie, Institute on Disability Project Coordinators Carol Tashie and Joanne M. Malloy, and high school administrator Stephen J. Lichtenstein describe how the best strategies for special education transition planning and general education graduation planning can be merged into a unified process for all high school students.

Acknowledgments

I could never adequately thank all of the people who have contributed to my ability to write and organize this book, but I will try nevertheless. First, I want to thank Bill Stainback, who made the fateful call in August 1994 to his Brookes editor suggesting that a book on high school restructuring and inclusion ought to be published and that I might be its author. Since 1987, my boss Jan Nisbet has tolerated my quirks and stubbornness so that I could find the balance I needed to balance my professional and personal lives. She continues to be a visionary and supportive leader. Helen Thornton, the project officer at the Office of Special Education and Rehabilitative Services (OSERS), U.S. Department of Education, supervising the grant that sponsored much of the work on which this book is based, gave me great latitude in interpreting the requirements of my project and gave me much thoughtful feedback on my ideas. Although I am sure the U.S. Department of Education does not agree with everything I have written herein, they recognize the importance of academic freedom and encourage innovation. Virginia Roach of the National Association of State Boards of Education honored me by writing the Foreword, in which she shares her unique national perspective on school reform and students with disabilities.

The contributors to this book represent the folks who are in schools every day trying to make them become places where all students are welcome and are supported to learn as much as they can. They were understanding about my need to use just the right word or phrase to convey a new way of thinking about the inclusion of students with disabilities in school restructuring efforts.

One of the most rewarding benefits of doing this book has been the professional collaboration that has developed between Douglas Fisher of the Interwork Institute at San Diego State University and me. It was almost accidental that we discovered how similar our experiences were at Souhegan and Santana High Schools. The contributions to the book made by Douglas Fisher, his colleague Caren Sax, and all the students and teachers at Santana High School helped ensure that this book would be relevant to people from all different kinds of schools and communities.

My colleagues at the Institute on Disability challenge me every day to expand my vision of what is possible for people with disabilities. Every idea I have is probably just an extension of something that

xxiv   Acknowledgments

somebody else thought of first. Karen Gifford, my secretary, is good
at everything that I am not and kept me organized and sane so
that I could concentrate on this work. Scott Beeler, my first editor at
Brookes, was so patient with my ever-changing chapter descriptions
and deadlines. He remained calm when I told him that the book was
a work in progress and that I would not really know what it would
look like until it was finished! He guided the book through all of the
steps of the publishing process with great skill and gentle encouragement. Paul Klemt, production editor, deserves a gold star for his me-
ticulous attention to the details that actually put the book in print.

From 1992 through 1996, I had the privilege of working at Souhegan High School in Amherst, New Hampshire, on an OSERS-
funded research project. Although I was terrified at the prospect of
working with teenagers and felt totally incompetent among such a
prestigious group of teachers and school reform advocates, they welcomed me into their break-the-mold classrooms as their roving conscience and critical friend in coping with the issues of heterogeneity
and inclusive education. Kim Carter, Sally Groves, Rick Lalley, Bob
Mackin, Marty Rounds, Allison Rowe, Judy Service, and Kathryn L.
Skoglund smoothed the way for me and helped me learn more in
those 4 years than I did in the 20 previous years in the field of education. Dan Bisaccio, Crista Burrel, Debbie Currie, Bill Dod, Kris Fach,
Cathy Fisher, Edorah Frazer, Linda Kelly, Jen Mueller, Bobby O'Sullivan, Eric Pohl, Colleen Roy, Paul Schlotman, Peggy Silva, and Regina
Sullivan (just to mention a few!) were particularly giving of their
knowledge, support, and hearts relative to all the students in their
classrooms. Jill Martin, who served as an intern with me at Souhegan
during the 1993–1994 school year, really made a difference in the lives
of the students there, and her presence was felt by them for many
years afterward.

Finally, thank you to the students! Since 1985, I have met hundreds of students all over the state of New Hampshire through my
work with their schools. The story of each one remains with me today
and is represented faithfully, I hope, throughout this book. In particular, the Souhegan class of 1996, with whom I spent their entire high
school career over the 4 years of the project, possess the greatest wisdom of all. Amro, Brad, Brandon, Dave, Joe, Kelly, Kevin, Michelle,
Mike R., Mike W., P.J., Rob, Ryan, and all the others convinced me
that young people know that inclusion is about *all* of us, not just
students with disabilities. Their experiences in a very unique school
and the values that they have about diversity are our hope for the
future—the future of not only education but our communities and
our world.

To my children—Katherine, Anne, and Abby
And to Byll with love

Restructuring
High Schools for All Students

1

Preparing the
Ground for What Is to Come

A Rationale for Inclusive High Schools

Susan Shapiro-Barnard

"Those of us committed to education are committed not only to effecting continuities but to preparing the ground for what is to come." (Greene, 1988, p. 3)

Molly

Molly is an eighth-grade student who takes all general education classes at the middle school in her town. Because she happens to have a disability, she is provided with a variety of supports. Both Molly and her parents expect that she will attend the local high school next year and continue to be supported in general education classes. However, they are worried that sharing these expectations at a school meeting will yield only a long silence. In the past, educators have supported Molly's participation in general education, but more recently they have shared concerns about the increased emphasis on content in high school classes. They do not believe that Molly will "get anything out of them." Plans are already under way for Molly to spend a portion of her day in the high school's special education room, where the curriculum is "more practical."

In almost all instances, conversations about whether high school students with disabilities should be educated in general education classes begin with the premise that they should not. Often that premise holds until people can gather together enough evidence to the contrary. So, Molly and her parents must come to the next meeting prepared to prove that she can learn in general education classes. It is hard to imagine that a student without disabilities would need to do the same.

Imagine for a moment that our judicial system presumed people guilty until proved innocent. What would happen if people were treated as criminals until ample proof of innocence was provided? There would be outrage, accusations of rights denied, lawsuits, and pleas for a more just system. Fortunately, our judicial system does not operate in this manner. It presumes people innocent until proved guilty because that is the least dangerous assumption.

Leaving the courtroom and stepping back into the classroom, imagine that our educational system presumed students unable to learn in general education classes until it was proved otherwise. What would happen if students were excluded from general education until there was ample evidence to support their inclusion? Unfortunately,

This chapter was supported in part by Grants H158A1003 and H086J50014 from the U.S. Department of Education, Office of Special Education and Rehabilitative Services and the New Hampshire Department of Education, Partnerships for Educational Innovations. The opinions of the author are not necessarily those of the U.S. Department of Education or the New Hampshire Department of Education.

there is no need for imagination here. This is not a hypothetical situation.

Every day, students with disabilities are excluded from the mainstream of high schools. Only 30% of students ages 12–17 attend general education classes as compared with 50% of students ages 6–11 years of age (U.S. Department of Education, 1995). The unwritten rule seems to suggest exclusion unless it is proved that inclusion is appropriate. Ironically, there is also a written rule that is more like the premise of innocent until proved guilty: the law. The Individuals with Disabilities Education Act (IDEA) of 1990 (PL 101-476) states that students with disabilities must be educated in general education classrooms with appropriate supports and services unless it can be proved that they are unable to learn in that environment with those supports and services.

What will happen when Molly and her parents attend the next meeting and present the ways in which she benefits from being educated in general education classes, provide examples of how creative supports are successfully being utilized at the middle school, and cite court decisions that strongly support inclusive education? Probably, Molly will go to high school and be supported to take general education classes, but something else will happen, too. The field of vision will be narrowed as the question of inclusive education—a question that embraces both the efficacy and the humanity of our schools—gets answered with a list of benefits for an individual student with disabilities. The issue of inclusive education is larger than that. It does make sense for students with disabilities; but then so too does it make sense for students without disabilities, entire school communities, and the future of public education.

OVERVIEW

This chapter provides a rationale for inclusive high schools. But inherent in this exercise—defending the reasons high schools should be inclusive—are two dangerous assumptions. The first is that it is necessary to prove that students with disabilities can and should be educated in general education classes. The second is that the merits of inclusive education can be judged solely by the benefits that accrue to students with disabilities. We have been here before and we have been here for too long—debating who can learn and who has the right to be in school and defending inclusion for only students with disabilities.

Certainly, there is work to be done to adequately ensure that students with disabilities have equal access to educational opportunities. However, the nature of that work has changed dramatically. It is no longer necessary to ask whether high school students with disabilities can learn in general education classes. Countless high school graduates throughout the United States have already answered this question. Instead, the task at hand is to better understand what students learn so that we can then determine how best to support them.

Although this chapter documents what students with disabilities learn in general education classes, it also advances a bolder, more encompassing thesis: that the only place where students with disabilities can learn what they need to learn to lead a productive adult life is the general education classroom and that inclusion benefits the entire school community. From this new point of view, we can begin to understand that school reform is incomplete unless it includes inclusive practices and values.[1]

WHAT ALL STUDENTS LEARN IN HIGH SCHOOL

Think about your own high school experience for a moment. What are the most important skills you learned? What lessons helped you become a successful adult? Perhaps you learned to manage time, organize materials, or work with other people. Perhaps you learned to read, to communicate ideas, or to locate resources for information. Or perhaps you learned to keep on going when the going got tough, to read people "between the lines," or to defend your own beliefs. Most likely, your ability to convert moles to grams and your skills with a food processor are not the basis for your success.

Many adults say that the most frequently used and highly prized skills gained during their high school years are habits of learning and working such as inquisitiveness, diligence, collaboration, and critical thinking; content area knowledge, because learning about the world helps many people to find their place in it; and basic academic skills such as reading, writing, and mathematics (Sizer, 1992). Each of the aforementioned skill areas is addressed in the following discussion about what high school students with and without disabilities learn in general education classes.

STUDENTS ACQUIRE HABITS
OF LEARNING AND WORKING

The ability to recite poetry from memory, recognize famous artwork, and recall the date of the French and Indian War used to be trade-

---

[1]*Inclusion* is defined as all students being educated where they would be educated if they did not have a disability (i.e., in age-appropriate general education classes in their neighborhood school), with necessary supports provided to students, educators, and families so that all can be successful.

marks of a well-educated person. But the world has changed, and new competencies have become important. The SCANS report, *What Work Requires of Schools* (U.S. Department of Labor, 1991), identified eight categories of attributes and skills related to success:

1. Identify, organize, plan, and allocate resources
2. Work with others
3. Acquire and use information
4. Understand complex interrelationships
5. Work with a variety of technologies
6. Perform basic skills (e.g., read, write, perform arithmetic and mathematical operations, listen, and speak)
7. Perform thinking skills (e.g., think creatively, make decisions, solve problems, visualize, know how to learn, and reason)
8. Display personal qualities (e.g., responsibility, self-esteem, sociability, self-management, integrity, and honesty) (pp. xvii–xviii)

In response to these newly identified competencies, many schools are realigning their graduation outcomes with the skills necessary for success in the world. For example, one of the guiding principles of the Coalition of Essential Schools, a collection of high schools committed to meaningful school reform, is depth over breadth (Sizer, 1992). A school committed to this principle would not require its students to learn the facts about all past wars. Instead, a teacher might pose a series of questions for consideration: How do wars start? How do they end? When is war just? What is worth dying for? Students would then be required to synthesize information about past armed conflicts to develop a deeper understanding of war. This approach, reflecting new educational priorities, emphasizes thinking skills, not memorization (C. Fisher, personal communication, January 1997).

Talk like this makes lots of people nervous, especially people who contend that a well-educated person is one who has obtained a common body of knowledge that has been compiled and agreed on by other well-educated people. There is no need to worry, however. No student would want to come to school if the agenda for 12 years consisted of only the skills identified in the SCANS report (U.S. Department of Labor, 1991). It would be dreadfully boring to work with others to think, organize, and understand the relationships between nothing. Skills will always be best taught through content.

Depending on whether the context is special education or general education, the word *skills* can refer to two very different sets of abilities. Students with disabilities have been learning how to water plants, use the bathroom, memorize definitions, and write a check for what feels like forever in special education classrooms. The perception accompanying this learning is that the most important skills for students with disabilities to gain are the skills that students without disabilities already possess. These intentions are good, but the outcomes are not. Take, for example, the students who, in the name of gaining functional skills, are never taught to read (Koppenhaver, Coleman, Kalman, & Yoder, 1991). (Is there a more functional skill than literacy?) This instructional emphasis fuels the creation of separate curricula and classrooms and ultimately a readiness checklist for a student's inclusion into general education. It should come as no surprise that some students are never included.

Of course, learning to balance a checkbook and use a fork and knife are important. But these skills are not more important than learning how to work with people, what to do to stay motivated, or when to ask a question. That is where our professional thinking gets muddled as educators feel compelled to choose between one set of skills and the other when planning a student's education. This should not be the case. Having a disability should not mean needing to choose between thinking about manners and learning to think, working on saying hello and working with classmates, or learning to use a knife and learning to use a word processor. When mastering a traditional list of functional skills is deemed more important than developing effective habits for learning and working, students with disabilities are set up to fail. Research and testimony say that a, b, and c are key ingredients for success; but students with disabilities are being taught x, y, and z.

STUDENTS LEARN CONTENT AREA KNOWLEDGE

Certainly there is nothing wrong—and lots right—with gaining knowledge for its own sake. Information about science, literature, history, business, health, and the fine arts is important. It is exciting, invigorating, and expansive—the very stuff of learning. Knowledge helps students identify areas of interest that may lead to future hobbies or provide career direction. It is what people think about, talk about, and write about. Therefore, it is important that schools do not abandon teaching knowledge for its own sake as they redefine learning for the 21st century.

However, the notion of getting through the curriculum has become anachronistic as the amount of information in the world has begun to grow faster than people can learn and absorb it. Perhaps there was a time when students could be taught all that was known about science, but that era is long past (Wiggins, 1989). Thus, educators recognize that teaching students how to gain knowledge by supporting their efforts to develop effective personal habits for lifelong learning is essential. Knowledge is important for its own sake, absolutely. It would be a sad day if people stopped studying insects, other cultures, and economic principles. But knowledge also holds the attention of students so that habits of learning and working can be acquired. It serves as both a vehicle for learning and a destination.

Recognizing the dual purpose of learning content area knowledge—for its own sake and for the sake of learning how to learn—is important especially as it pertains to students with disabilities. Students with disabilities are often denied access to general education classes on the basis that they will be unable to learn the content being taught. Think back to Molly's team for a moment. Many of the educators were concerned that the general education curriculum would not be meaningful for her, so a special education class was recommended.

Ironically, the reasons for suggesting a special education class—Molly's alleged need for more practical learning—strongly justify Molly's taking general education classes. Like all students, Molly needs to learn to work independently and with her peers, to manage time and materials, to contribute thoughts and hear the thoughts of others, and to solve problems and rethink solutions—in short, to function in the real world. So, if it is true that the process of learning provides all students with lifelong skills for working and learning, then the argument for excluding Molly on the basis that she needs a more practical curricular emphasis proves obsolete. The content area knowledge taught in heterogeneously grouped general education classrooms supports all students to acquire important habits of working and learning. The very stuff that Molly needs.

Is this the only reason Molly should be included in general education classes? Is it only the acquisition of skills that warrants the learning of knowledge for students with disabilities? Goodlad and Oakes (1988) challenged educators: "We must rid ourselves of the dangerous notion that individual differences, such as in interests and rate of learning, call for substantially differentiated curriculums" (p. 19). Like others in the field who criticize the practices of ability grouping and tracking (e.g., Wheelock, 1992), Goodlad and Oakes argued that our schools and the students within them are too often organized based on the misconceptions that educators hold about learning and who can do it. On making knowledge accessible for all students, Goodlad and Oakes stated,

> It is helpful for both the public and the professionals to understand that the general laws of the land imply equal access not only to schools but to the education schools are supposed to provide. Further, state documents on schooling almost always include the concept of equity in some form and

admonish school boards and educators . . . to eschew practices that discriminate against students because of their race, ethnicity, or religion. (1988, p. 20)

Disability must be added this list. The inextricable linking of a student's disability with the student's access to knowledge is unsound educational practice. All students have the right to attain knowledge. Even those who do not yet have a reliable mode of communication. Even those whose behavior greatly challenges us on a daily basis. Even those who have been labeled as having mental retardation. Not because research has proved that all students can learn all things, but because research has not proved that all students cannot. To assume that someone cannot learn something is to assume that there is no other way to teach it. It suggests a false precision for evaluating the knowledge and skills that a student has gained. It assumes that there is an accurate tool for measuring human growth, which of course there is not. An English teacher once commented,

> When I first learned that Lars would be in my sports literature class, I was nervous. I didn't know what to expect from him, nor did I know how to get this information. He had a little board that he used to communicate. At first I felt he would be better off in a resource room learning how to use that board than he would be in my class reading and writing about football. He never seemed to be listening or interested in our class discussions. But one day Lars starting pointing to letters on the board. Apparently, he is a big fan of the Patriots.

This story exemplifies a decision-making model called "the criterion of the least dangerous assumption" (Donnellan, 1984, p. 141). The theory underlying this model is that, in the absence of reliable and valid data about students' capabilities, the least dangerous assumption should be made. In other words, the assumption that should be made is the one that will do the least amount of harm, should it later be realized that the assumption was wrong.

A case in point related to the gaining of knowledge: It is sometimes difficult to determine whether a student with disabilities is actually learning content area knowledge. Therefore, in the absence of reliable and valid data, an assumption must be made. There are two options. First, it can be assumed that a student cannot learn knowledge, and subsequent decisions about course selection and learning priorities can be based on this assumption. But what if the assumption proves to be incorrect? What if the student does not enroll in academic classes, because it is assumed that he or she is unable to learn that kind of knowledge, and then it is discovered at some time in the future that the student could have learned this information? What has been lost? Most people answer, "The student's education," "The opportunity to go to college," or "12 years." Fortunately, there is another option. Educators can assume that a student can learn content area knowledge and therefore support the student to do so. What is lost if this assumption proves to be incorrect? The answer most people give is, "Nothing."

That is what makes the assumption of competence less dangerous than the assumption of inability. That is why all students must be included and supported to learn. However, there are still those who answer that time, money, and effort are lost in the second scenario and that these precious resources could have been better spent educating another student. There is nothing about this thinking that is not terrifying. And there is no sentiment further from the foundations of public education. Scores of students pass through the doors of public schools every day. Some leave school and go to work in movie theaters. Others cure diseases. A few eventually commit crimes. What are the criteria for resources being well spent? Are time and money wasted when high school graduates end up in jail? When high school graduates do not go on to college? When high school graduates do not vote?

People do not enter the field of education for the school lunches. People become teachers because they care about students and learning and because they are able and willing to believe in young people's potential. To teach is to take a leap of faith—sometimes small, sometimes not so small—and to believe that all students can learn and are therefore worthy of being taught. There is no way to predict the outcomes of education for any student. (If there were a way, would we use it?)

Students with disabilities have spent years trapped in special education classes, remedial classes, and/or lower-level general education classes where functional curricular goals (e.g., hand washing) have been prioritized to the exclusion, in some cases, of other learning. This is inappropriate. Students with disabilities have the right to learn meaningful functional skills as well as gain knowledge, to utilize that knowledge to gain skills for learning and working, and, as discussed in the following section, to learn basic academics. Ability grouping and tracking have harmed students with disabilities greatly because their right to gain this wide variety of skills—skills that are best acquired in general education classes—has been put on hold, at least until the goals listed on the individualized education program are mastered.

STUDENTS LEARN BASIC ACADEMIC SKILLS

Frank

Frank is a 52-year-old man who has a lot of interests and a lot of labels. He lives alone in an apartment but receives numerous supports and services to assist him with the demands of daily living. Last month a worker from an adult services agency taught him how to use the microwave oven in his kitchen. Prior to that, he learned to program his videocassette recorder. Frank was asked what he would like to learn next. His answer, without any hesitation, was, "I want to learn to read."

Literacy is a national goal for all Americans. The U.S. educational agenda set forth in Goals 2000: Educate America Act of 1994 (PL 103-227), states that, by 2000, "every adult American will be literate." Most people learn to read in school. Frank attended a school. Why didn't he learn to read? To begin with, no one expected him to read. In addition, no other students at his school were reading.

In a keynote address at the 1996 National Equity and Excellence Conference, Deborah Meier, former principal of Central Park East Secondary School in New York City and author of *The Power of Their Ideas* (1995), described her experience of learning how to drive a car. She explained that, like many children, she spent endless childhood hours in the family car, where she had the opportunity to watch her parents driving. Although she was not yet old enough to drive, there was always the expectation that she would someday do so. No one doubted that. Meier suggested that these two conditions—the opportunity to watch an expert and high expectations—are two conditions necessary for learning (Meier, 1996).

Meier also talked about baseball. As a child, she attended many professional games, and, although she had countless opportunities to watch the experts, she never learned to play baseball. Why? She argued that, unlike the expectations that were held for her brother, no one expected that she would ever play. The first condition for learning was met, but not the second. Perhaps the reason Meier did not learn to play baseball is the same reason some students with disabilities do not learn in general education classes. The models are in place, but the expectations for learning still tend to remain low. Once again, the first condition for learning is met, but the second is not.

When students with disabilities are educated in special education classes, both conditions for learning are usually absent because there are few experts to watch and learn from, and expectations for learning are low or nonexistent. If literacy skills are addressed at all, then there is usually only a sincere hope, not a solid expectation, that students will someday be able to read well. Hence Frank's dilemma.

Reflecting on the way in which people learn to read, Smith wrote,

> That we learn from the company that we keep is common everyday wisdom. Every parent knows that children learn to talk exactly like their friends. They also learn to dress and behave and perceive the world in exactly the same way their friends do. It is impossible to prevent them from doing so. No matter how much of their day children hear their parents or their teachers talking, they will not learn to talk as their parents or their teachers talk—at least not as long as they see themselves as being more like their friends than like their parents or teachers. . . . I have characterized this coming to be like the company we keep as "joining the club." Children learn to talk by their membership in the "spoken language clubs" made up of the people they will come to talk like: first family, then friends. And children learn to read and write if they join the "literacy club," literally identifying themselves with people who read and write. (1992, p. 434)

Students learn basic academic skills when they are expected to do so, when there are adequate models around them, and when necessary supports and modifications are in place. These factors are not present in the special education classroom.

HOW INCLUSION BENEFITS
ENTIRE SCHOOL COMMUNITIES

To say that inclusive education benefits school communities—by improving the lives of students with disabilities, more efficiently allocating resources to support a greater number of learners, and merging the systems of special education and general education—would seem to state the obvious. Heaps of evidence and endless examples of these outcomes can be found in schools throughout the United States. To say, however, that inclusive education benefits school communities by creating a culture where belonging is a necessary condition for quality education does not seem to state the obvious, though increasingly it is recognized as stating the truth (C.M. Jorgensen, personal communication, June 1994; Kunc, 1992).

Inclusion Is Not Merely an Instructional Practice

Once upon a time, there was a high school where all students were included and school reform and restructuring efforts were well under way. But students were mean to one another. They came to school afraid of being picked on for their differences. It was a high school that carefully crafted structures, schedules, and assignments but forgot about climate. All students were educated together, more because they were organized that way and less as a result of diversity being valued.

This story is a reminder that inclusive learning communities are not created simply by employing state-of-the-art instructional practices. Attention to the culture of the learning community is equally important because innovative structures and strategies are greatly discounted in an atmosphere that continues to reward sameness and conformity. In an atmosphere that continues to see difference as a liability. In an atmosphere that continues to believe only some people are different. For many years, students with and without disabilities have been sorted based on personal characteristics—some that are valued in school (e.g., having strong linguistic intelligence) (Gardner, 1983) and others that are not (e.g., having Down syndrome). Inclusive schools undo these artificial divisions by embedding into the school culture a value that "no one is perfect, but everyone is okay" (Dillon et al., 1993, p. 29).

Schools looking toward the future do not need educators who simply agree that diversity is a good thing, because these educators will organize disability awareness weeks and contain diversity in curricular units. Schools need educators who value diversity as a result of their own life experience, who understand that "diversity is in everyone's best interest" (N. Kunc, personal communication, November 1996).

Perhaps inclusion will continue to be seen as just another educational philosophy until those who do not yet embrace it are themselves discriminated against. Perhaps it is only at this point that inclusion moves out of the educational realm and into the realm of social justice. Perhaps I do not care if you are devalued for communicating with a computer until I am devalued because I am female. Or gay. Or old. Or of Asian descent. Or overweight. Or simply not like you.

Inclusive education benefits school communities by bringing attention to the issue of belonging and by reminding us that the capacity of schools to host meaningful learning opportunities parallels our attention to this matter. Even if there were no students with disabilities, the culturing of inclusive schools would still be important because the entrance of students with disabilities into general education classes does not signify the presence of diversity in the school; it recognizes and affirms the diversity that has always existed. As a result, people are less bound by false ideals of normalcy, are less fearful of expressing their own uniqueness, and thus are more able to learn.

CONCLUSIONS

Have you ever walked into a McDonald's restaurant and asked for a grilled cheese sandwich? They will tell you it's not on the menu. If you tell them that what you really want is just a piece of cheese melted on a bun, they will say they are sorry, but they cannot do that. You offer to buy a cheeseburger but ask them to hold the burger, and they will say okay but look very nervous.

Change is hard. Changing schools is harder. When change hovers nearby, the structures and systems in schools that are most protected are usually those most in need of alteration—the issues we gloss over with rhetoric. We fly banners from the flagpole that invite celebrations of diversity. We announce to parents that we believe all students have unique gifts and talents. Then we walk back into the classroom and prepare students to take standardized achievement tests so that we can see which kids have been filled up with the most information.

Struggles in education are not limited to disability-related initiatives. We need to do more than repair special education; we need to transform general education. History reminds us that we have changed schools before and that we will change them again, but this time there is a notable difference. We are restructuring education for all students, not just most of them, and our efforts are proving successful.

This chapter has described both the learning that occurs in general education classes and the importance of that learning for all students, even those with long labels and thick student files. It has proposed that inclusive education benefits entire school communities, not only students with disabilities, most significantly through the creation of a school culture that values diversity. And though the work of building inclusive high schools is well under way, it is far from completed. Molly is still a high school student with a disability who is included. Can she someday be just a high school student?

In the chapters that follow, strategies for making an inclusive vision a reality are shared, including changing the role of special educators, developing inclusive curriculum, creating an environment in which social relationships can flourish, embedding self-determination into the general education curriculum, abolishing separate community-based instruction for students with disabilities in favor of community learning experiences for all students, and establishing an inclusive graduation planning system.

REFERENCES

Dillon, A., Tashie, C., Shapiro-Barnard, S., Schuh, M., Jorgensen, C., Dixon, B., & Nisbet, J.A. (1993). *Treasures: A celebration of inclusion.* Durham: University of New Hampshire, Institute on Disability.

Donnellan, A. (1984). The criterion of the least dangerous assumption. *Behavioral Disorders, 9,* 141–150.

Gardner, H. (1983). *Frames of mind: The theory of multiple intelligences.* New York: Basic Books.

Goals 2000: Educate America Act of 1994, PL 103-227, 20 U.S.C. §§ 5801 *et seq.*

Goodlad, J., & Oakes, J. (1988). We must offer equal access to knowledge. *Educational Leadership, 45,* 16–22.

Greene, M. (1988). *The dialectic of freedom.* New York: Teachers College Press.

Individuals with Disabilities Education Act (IDEA) of 1990, PL 101-476, 20 U.S.C. §§ 1400 *et seq.*

Koppenhaver, D., Coleman, P., Kalman, S., & Yoder, D. (1991). The implications of emergent literacy research for children with developmental disabilities. *American Journal of Speech Language Pathology, 1,* 38–44.

Kunc, N. (1992). The need to belong: Rediscovering Maslow's hierarchy of needs. In R.A. Villa, J.S. Thousand, W. Stainback, & S. Stainback (Eds.), *Restructuring for caring and effective education: An administrative guide to creating heterogeneous schools* (pp. 25–39). Baltimore: Paul H. Brookes Publishing Co.

Meier, D. (1995). *The power of their ideas.* Boston: Beacon Press.

Meier, D. (1996, January). *Keynote address.* Paper presented at the 1996 National Equity and Excellence Conference, Nashua, New Hampshire.

Sizer, T. (1992). *Horace's school: Redesigning the American high school.* Boston: Houghton Mifflin.

Smith, F. (1992, February). Learning to read: The never-ending debate. *Phi Delta Kappan, 73,* 432–441.

U.S. Department of Education. (1995). *Seventeenth annual report to Congress on the implementation of the Individuals with Disabilities Education Act.* Washington, DC: Author.

U.S. Department of Labor. (1991). *What work requires of schools: A SCANS report for America 2000.* Washington, DC: U.S. Government Printing Office.

Wheelock, A. (1992). *Crossing the tracks: How "untracking" can save America's schools.* New York: New Press.

Wiggins, G. (1989). The futility of trying to teach everything of importance. *Educational Leadership, 47,* 44–48.

2

Equity and Excellence

Finding Common Ground Between Inclusive Education and School Reform

Robert L. Fried and Cheryl M. Jorgensen

Here is a scene that one might find in any community where people are trying to determine what 12 years of schooling should add up to for their children: A committee of faculty, staff, and parents is trying to redefine the school's diploma in performance language. Everyone agrees that all students should be challenged to perform the best work they can do, that all students need to learn to work well individually and together, and that a diploma based on students' demonstrating and applying what they have actually learned is better than one based on rote memorization and Carnegie units. The committee also agrees that students should work hard to become proficient in key skills and competencies such as reading, writing, and using math and science for solving problems.

Despite large areas of agreement, the group has reached an impasse on deeply held but divergent views on whether one set of academic standards can be fairly applied to all students. What stymies them most is the diploma itself and what it represents. Within this group, the special education teacher, the principal, and a parent of a student with a learning disability want to make sure the new diploma respects the diversity of students and their learning styles and rewards each student for doing his or her best. These three oppose new graduation standards that discriminate against students who might never achieve some of the new, tougher requirements being proposed.

"I don't want my boy to wind up with a diploma that's got big asterisks all over it—you know, the 'Dummy Diploma,'" a parent says.

The principal supports her by saying, "We want to reward hard work and sincere effort and allow all youngsters to find different ways to show us the best they can do."

But the English teacher, the science department head, and a parent who has volunteered in programs for high-achieving students want more academic rigor in the diploma process. They bemoan the lack of intellectual challenge for students, many of whom now take advanced placement courses only because such courses look good on college applications. To them, studying subjects like Shakespeare, physics, or the Federalist debate represents a bulwark against those who would turn our education system over to a bunch of technocrats and process junkies, throwing out the classics and replacing them with software and slogans.

In some communities, this debate is fraught with deep political, religious, or cultural divisions. Elsewhere, as above, it is a discussion

This chapter was supported in part by Grant H023R20018 from the U.S. Department of Education, Office of Special Education and Rehabilitative Services.

among allies in the struggle against the status quo, which both sides agree provides neither high standards nor respect for diversity. Although each side is willing to honor the ideals of the other, finding a way to combine them into a diploma package is difficult, to say the least. One reason for the difficulty is that what parents and teachers want for students falls into three complex and interconnected realms:

1. Academic content (i.e., cultural, historical, scientific information)
2. Essential skills (i.e., ways of gaining access to and working with information, ideas, and people)
3. Attitudes and values (i.e., character development and habits of mind) that reflect a diversity of abilities and allow multiple paths for students to demonstrate their achievement

Another equally thorny problem is that the goals of high standards and high achievement appear to clash with those of full equity and respect for the diverse learning styles and abilities of all students. It is hard to devise a performance-based diploma that does justice to both.

Although the scenario depicted is fictitious, it does represent attitudes that exist in communities all over the United States. In fact, during the 1993–1994 school year, a statewide New Hampshire task force sponsored by a federal school restructuring and inclusion grant was convened to grapple with these very issues in the hope of finding a solution that would not require a compromise of anyone's ideals. The group was composed of parents, teachers, college faculty, as well as consultants who were working with school districts involved in significant restructuring efforts in both general and special education. This chapter recounts the yearlong discussions of the task force members and illustrates the necessity for both "sides"—those advocating for general education reform and those concerned with inclusion—to merge their conversations for the benefit of all students.

INITIAL TASK FORCE MEETINGS MIRED IN DEBATE

Each member who joined the task force was committed to collaborating with other individuals and organizations that had students' best interests at heart, so that their combined power might have a chance to make real change happen in public education, despite powerful community resistance to new educational ideas and paradigms. As partisans for different kinds of change, they quickly discovered that they were marching to the beat of different drummers.

As administrators of the sponsoring grant, staff from the University of New Hampshire (UNH) Institute on Disability tended to view the issue of school reform primarily through the lens of students with significant disabilities. They advocated for membership of all students, regardless of the nature of their disability (and with adequate educational support), into the general education classes to which they would be assigned if they had no disability. Despite the fact that they acknowledged that not all existing classes are high-quality learning environments for students with or without disabilities, inclusion advocates argued that real equity is not found in a perfect education but in a typical education for all students.

It was common to hear an advocate of inclusion say, for example, "Kids with disabilities have the same right to be in class with a mediocre teacher as any other kid. Let's get them all in class together, as an integral part of the regular school community. Then we can work to make those classes as good as they can be for all students."

Advocates of curricular reform and high performance standards acknowledged that a small percentage of students may never be able to reach those standards by the time they are ready to graduate. A typical comment was, "I'm sure we can find some way to acknowledge the small percentage of kids who try hard but, through no fault of their own, cannot reach the newer and higher standards. We can't abandon the concept of diploma accountability and the positive pressure it will place on the whole system just because a few kids will end up with an asterisk on their diplomas."

The first few task force meetings produced many sharp exchanges. As advocates used to defending their reforms against traditionalists within school systems, they had little patience with those who claimed to be reformers but seemed so ready to compromise on what the other side saw as *the* critical issue (i.e., full inclusion on the one hand, higher performance standards on the other). As one member put it, "We each saw ourselves as zealots for change—our kind of change—and we naturally assumed that what was crucial to our constituency must be good for everybody else in the school."

Two factors saved the effort from early disintegration. One was a fascination with the debate itself. It was, after all, refreshing to lock horns with articulate change advocates rather than with school-based resisters. A task force member reflected, "As frustrating as our sessions got, as little progress as we seemed to be making in those first few meetings, something kept us coming back. What that 'something' was, we often weren't sure. Maybe it was all the idealism."

The second factor that kept the conversation going was that a systematic plan for moving the task force meetings forward was designed by the facilitators. Rather than continuing to focus on differences, the facilitators suggested that the group take a time-out from arguing about areas they knew were difficult to resolve and first try to establish educational principles that both groups could support.

PRINCIPLES OF SCHOOL REFORM AND INCLUSIVE EDUCATION WERE DEVELOPED

The first step in this process was the development of clearly stated principles of both school reform and inclusive education. These principles, refined over the course of several meetings, are depicted in Table 1. When these lists were finalized, the group could see that there

Table 1.   Principles of school reform and inclusive education

Some principles of school reform
1. Schools should focus on helping adolescents use their minds well.
2. Students must master a number of essential skills and be competent in certain areas of knowledge.
3. The governing outlook of schools should be "student as worker."
4. Curriculum and pedagogy should be driven by desired student outcomes.
5. Graduation from high school should not be an expectation of students who merely "spend time" in school but should be awarded based on achievement of rigorous, performance-based learning outcomes.
6. Staff should be generalists first and specialists second. The dominant pedagogy should be coaching. Teaching style and time allotted to achieve mastery should be individualized.
7. Schools should become democratic societies in which individuals share in decisions, accept consequences, and expect justice.
8. Schools should be communities of learners where a spirit of inquiry, reflection, and risk taking prevail.

Some principles of inclusive education
1. Schools should demonstrate respect for each student's gifts and talents.
2. All students can learn.
3. All students benefit from learning together with students who are different from themselves, including those of different races, cultures, genders, talents, temperaments, and experiences.
4. Students with disabilities should be assigned to classrooms and schools using the same decision guidelines applied to typical students.
5. Academic awards and honors should be attainable by any student who demonstrates achievement and effort that exceeds his or her own and others' expectations.
6. Schools should provide enough support to teachers to enable them to provide a quality education to all students in their classrooms without harming any student in those classrooms.
7. Students with disabilities should have the opportunity to make choices similar to those afforded students without disabilities and should be active in school governance, such as the student council.
8. Students with disabilities should be allowed to participate in activities that provide them with an opportunity to fail as well as those offering an opportunity to succeed.

were areas of confluence as well as areas of contrast on the two lists. Finding these areas of agreement was heartening: Everyone believed that all students can learn, that schools should become democratic societies, and that schools should be supportive communities of and for learners.

A list of commonly held principles began to emerge, and the areas of disagreement came into clearer focus. The inclusion advocates continued to say that "if there were only one set of performance standards, some students would be automatically disqualified from receiving a diploma because of the severity of their disabilities." They emphasized the need for "a diploma to which all students can aspire, one that recognizes the achievement of a student's individual goals and his or her best effort."

The restructuring people responded, "Without common high expectations, we'll never have true accountability. Right now, in communities where poor and minority kids are shunted into low-level classes, parents are told their kids are doing 'just fine' and are 'working at their capacity.' But they end up with worthless diplomas."

Easy answers were elusive. At one point, a school reform advocate proposed that students' academic accomplishments be reflected in their diplomas by adding the phrase *with modification* for students with learning disabilities.

"No!" came the retort from the inclusion advocates. Their position was that going through graduation is more than a rite of passage earned by students who try to do their best. It is a public acknowledgment that the school has honored the students' hard work and achievement, even if some students' talents are different from the norm. They believed that backing down on the issue of the same diploma for all students would only continue the pattern of consigning people with disabilities to the margins of society. In a school that embraces personalization and recognition of individual talents, every student's diploma should signify something unique.

NEW VIEWS BEGAN TO EMERGE

By midpoint in the year, the inclusion advocates came to appreciate, albeit cautiously, the power of standards as an intellectual focus for school reform and agreed that most students with learning difficulties would benefit from implementation of those standards as long as there was also a comprehensive system of supports. The restructuring advocates began to see the benefit to the school climate of students learning together with others who represented a spectrum of diversity, including race, culture, gender, age, talent, temperament, and experi-

Table 2. Qualities and beliefs of restructured and inclusive schools

1. All students are valued members of society and of their school communities. *All students* means every single student.
2. Schools help students to think clearly, develop their intellectual and creative potential, and in general learn to use their minds well.
3. Schools respect each student's gifts and talents by recognizing and honoring demonstrations of effort and achievement.
4. Schools see themselves as communities of learners in which a spirit of inquiry, reflection, and risk taking prevails.
5. All students benefit from learning together with others who represent a spectrum of diversity, including race, culture, gender, age, talent, temperament, and experience.
6. Knowledge is as varied and interwoven as human experiences. This principle is reflected in the interdisciplinary nature of the curriculum.
7. Teachers view themselves first as educators of students and second as specialists in a subject area. They are excited about learning and enthusiastic in their work with students.
8. Class sizes are small enough so that teachers can personalize instruction. At the high school level, this means that no teacher has to work with more than a total of 80 students per semester.
9. Schools are democratic societies in which students share in decisions regarding governance, curriculum, and goal setting.
10. All students benefit from opportunities to receive, as well as to provide, assistance and service to others and to their community.

ence. Table 2 represents the growing number of areas of common agreement.

UNRESOLVED DIFFERENCES PERSISTED

Despite the satisfaction of developing the list of common principles (see Table 2), many believed that the group was still stalled. Table 3 depicts several areas in which proposed language met with serious concern.

The extent of the impasse was reflected in the questions that were lobbed back and forth across the conference table:

"What about students with severe disabilities who may never demonstrate what most folks see as competence in language arts and math?"

"What is a *core curriculum*? Do you really believe that all students should take the same courses?"

"How can our schools be held accountable for quality if there are no benchmarks that assess students' learning and teachers' teaching?"

"Can we really expect teachers to personalize instruction in a heterogeneous class of 25 or 30 students?"

"Does *all students* include those kids whose behavior can throw an entire class into turmoil?"

"Must we eliminate tracking and ability grouping altogether? What about courses that require prerequisites, especially in math and science?"

"Sure, outcomes are important. But shouldn't teachers be free to focus on areas such as citizenship, that aren't tied to a measurable 'educational outcome'?"

The temptation was great by this time to give up, to agree to disagree and retreat to the security of partisan camps: "Inclusion advocates over here; you restructuring people, over there!"

A BREAK IN THE IMPASSE

A break in the impasse came about when two members of the group who had assumed the roles of co-facilitators met over lunch. They spent several hours working on draft language of what they were now calling the "prickly" issues (see Table 3). But they were able to move the discussion ahead only when they had identified what the underlying concerns for both sides were. Such convergence did not come easily. What made it possible to begin to break the logjam on points like these was a mutual realization that unless the issue of performance expectations and curriculum standards becomes an ongoing part of a school's conversation, the probability is great that little significant progress will be made in improving what most students actually get from their years of compulsory schooling. By the same token, unless the needs, talents, and social acceptance of students with disabilities and other challenges are an ongoing part of a school's conversation,

Table 3.   Principles that appeared to defy consensus

1. Education programs for all students are based on a core curriculum. A variety of instructional strategies are necessary to help students achieve success within the core curriculum.
2. As students progress through key transition points in the K–12 curriculum, they demonstrate competence in areas that include language arts and mathematics.
3. Students work to master a number of essential skills and to be competent in certain areas of knowledge. High school diplomas are awarded based on a student's achievement of performance-based learning outcomes.
4. All students are educated in heterogeneous classes in the schools to which they would normally be assigned.
5. Teachers understand the diversity in students' styles of learning and apply that understanding in the classroom. They personalize instruction and the conditions under which students work to achieve mastery.

the probability is great that other unconventional students will like-wise be discriminated against or ignored.

Here was an accommodation that did not require a compromise of principles. When the two facilitators shared this mutual recognition with the larger group, it allowed the members to expand and cate-gorize their list of shared principles in a manner that would be ac-ceptable to a broader group of advocates for inclusion and school reform. The full list of agreed-on principles is included in Table 4.

THE TASK FORCE CONCLUDES ITS WORK

By July 1994, 11 months of deliberations had brought the group a long way toward a meeting of the minds regarding inclusion and school reform. Four points of disagreement remained: heterogeneous group-ing of students in all classes, standards of performance assessment, students who did not achieve as expected, and the characteristics of the diploma. Statements designed to resolve those issues are presented in Table 5, although this task force did not come to a final consensus on them.

Why Are There So Many Unresolved Questions?

One would think, with the list of principles held in common by the advocates of curriculum restructuring and the champions of full in-clusion (see Table 4), that the group members would all have ex-pressed a collective sigh of relief and congratulated themselves on achieving a level of accord that once seemed impossible.

They knew that they had been part of a discussion that is too often missing from public education. Teachers especially have little time within their school day to reflect on their own practice with their colleagues, much less debate some of the beliefs and assumptions about education that reflect the values of the society as a whole. They also realized that in building a bridge between the inclusion and re-structuring movements, they had taken on the many unresolved is-sues within each movement (e.g., concerns about including students with serious emotional difficulties, debates about how much Shake-speare to require, whether there are any reliable standardized mea-surements to assess what students actually know and can do).

But, after almost a full year of deliberations, the group was ready to disband. They had broadened their own understanding of inclusion and school reform, yet there was a reluctance to patch together a shaky consensus on the toughest issues. So, they ended their work with a list of questions, depicted in Table 6, to bequeath to teachers and parents who struggle on a daily basis with making their schools

Table 4.   A synthesis of common educational principles and beliefs

Principles related to how people work and learn together

1. All students are valued members of society and of their school communities. *All students* means *every single student.*

2. All students are educated to live, work, and play in diverse communities.

3. All students benefit from learning together with others who represent a spectrum of diversity, including race, culture, gender, age, talent, temperament, and experience.

4. All students benefit from opportunities to provide as well as to receive assistance and service to and from others in the community.

5. Schools work hard to strengthen relationships among students, families, the community at large, and the school. When students are young, their families are active partners in creating and evaluating students' educational programs. Increasingly, as students age, they advocate for themselves.

6. Schools are democratic societies in which students share in decisions regarding governance, curriculum, and goal setting.

7. Schools establish clear expectations for behavior based on respect, trust, and decency that provide explicit consequences and fair judicial procedures.

8. Collaboration between and among students, educators, and support staff takes place as a regular part of every working day.

Principles related to how schools are organized and the roles people play

1. Teachers view themselves first as educators of students and second as specialists in a discipline. They are excited about learning and enthusiastic in their work with students.

2. Class sizes are small enough so that teachers can personalize instruction. At the elementary school level, the target teacher–student ratio is 1:20. At the secondary level, the target ratio is 1:80.

3. Teachers and other school staff have ongoing support and training to enable each student to be successful.

4. Teachers understand the diversity in students' styles of learning and apply that understanding in the classroom. They do personalize instruction and the conditions under which students work to achieve mastery so that students' unique talents and abilities are developed and appreciated.

5. School principals and staff have the chief responsibility for site-based decisions about curriculum, teaching methods, and use of time for all students.

6. Schools see themselves as communities of learners in which a spirit of inquiry, reflection, and risk taking prevails.

7. Schools help students think clearly, develop their intellectual and creative potential, and, in general, learn to use their minds well.

8. Schools respect each student's gifts and talents by recognizing and honoring demonstrations of effort and achievement.

**Principles related to curriculum,
performance, assessment, and achievement of students**

1. All students can learn.

2. All students are provided with necessary supports to learn and be successful.

3. Students work to master a common set of districtwide, performance-based learning objectives in essential skills and areas of knowledge that have been delineated by the faculty with parent and community input as critical to students' success in life. These performance objectives are reflected in the ways that schools are organized, time and staff are used, and student mastery is assessed.

(continued)

Table 4.   (continued)

4. The curriculum represents an effective educational program for students to master performance objectives. It includes areas that best represent what the school and community expect students to know (e.g., understanding, information), to be like (e.g., values, attitudes, habits of mind), and to be able to do (e.g., skills, practices). Options and choices are provided for students in the manner in which they demonstrate mastery and in other areas in which they choose to become proficient.

5. Curriculum development and assessment are guided by "depth over breadth."

6. Knowledge is as varied and interwoven as human experiences. This principle is reflected in the interdisciplinary nature of the curriculum.

7. Student success within this curriculum is achieved through intellectual, interpersonal, and experiential strategies that enable students to acquire essential skills and knowledge and to develop character and values. Learning is an active rather than a passive experience, with students being responsible for performing the intellectual work of the curriculum and teachers supporting, coaching, and facilitating students' endeavors.

8. The primary work of the curriculum is accomplished by students' actively thinking through, experimenting with, speculating about, researching, debating, discussing, and responding creatively to the ideas and issues contained within the curriculum. Didactic instruction (i.e., lecturing) plays a part in an overall approach to teaching, but most essential content knowledge is acquired by students working with information and applying it in performance and problem-solving contexts.

places where all students are welcomed and supported to achieve the highest standards possible.

CONCLUSIONS

The task force completed its work in 1994. Although it is impossible to establish a causal relationship between this group's work and the current state of the state of New Hampshire relative to inclusive education and school reform, a number of significant changes did occur that have a potential impact on every student in New Hampshire and not just those with disabilities.

One of this chapter's coauthors testified in the landmark lawsuit brought by five New Hampshire school districts that challenged the state's funding of public education through property tax revenues. He brought his conviction about the rights all students have for a quality public education to the forefront of those deliberations.

In addition, the first national equity and excellence conference was held in New Hampshire in January 1996. At that conference, 400 teachers and administrators from all over the United States focused on the issues of school reform and inclusion of students with disabilities in presentations made jointly by experts in both fields. Because of the resounding success of that endeavor and the participants' hunger for continued opportunity to collaborate with colleagues tackling both issues at once, a second conference was planned for October 1997.

Table 5.   Proposed principles designed to resolve persistent differences

1.   Students are heterogeneously grouped within the curriculum in classes that pro-
     vide a challenging learning experience for all students. As they advance toward
     achieving their graduation requirements, students select additional courses and
     activities based on interest, with access open to all who wish to participate.
2.   Students are expected to demonstrate competence in curriculum objectives as
     they progress through transition points in primary, elementary, middle, and high
     school grades. These assessments are critical to ensure that the student, staff,
     and parents are aware of the student's progress, given his or her learning style
     and talents.
3.   For any student who does not achieve the stated competencies at these transi-
     tion points, a concerted effort is mounted by the student, teachers, and parents
     to improve areas of inadequate performance. These efforts should not jeopardize
     the student's social acceptance and self-esteem. At each of the transition points,
     the student receives formal recognition of his or her achievements.
4.   Students earn certificates of mastery when they complete the district's
     performance-based learning objectives. They are then prepared to pursue post-
     secondary education or to begin their working careers. Students may require
     varying amounts of time to achieve these certificates.

The UNH Institute on Disability has infused thinking about fundamental school reform into the fabric of its work in education at all
levels. Project coordinators are working closely with New Hampshire
Department of Education staff on issues relating to curriculum frameworks and the statewide assessment program. These same staff participated in reviews of local districts' applications for consolidated federal funding in areas such as Title I, migrant education, special
education, and English as a second language. A statewide educational
summit was held in October 1996, which was attended by local and
state leaders in both general school reform and inclusion. We have
come to realize that school reformers and inclusive education advocates share a passionate concern for the future of all children and that
only through finding common ground with one another on the details
of day-to-day educational practice will our visions become reality.

The debate about equity and excellence influences the lives of
students and teachers at the local school level. What might a school
that manages to challenge and include all students look like? In Chapter 3, the foundations of restructuring and inclusive schools are presented through examples from a number of schools across the United
States.

Implementation Suggestions for Teachers

1.   Become familiar with some of the literature on school restructur-
     ing and inclusion. The authors recommend *Horace's School: Rede-
     signing the American High School* (Sizer, 1992); *The Power of Their
     Ideas: Lessons for America from a Small School in Harlem* (Meier, 1995);

Table 6.   Topics for the next conversation

1. How can we decide what kind of knowledge we expect all students to possess, realizing that there is hardly a single fact, date, formula, or term that all successful or educated people do, in fact, know? Is there any specific knowledge required by everybody?

2. What kind of distinction ought we to make between the a) knowledge that we want our children, as they grow toward adulthood, to acquire about the cultures that define us as a nation (e.g., historical, scientific, sociopolitical, literary, artistic, linguistic) and b) specific knowledge (i.e., cultural literacy) that some people feel we should require all students to learn in school?

3. Does it even make sense to press for student mastery of traditional areas of knowledge, or disciplines, as they currently exist in secondary schools (e.g., English, social studies, math, science, the arts), since the application of such knowledge increasingly tends to be interdisciplinary and problem centered?

4. How can we find ways to personalize every student's learning agenda without running the risk that some schools or districts will use this as an excuse to permit low standards to be set for students from disadvantaged families who are not able to advocate well for their fair share of educational resources and opportunities (e.g., gifted programs, honors courses)?

5. Similarly, how can we set high and challenging standards for all students, based on our best guess of the skills, knowledge, and attitudes that people will need in their lives, without putting the attainment of such standards out of reach for some students with disabilities?

6. How do we balance, on the one hand, the need to be fair to and supportive of students who come to school with a range of academic and social strengths and weaknesses with the desire, on the other hand, to help a much greater percentage of such students to work hard to master essential skills that may require sustained effort on their part?

7. How can we advocate strongly for our vision of educational equity and excellence for the future while keeping faith with present-day educators who are struggling often against serious opposition to make more modest reforms that may pave the way for our vision to be realized?

The Passionate Teacher: A Practical Guide (Fried, 1995); *Inclusion: A Guide for Educators* (Stainback & Stainback, 1996); *No Pity: People with Disabilities Forging a New Civil Rights Movement* (Shapiro, 1993); and *Keeping Track: How Schools Structure Inequality* (Oakes, 1985). Read literature by people with disabilities and their families to get a first-person perspective on the experience of disability. Suggestions include *Nobody, Nowhere: The Extraordinary Autobiography of an Autistic* (Williams, 1992), written by a woman who has autism; *I Raise My Eyes to Say Yes* (Sienkiewicz-Mercer & Kaplan, 1989), written by a woman who lived most of her life in an institution and was discovered to be intelligent; and *Circles of Friends: People with Disabilities and Their Friends Enrich the Lives of One Another* (Perske & Perske, 1988).

2. Examine your own attitudes and beliefs about diversity, competition, learning, community, and education.

3. Organize a discussion group of teachers—general education and special education—to discuss some of these topics. Make participation low risk by establishing ground rules of confidentiality and keeping your discussions internal for a while.
4. Bring issues relating to students with disabilities to larger discussions in your school about raising standards, equity, and teaching.

Leadership Suggestions for Administrators

1. Ensure that students with disabilities are considered in each and every discussion about, for example, standards, graduation requirements, improving student performance, and assessment.
2. Invite special education administrators to be part of every administrative team meeting.
3. Support teachers to organize their own reflective inquiry groups and provide them with resources to consider questions of equity and excellence.

REFERENCES

Fried, R.L. (1995). *The passionate teacher: A practical guide*. Boston: Beacon Press.

Meier, D. (1995). *The power of their ideas: Lessons for America from a small school in Harlem*. Boston: Beacon Press.

Oakes, J. (1985). *Keeping track: How schools structure inequality*. New Haven, CT: Yale University Press.

Perske, R., & Perske, M. (1988). *Circles of friends: People with disabilities and their friends enrich the lives of one another*. Nashville, TN: Abingdon Press.

Shapiro, J.P. (1993). *No pity: People with disabilities forging a new civil rights movement*. New York: Times Books.

Sizer, T. (1992). *Horace's school: Redesigning the American high school*. Boston: Houghton Mifflin.

Stainback, S., & Stainback, W. (Eds.). (1996). *Inclusion: A guide for educators*. Baltimore: Paul H. Brookes Publishing Co.

Sienkiewicz-Mercer, R., & Kaplan, S. (1989). *I raise my eyes to say yes*. New York: Avon Books.

Williams, D. (1992). *Nobody, nowhere: The extraordinary autobiography of an autistic*. New York: Times Books.

3

Philosophical Foundations of Inclusive, Restructuring Schools

Douglas Fisher, Caren Sax, and Cheryl M. Jorgensen

In the United States, the educational system is expected to contribute to the preparation of children for the demands of adult life. This value is deeply embedded and is considered an inalienable right. In excerpts from her junior decathlon speech, LaSheieka Little, a student at Santana High School in California, provided this view of how her school extended this right to all students, including those identified with significant disabilities, within general education classes:

> Every day it brings me great enjoyment when I walk through the halls of Santana High School and see many different types of teens. But the reason I smile is because students with disabilities are treated no differently than any other student. At Santana, students with disabilities have the opportunity to be included in and actively participate in general education classes with the rest of the student body.
>
> What is inclusion? Inclusion is when students with disabilities become part of our learning environment. They become involved in classwork, although sometimes their assignments are modified to [accommodate] their needs but [remain] focused on what the class is learning. It is when students with disabilities become members of the school.
>
> In one of my classes, I met Jesse, who uses a wheelchair and is unable to communicate with words. I knew that she was learning because she began to smile and raise her head when you said something or did something that she liked. If Jesse had been confined to one room, she would not have been exposed to many different people and would have never raised her head. That was her way of responding.
>
> The truth is that students with disabilities have been excluded for so long [that] we did not know what to expect. Because of inclusive education, we have learned that students with disabilities have the same rights and feelings [as other students]. We have also learned to get to know one another and therefore build better understandings and friendships.
>
> People are often afraid of what's different. Inclusive education gave us a chance to realize that people are people and that no one should be excluded because of a disability. I know it will bring better friendships and good will because I now have friends I would have never had.
>
> We as a people need to come together, no matter how different we are from one another. You as a parent would not want your son or daughter to miss out on his or her life because of a disability. At our school, students with disabilities have the chance to be involved in club activities, the yearbook, and sports. With inclusive education, we learn and grow as a people. The point I'm trying to make is that inclusion works! Not only for students with disabilities, but for us as a people.

As communities become increasingly diverse and society becomes more complex, schools must respond with innovative strategies and comprehensive initiatives, not only to prepare students to be economically productive but also to instill in them the respect for diversity that LaSheieka expressed.

This chapter was supported in part by Grants H023R20018 and H086V40007 from the U.S. Department of Education, Office of Special Education and Rehabilitative Services.

Although the essential components of an inclusive school have been documented for 10 years and there is a growing body of scholarly work that addresses school reform, few descriptions exist of schools that are attempting to address *both* of these initiatives simultaneously and in a coordinated way (Benjamin, 1989; Fullan & Steigelbauer, 1991; Glasser, 1990; Goodlad, 1984; Lipsky & Gartner, 1989; National Commission on Excellence in Education, 1983; Patterson, Purkey, & Parker, 1986; Sizer, 1992; Stainback, Stainback, & Forest, 1989; Villa, Thousand, Stainback, & Stainback, 1992). Furthermore, identifying successful practices that are applicable across geographic areas and socioeconomic differences is particularly difficult.

Since 1992, we have been working in high schools that are responding to the dual challenge of equity and excellence. These schools, representing urban and rural communities from several different states, have made the inclusion of students with disabilities a priority within their broader school restructuring efforts. After reading one another's work and attending each other's conference presentations, we were anxious to compare notes. As we shared our successes and frustrations, we noticed the similarities in our experiences. Realizing that our common experiences might help others engaged in similar work, we recorded our observations, focusing initially on just two school sites. One of the schools was in a rural, middle-class, Caucasian community in a small state. The other was in an urban, ethnically diverse community in a large state. Although our stories came from schools in opposite corners of the United States, common themes began to emerge. To ensure that the themes represented more than coincidence between two schools, we tested our ideas by talking with other colleagues. Based on these conversations and more fine-tuning of our original ideas, we agreed on eight principles and practices that are characteristic of inclusive, restructuring schools. These principles and practices are as follows:

1. Decisions about inclusive education and school reform must originate in administrative vision that is unwavering in the face of uncertainty and the difficulties of putting principles into practice.
2. Inclusion of students with disabilities must be solidly based within general education reform efforts.
3. Support for teachers and administrators during the change process must be provided through internal structures and through association with an outside "critical friend."
4. Social justice issues, including disability, must be infused throughout the curriculum.
5. Creative use of time through implementation of innovative school schedules is essential.

6. General and special education teachers with new job descriptions that reflect shared responsibility for all students must collaborate to design the curriculum, teach, and evaluate students.
7. Tracking has been eliminated, and most classes are heterogeneously grouped.
8. The curriculum must be thematic, performance-oriented, constructivist, and based on high achievement standards for every student.

This chapter elaborates on the first four principles that represent the underpinnings of a school's climate and its guiding philosophy. Chapter 4 describes the rationale for and interrelationships among innovative scheduling, changing teachers' roles, and heterogeneous grouping. Chapter 5 presents the elements of an inclusive curriculum design model that is thematic, performance oriented, and based on high standards. Finally, Chapter 6 showcases examples of units and lessons that were designed for inclusive high school classes.

Caitlyn's Story

In the spring of 1992, the father of a 14-year-old girl who experiences severe disabilities contacted a consultant from the Institute on Disability at the University of New Hampshire (UNH) to obtain assistance in moving his daughter from a segregated, regional educational program back to her home high school. Because inclusion of students with severe disabilities is practically nonexistent in their state, this family had to rely on a consultant who lived more than 3 hours from their community to help plan their daughter's educational program.

Although the school staff were initially very reluctant to consider the family's wishes, they agreed to "give it a try" as long as Institute staff were available to provide training and technical assistance. Institute staff and high school personnel worked collaboratively to plan for Caitlyn's return, and, in September 1992, she proudly became a "regular" ninth grader at her large suburban high school. Caitlyn's transition was an example of everything that we thought we knew about making inclusion work well. Substitute teachers were provided so that teachers could be involved in the design of her educational program right from the start. A group of her future ninth-grade classmates were included in the planning, not as peer buddies or as a circle of friends, but as experts on what the typical high school experience is like from the perspective of students and to help brainstorm the supports that Caitlyn would need. A teacher was identified to serve as the coordinator of Caitlyn's program, and she was both competent and personable. With support from the Institute staffperson, she worked hard during the spring and right before school opened to make sure that classroom teachers understood the rationale for Caitlyn's presence at the school and how they might include her as an active participant in their classes. Caitlyn tried out for cheerleading, and, although she did not make it, she did join the pep squad that performed sideline cheers at every game.

After a few months of school, the Institute consultant approached the principal and special education director about returning five other students with severe disabilities to the high school. A similar planning process was begun, and in the fall of 1993—just 1 year after Caitlyn came back—all students with severe disabilities who lived in that community were full-time members of general education classes in their home high school. Interviews with teachers and students in the school indicated that though some teachers had serious doubts about the wisdom of what was happening, the teachers and students who were directly involved were generally pleased. By midyear, the Institute consultant was no longer a regular visitor to the school and assumed that all was well.

Late in the school year, a number of changes occurred at the school. The special education director and the superintendent submitted their resignations. A new special education director was hired who had no experience with inclusive education, and he began discussions with staff about establishing a self-contained classroom for Caitlyn and the five other students with severe disabilities. In a panic, parents of the students began calling the Institute consultant, and, despite her efforts to advocate for the students' continued inclusion, all six students were slated to go into the self-contained program in the fall of 1994. A local taxpayer's association worked hard for their favorite school board candidates, whose main platform issues were a back-to-basics curriculum and reduction in the special education budget by eliminating a number of teacher's aide positions. Because of these changes, the high school's inclusion facilitator also resigned in the spring of 1995. The six students, who should have graduated with their classmates in 1996, were still attending the school-based, self-contained program when this book went to press, and the school's out-of-district budget had actually risen since 1994 because more students had been placed in regional and residential programs.

The newly hired superintendent promised the school board and community that raising students' performance on the state-wide assessment test was his primary goal, and, for the time being, the inclusion of students with disabilities was not on the agenda.

Although this story is a worst-case scenario, the experience of many students who have disabilities and their parents is that inclusive education is dependent on the commitment and activism of a few individuals within a school, making these students vulnerable to changes in local and state politics and policies. Year after year, parents report that they have to start all over again, convincing each new crop of teachers that their child has a right to be included, educating yet another cadre of team members about their child's personality and learning needs, and feeling like several months of every school year are lost to start-up time. *It has become clear that unless inclusion of students with disabilities is firmly embedded within a school's mission and philosophy, and unless inclusive practices are viewed as fitting in with teaching practices that are effective for a large percentage of the student body, it will inevitably fall by the wayside along with other innovations that had short-term appeal but did not affect the hearts of teachers, administrators, and the community.* This chapter provides examples of four essential principles or practices that promote inclusion within broader efforts to improve education for all students.

DECISIONS ABOUT INCLUSIVE EDUCATION AND SCHOOL REFORM MUST ORIGINATE IN ADMINISTRATIVE VISION THAT IS UNWAVERING IN THE FACE OF UNCERTAINTY AND THE DIFFICULTIES OF PUTTING PRINCIPLES INTO PRACTICE

Perhaps the single most important element related to the long-term success of both school reform and inclusive education is administrative vision and commitment. At Souhegan High School in Amherst, New Hampshire, that vision guides daily action as well as long-range planning. (A thumbnail sketch of Souhegan follows, and the Amherst and Souhegan School Districts Mission Statement and Philosophy is presented in Figure 1.)

A Thumbnail Sketch of Souhegan High School

Souhegan High School in Amherst, New Hampshire, is a member of the Coalition of Essential Schools. Opened in 1992, it is located in a quaint New England village 1 hour north of Boston and is a racially homogeneous Caucasian school. There are ap-

---

Amherst and Souhegan School Districts Mission Statement and Philosophy

The Amherst and Souhegan school districts aspire to be a community of learners born of respect, trust, and courage. We consciously commit ourselves:

- To support and engage an individual's unique gifts, passions, and intentions
- To develop and empower the mind, body, and heart
- To challenge and expand the comfortable limits of thought, tolerance, and performance
- To inspire and honor the active stewardship of family, nation, and globe

To this end, the Amherst and Souhegan school districts have determined that the skills and resources of special education will be accessible by all staff and students and available to assist any student with exceptional needs. To the maximum extent possible, all of our students are educated within the regular class. Special education support takes many forms: direct instruction to students, consultation to classroom teachers, direct instruction within the classroom to small groups or whole class, diagnostic teaching (or placement), assessment of learning and teaching styles. Although the majority of our special needs students meeting [identification] criteria are [identified] in these districts, it is not necessary to [be identified] to receive services. It is increasingly clear that special education services delivered in isolation are not effective. We strive to be an inclusive system: inclusive of all students and all teachers. In this way, we will develop students who are independent learners, who understand their educational needs, and who can advocate for themselves within the academic environment. Our goal is to become a community of learners in the truest sense of those words.

Figure 1.   Amherst and Souhegan School Districts Mission Statement and Philosophy. (Reprinted by permission from Souhegan High School.)

proximately 800 students in Grades 9–12, and 17% are identified as having educational disabilities. Although there are a few students placed in out-of-district programs, almost all students who ought to attend Souhegan do. There are no separate programs or classrooms for students with disabilities. Except for sequential courses in mathematics and modern languages and the usual advanced placement classes, all others are heterogeneously grouped. At Grades 9 and 10, students and teachers are organized by teams governed by a flexible block schedule. Special education teachers are full-time members of the ninth- and tenth-grade teaching teams.

At Grades 11 and 12, the school day is more traditionally organized, although there is a double-period humanities block team-taught by English and social studies teachers. One special education teacher supports students and teachers at eleventh grade, and another works with twelfth-grade students and teachers.

Although Souhegan opened its doors as an untracked, heterogeneous, inclusive school in 1992, there have been many challenges to this philosophy from a few teachers at the school, from some students, and from community members. The school administration's response to these challenges illustrates the importance of vision in influencing practice.

During the 1993–1994 school year, a group of parents of students who would have been in honors classes in a traditional high school lobbied to place a referendum on the annual town meeting ballot that would have required Souhegan to establish ability-grouped academic tracks. (In most smaller New Hampshire communities, the annual town meeting is the forum through which every citizen can participate in passing the community and school operating budgets. Important policy issues are often decided through special articles or referenda.) These parents argued that high-achieving students were being held back by heterogeneous classes. Vigorous debates ensued at school board meetings leading up to the annual town meeting. Parents presented research that they believed substantiated their views. Souhegan's administrative team and many faculty also presented their views about the pedagogical soundness of heterogeneous grouping and the harmful effects of tracking. A few students argued on behalf of ability grouping, but the majority spoke about how they believed that their motivation, self-esteem, and academic achievement had improved as a result of their inclusion in heterogeneous classes. After a final, heated, open debate attended by a record number of the town's citizens, the referendum vote was taken. When the ballots were counted, 83% were in favor of maintaining the current system, a strong affirmation of Souhegan's administrative commitment and the teachers' instructional practices.

Although the number of parents arguing against heterogeneous classes grows smaller each year, Souhegan administrators continue to gather standardized achievement test data. Souhegan High School has the highest rate of participation in the SAT program, and their students rank second among all high schools in the state on both the SAT and the New Hampshire Statewide Assessment Test. In addition, SAT scores have remained stable throughout all 4 years of Souhegan's operation. Principal Bob Mackin commented on his role in advocating for inclusion:

> The principal is really a role model. I have to be solidly behind inclusion and keep people coming back to the table to figure out solutions even when the going gets tough. This year some of the math teachers came to me and wanted to remove a group of kids from our math program because they were having difficulty passing Math I. I asked them, "If we pull these kids out, will they acquire the skills to move on to Math II?" The teachers admitted that they probably wouldn't. While I understand that there will be some variability in the skills that our kids leave Souhegan with, I'm not willing to establish a totally different set of standards for students with

disabilities. I think that we need to hold them to high standards and through the curriculum and the support we provide, push them to reach those standards.

Kathryn L. Skoglund has been the director of special instructional services in the Amherst School District since 1985 and was instrumental in the development of Souhegan's inclusive philosophy. Her comments reflect a view from the trenches about what it takes to keep inclusive education at the forefront of the school restructuring conversation.

It may seem easy to talk about what is necessary for effective inclusive education, particularly at a school like Souhegan High School, where we started from scratch and hired staff with the Souhegan High School Mission Statement engraved in our minds. However, there still exist hurdles for inclusive education, even here. It is difficult to maintain the inclusive momentum unless the focus is constant and overt. At Souhegan, faculty and staff have a lot on their plates, a kind of educational smorgasbord. It is easy for inclusion to become lost in the midst of all other activity unless the administration maintains it as a primary agenda item.

Without constant support and an atmosphere of trust, it is easy for teachers to return to what is known and familiar. It is imperative that those of us who are involved in successful inclusionary practices take the time to gather data, particularly from a longitudinal perspective, that show where the successes are and why they are occurring. We must report our findings in ways that are clear to our teachers, our community, and our school board members.

We must talk and talk and talk—about kids, about curricula, about schedules, about pedagogy, about shortcomings, about strengths, about planning, about problem solving, about miscommunications, and about disagreements.

INCLUSION OF STUDENTS
WITH DISABILITIES MUST BE SOLIDLY
BASED WITHIN GENERAL EDUCATION REFORM EFFORTS

Performance-based standards, portfolio assessments, senior exhibitions, student-centered learning, multiculturalism, service learning, and school-to-work programs—there is certainly no shortage of general education reform initiatives! The challenge for schools is to adopt those new practices that support the core values and long-range plans that reflect community needs and effective practices. Unfortunately, students with disabilities have not been included as an integral part of most school reform efforts. If they are included at all, it is often as an afterthought or in response to advocacy from special educators or parents.

How does a high school address the needs of a diverse student population while implementing an innovative reform effort? At Santana High School, just east of San Diego, the community responded to this challenge by establishing a number of expected schoolwide learning results or standards (Table 1) to address historically high dropout rates, segregated special education classes, low academic achievement, and graduates underprepared for their careers. (A thumbnail sketch of Santana High School follows.) The performance measures that align with the standards are interpreted in such a way that all students can achieve them, albeit with different kinds and levels of support.

The implementation of these new standards required a number of adjustments to the traditional operation of the school, including changes in the curriculum, instructional methods, perceived ability tracking, departmental structures, and the bell schedule. The staff discovered that changing any one of these elements affected all of the others. For example, as teachers changed how they delivered their curriculum, the traditional 54-minute period schedule was adjusted. The composition of teaching teams changed from a departmental focus to one that was interdisciplinary and theme based. Given the history of inclusive education at this school, special educators were expected to be part of the planning and implementation teams from the

Table 1.   Santana High School expected schoolwide learning results

Students will become . . .

EFFECTIVE COMMUNICATORS WHO . . .
- Read, write, speak, and listen reflectively and critically for a variety of purposes and audiences
- Can perform in both collaborative and individual environments
- Are exposed to strategies for resolving conflicts

SELF-DIRECTED LEARNERS WHO . . .
- Gather and utilize information and demonstrate strategies to solve problems
- Coordinate time management and organizational skills
- Create intellectual, artistic, practical, and physical products

EFFECTIVE USERS OF TECHNOLOGY WHO . . .
- Access, research, and organize information for personal, educational, and career purposes

INVOLVED CITIZENS WHO . . .
- Examine and respond to social, health, and environmental issues
- Can identify the positive aspects of diversity

KNOWLEDGEABLE, EFFECTIVE CANDIDATES FOR THE WORLD OF WORK WHO . . .
- Recognize the relationship between school and the workplace
- Set short- and long-term goals and work progressively toward their achievement
- Possess the requisite skills for the examination of a variety of career options

start. This ensured that students with disabilities were explicitly part of this school's reform agenda. One of the most controversial educational debates at Santana and elsewhere centers on tracking or grouping of students by their perceived ability (Oakes, 1985; Wheelock, 1992). A group of Santana science teachers who had positive experiences with heterogeneous classrooms that included students with disabilities decided to detrack their courses. The decision to detrack sciences led to the adoption of a new approach to science education. The discrete sciences of biology, chemistry, physics, and geology were coordinated into a 2-year thematic sequence. Thus, all ninth-grade students, regardless of their perceived ability, enrolled in "Science and Me," which included aspects of each of the discrete sciences as they relate to the individual.

A Thumbnail Sketch of Santana High School

Santana High School is located about 20 miles east of San Diego in southern California. Current enrollment is more than 1,800 students, representing the cultural and linguistic diversity of the community. Santana is a member of the Second to None school alliance, a high school reform initiative in California. Prior to 1992, the school had 28 students identified as having significant disabilities who received their instruction in special day classes and community-based environments. Presently, all students with significant disabilities attend general education classes for the entire school day. A block schedule whereby students attend three 90-minute classes daily for a 9-week quarter was instituted in 1994, and, as a result, teachers have initiated thematic instruction and cooperative learning strategies. This alternative school-wide schedule provides a common planning period for teachers at the end of each school day. Over time, as the curriculum has become more integrated, related services, including speech and physical therapy, have been incorporated into daily schedules. Santana was recognized for its accomplishments by *Exceptional Parent* magazine with an education award in 1996.

SUPPORT FOR TEACHERS AND ADMINISTRATORS DURING THE CHANGE PROCESS MUST BE PROVIDED THROUGH INTERNAL STRUCTURES AND THROUGH ASSOCIATION WITH AN OUTSIDE "CRITICAL FRIEND"

Common to every single school that has sustained a major change in educational philosophy and practice is their commitment to support teachers during the change process and their association with one or more outside-the-school "critical friends" (Olson, 1994). At Souhegan High School, that support has been provided through a number of different strategies and forums, including the following:

1. Traditional staff development and in-service training
2. Association with the UNH Restructuring and Inclusion Project
3. Membership in the Coalition of Essential Schools and the Annenberg Institute for School Reform
4. Provision of time and support for teachers to engage in reflective inquiry about their curriculum and their teaching practice

Two of these elements, reflective inquiry and association with a critical friend, have been particularly useful in ensuring the effective implementation of Souhegan's commitment to inclusion and heterogeneous grouping.

Curriculum Tuning, a Reflective Inquiry Process, Evaluates Curriculum Design

Curriculum tuning provides teachers with a structure for getting constructive feedback on curriculum as it is in the process of being designed and on the effectiveness of teaching by evaluation of students' end-of-unit exhibitions or demonstrations (Allen, 1995). The basic structure of tuning is relatively simple and consists of the following format. A teacher or teaching team asks a group of colleagues for feedback on a curriculum idea or on end-of-unit student work. He or she (or they) is the "tunee" and two to four colleagues invited by the tunee are the "tuners." Prior to the tuning meeting, the tunee disseminates a one-page description of the unit or the student work that will be tuned. The tuners are responsible for familiarizing themselves with this material prior to the tuning session. A facilitator not participating as a tuner keeps the group focused and structured according to the protocol, and someone not participating directly in the tuning functions as a debriefer at the conclusion of the session. At the appointed time for the tuning, all of the participants gather in a classroom or conference room and promise to devote a minimum of 40 minutes to the discussion. The tuning protocol is presented in Table 2.

The notes from an actual tuning session illustrate how the process works with real teachers and a real curriculum. Souhegan ninth-grade science teacher Chris Balch had an idea for teaching students about the environmental impact of careless disposal of toxic products com-

Table 2.   Tuning protocol

1. *Introduction by the facilitator* (10 minutes): The facilitator explains the protocol, and participants introduce themselves.
2. *Tunee presentation* (5–10 minutes): The teacher asking for feedback presents a brief description of the unit or examples of student work. He or she may bring books, articles, equipment, or other learning resources if they will enhance the tuners' understanding of the lesson. During this presentation, the tuners take notes as necessary.
3. *Clarifying questions* (5 minutes): The tuners then have the opportunity to ask one to three concise clarifying questions to enable them to get a clear understanding of the unit or student work being presented. These questions should not be thinly disguised feedback or judgments and should need only a brief answer by the tunee.
4. *Tuners record warm and cool comments* (5–10 minutes): The tuners then record warm (i.e., complimentary) and cool (i.e., questioning or challenging) comments or questions. The tunee can express a preference for the cool comments to be phrased as questions or as direct statements and recommendations.
5. *Tuners share cool and warm comments with tunee* (10 minutes): There are two choices for how the tuners' comments can be communicated with the tunee. The first choice is for the tuners to share their warm and cool comments directly with the tunee in a round-robin fashion. The second format allows the tuners to have a conversation aloud among themselves in which they discuss the unit or work being presented, focusing on both warm and cool comments, additional ideas for the unit, or other feedback. During this portion of the tuning, the tunee takes notes and does not interact with the tuners.
6. *Reflection/response* (10 minutes): At the conclusion of the feedback period by the tuners, the tunee then has a "conversation with him- or herself" aloud or with his teaching partner about selected warm and cool comments. A critical point is that the tunee can respond to any or all of the comments but does not have to justify why particular comments were ignored. This protocol gives tunees the power and prerogative of choosing just those comments that seem most useful at the present time.
7. *Debrief* (10 minutes): At the conclusion of the formal tuning, the debriefer asks the participants to reflect on their contributions and the usefulness of the process. He or she gives participants feedback on their communication skills and whether they were appropriately self-critical.

monly found around the home, garage, and garden. He asked for some specific feedback on the sequencing and timing of activities and suggestions for activities that would illuminate this issue. He also wondered which types of organisms would be appropriate to survey and the measurement tools that would identify those organisms.

The Tunees: Chris Balch, ninth-grade science teacher, and Fran Harrow, school nurse (his teaching partner for some units during the semester)
The Tuners: Diane Glidden, Bruce Shotland, and Paul Schlotman, science teachers
The Facilitator: Allison Rowe

The Debriefer: Jennifer Mueller
The Unit: "The Danger Zone at Home," describing how toxic waste
  pollution occurs in your home and its effect on living systems

Description of Lesson

Chris: I don't have it all worked out yet, but here's how I think the
           unit would go. Students would brainstorm a list of the toxic
           substances present in their homes. They would design and
           conduct a home survey of which substances are actually pres-
           ent. After sharing the survey results in class, they would talk
           about how those substances are commonly disposed of. I
           would facilitate a discussion of the environmental impact of
           disposal methods. Students would then do a pond survey to
           see what living systems exist there. They would research the
           concentrations of toxins that might actually be dumped into a
           pond. They then might do a sequential dilution of the toxic
           substance and test the impact on pond life that has been
           brought into the classroom laboratory.

Clarifying Questions

Bruce: How long will this unit take?
Chris: 3–4 days.
 Paul: What do you want them to get out of this? What are your
           learning outcomes?
Chris: Well, I haven't gotten to the point where I have written down
           all of the skills that I want them to have. I wanted to get your
           feedback first. But generally, I want them to refine their field
           research skills within a real-life application.

Discussion Among Tuners

In this instance, the tuners had a free-flowing discussion while Chris
and Fran took notes.

Would probably take longer than 3–4 days to do justice to it. After you do
the house survey, you could have them do an LD 50 using brine shrimp.
You could graph concentration versus kill ratio. What are the ethical con-
siderations of killing the brine shrimp for the sake of this experiment? This
seems to be a great unit for students with diverse learning styles. It has
hands-on activities, real-life implications, and lots of opportunity for some
critical analysis, and consideration of multiple points of view and competing priorities. Don't forget about "casual chemicals": substances that don't
necessarily have warning signs. This project is great. Ties into Project 2061.
Could be a full-year project in which you poison brine shrimp and then
feed them to guppies to see the impact on the food chain. Good opportunity
to teach them about the entire watershed system and how dumping affects
all parts of it. It would be more authentic to study a real pond that has

toxic substances and watch it throughout a year to see the impact on the actual pond life. If you are going to put the effort into this activity, it should really be beefed up and part of a more comprehensive unit so that kids don't just think it's an isolated activity.

Allison (as facilitator):   I think Chris and Fran are still asking about the timing issue. Could it be a small unit and still retain its usefulness and authenticity?

The tuners each responded "no"—they did not think that the unit would be authentic in an abbreviated form.

Tunees Reflect on Feedback

Chris's and Fran's reflections: I guess it would definitely take longer than 2 or 3 days. If we don't include the pond water survey and do only the home toxins testing, then that will be about 4 days by itself. We could still fit in the LD 50 test. I think using the real pond would make it authentic and meaningful to the kids. I like the hard data collection LD 50 test. Graphing concentrations versus percentage of survival and kills. The ethics question is interesting. We could have someone from a testing laboratory that does not use animals talk to the students about the limitations and advantages of using computer models or nonanimal systems. Finding a real toxic pond would be great.

Whole-Group Discussion of Process

Jennifer, the debriefer, then asked the participants to reflect on their participation and the usefulness of the process. Their comments included the following:

> You can get a lot of curriculum ideas early on even without a lot of prior preparation. Using tuning during the design process makes it more of a collaborative activity than a critical one. Using a protocol helps people stay focused on curriculum. It's a way to share information about what your colleagues have done. Interdisciplinary curriculum develops naturally when people share.

Issues relating to heterogeneous grouping or inclusion can be brought out during a tuning or can be the focus question that brings people together. At Souhegan, a special education teacher asked a group of

colleagues to "tune" her role on a teaching team and provide suggestions for how she might increase her effectiveness as a teaching
partner.

Association with a Critical Friend

The second strategy for advancing a systematic change process, and
one that was critical to Souhegan's inclusive education commitment,
was their association with the UNH Institute on Disability through a
federal research grant. The notion of a *critical friend*, or someone who
is an "outsider on the inside," is a foundation of the Coalition of
Essential Schools' work with their member institutions (Olson, 1994).
A critical friend, though not a part of the day-to-day activities of the
school, is known and respected by the faculty and administration. He
or she spends time at the school, not just in meetings, but in classrooms, watching and talking to teachers and students to get an understanding of the explicit culture of the school as it is reflected in
curriculum, teaching, and policies, as well as the implicit culture and
climate of the school that can be sensed after a period of time on site.
A critical friend is a part of important conversations at the school. He
or she listens carefully, clarifies people's comments, and provides context to the discussion by supplying information about other schools'
experiences and what is being discussed in the research literature.
After trust is established and the critical friend's expertise acknowledged, gentle questions can guide teachers and administrators to
deeper levels of reflection and toward new ways of solving dilemmas.

The association of one of this chapter's coauthors (Cheryl M. Jorgensen) with Souhegan High School exemplified this critical friend
role. During the first few months of the federally funded research
project that was housed at Souhegan, Cheryl spent 2 or 3 days per
week on site, just roaming the halls, eating lunch with teachers and
students, attending general faculty meetings, and, when invited, visiting classrooms. Gradually, teachers extended her an invitation to attend team meetings. Again, at first, she just listened and facilitated
discussions that were stuck. Soon, teachers began to ask her opinion
about issues specifically related to students with disabilities. She provided brief answers to their queries initially but gradually became a
more vocal participant in discussion of overall curriculum design and
personalization for all students.

Teachers' and administrators' comments about Cheryl's role illustrate the power of the critical friend in introducing an innovation
(i.e., inclusion), solving problems relating to its implementation, and
institutionalizing its principles and values into the culture and daily
operation of the school.

A modern language teacher: Cheryl didn't so much tell us what we should do, she just kept asking questions and guiding us toward finding the answers that would work for us.

The principal: Cheryl served as our "roving conscience" relative to inclusion. Because she was present so much in our school, we began to think about how everything we did was going to affect students with disabilities.

A science teacher: When I found out that I was going to have students with significant disabilities in my class, I really panicked. It wasn't that I didn't want them there, but I just didn't have any idea about what I could offer them . . . what they were supposed to get out of being in my science class. After having Cheryl work with our team last year, I now think automatically about how I'm going to design a unit that addresses all of the kids in my class.

SOCIAL JUSTICE ISSUES, INCLUDING DISABILITY, MUST BE INFUSED THROUGHOUT THE CURRICULUM

Out of frustration with the increasing racial tension at Santana High School, a tenth-grade English teacher proposed a new unit on social justice. Her colleagues were interested in the concept but understood that adopting this 9-week unit for the entire tenth grade required a revision in the core literature selection. While discussing the choices for reading material, the teachers and several inclusion project consultants—this school's critical friends—realized that, if the purpose of the unit was to focus on human rights and how a just society treats its citizens, then they needed to include information on all citizens. As a result, the focus of the unit expanded to include issues of disability, gender, sexual orientation, and socioeconomic status.

The Social Justice Project was introduced to the first group of students, who were required to choose and research a social problem in their community, such as domestic violence, homelessness, voting rights, or immigration. Students were required to conduct two interviews. The first interview was designed to find out how one of their own family members felt about this subject. The second interview, with a key person from a social services agency, focused on possible solutions to the social justice issue. In addition to an oral presentation on their findings, students wrote reports and helped design their own plan for how a "just" city should be organized.

After participating in the unit, students generalized the lessons they learned to additional subject areas. Some asked their teachers to relate some of these social justice issues to other problems and areas of study. For example, one senior in his twelfth-grade Shakespeare class asked about people with disabilities playing the role of court jesters. He had difficulty reconciling such treatment of people in an era of perceived cultural enlightenment. Over time, additional examples of infusing social justice issues into the curriculum included a core reading requirement of Steinbeck's (1937) *Of Mice and Men*, a "film as literature" class that examined the role of individuals with disabilities and women in media, a science class project in which students modified a laboratory chair for a student with multiple disabilities, a child development class that included an open discussion and paper on the birth of a child with a disability, and a psychology class that focused on conflict resolution and race and human relations.

The cumulative effect of these and similar experiences is an acceptance of all students, including those with disabilities, as members of the school community. In an inclusive, restructuring school, students are continually encouraged to examine their values, beliefs, and behaviors. We were convinced that this practice—a focus on social justice issues—was essential when LaSheieka shared her decathlon speech. When she becomes the physician she wants to be, LaSheieka's high school experience will remain with her and she will be well prepared for the multicultural world in which she will practice.

In Chapter 4, three nuts-and-bolts issues related to school restructuring and inclusive education are discussed: creative use of time, roles of general and special education teachers, and heterogeneous grouping. Implementation suggestions for teachers and administrators related to Chapters 3 and 4 are found at the end of Chapter 4.

REFERENCES

Allen, D. (1995). *The tuning protocol: A process for reflection.* Providence, RI: Coalition of Essential Schools.

Benjamin, S. (1989). An ideascape for education: What futurists recommend. *Educational Leadership, 47*(1), 8–14.

Fullan, M., & Steigelbauer, S. (1991). *The new meaning of educational change.* New York: Teachers College Press.

Glasser, W. (1990). *The quality school.* New York: HarperCollins.

Goodlad, J. (1984). *A place called school.* New York: McGraw-Hill.

Lipsky, D.K., & Gartner, A. (Eds.). (1989). *Beyond separate education: Quality education for all.* Baltimore: Paul H. Brookes Publishing Co.

National Commission on Excellence in Education. (1983). *A nation at risk: The imperative for educational reform.* Washington, DC: U.S. Government Printing Office.

Oakes, J. (1985). *Keeping track. How schools structure inequality.* New Haven, CT: Yale University Press.

Olson, L. (1994, May 4). Critical friends. *Education Week,* 20–27.

Patterson, J., Purkey, S., & Parker, J. (1986). *Productive school systems for a non-rational world.* Alexandria, VA: Association for Supervision and Curriculum Development.

Sizer, T. (1992). *Horace's school: Redesigning the American high school.* Boston: Houghton Mifflin.

Stainback, S., Stainback, W., & Forest, M. (Eds.). (1989). *Educating all students in the mainstream of regular education.* Baltimore: Paul H. Brookes Publishing Co.

Steinbeck, J. (1937). *Of mice and men.* New York: Modern Library.

Villa, R.A., Thousand, J.S., Stainback, W., & Stainback, S. (Eds.). (1992). *Restructuring for caring and effective education: An administrative guide to creating heterogeneous schools.* Baltimore: Paul H. Brookes Publishing Co.

Wheelock, A. (1992). *Crossing the tracks: How "untracking" can save America's schools.* New York: New Press.

4

Innovative Scheduling, New Roles for Teachers, and Heterogeneous Grouping

The Organizational Factors Related to Student Success in Inclusive, Restructuring Schools

Cheryl M. Jorgensen, Douglas Fisher,
Caren Sax, and Kathryn L. Skoglund

Although the philosophy and values discussed in Chapter 3 form a strong foundation for school reform, there are a number of nuts-and-bolts practices that must also be changed in order for the vision of reform based on those values to become reality. These practices include the creative use of time through a restructured school schedule, new roles for general and special education teachers that reflect shared responsibility for all students, and the elimination of tracking and ability grouping. Not only does each of these practices affect student success and belonging, but all three are interrelated in their contribution to a positive school climate.

This interrelationship is evident in the following description of Heritage High School, a fictitious but representative school in which the philosophical and organizational separation of general and special education stands in the way of the achievement of equity and excellence. Heritage's schedule, teacher roles, and tracking are critiqued, followed by a discussion of how changes in these practices would promote educational improvement for all students.

A DESCRIPTION OF HERITAGE HIGH SCHOOL

Heritage High School's school year is 180 days long, and a 6-week summer session is offered for students who fail a class during the academic year. The school day is divided into 7 instructional periods, each about 50 minutes long. Each of Heritage's 1,800 students is enrolled in an academic path. These paths include honors, college prep, general, tech-prep, and special education. Class sizes in the honors and special education tracks are small—between 12 and 15 students. College preparation classes have about 25 students, and some general track classes have 30 students. The schedule is arranged in such a way that a student who wants to enroll in a course or two outside of his or her primary track often has difficulty scheduling it. The grading system ranges from F to A+; most teachers scale or curve their grades. In some honors classes, grades are given a premium weighting when it is time to calculate students' cumulative grade point averages. In an honors class, a B− is actually calculated as a B to acknowledge that a student in an honors class would probably get a higher grade if he or she had not taken on the challenge of honors work.

Behind the student parking lot is an alternative school housed in two modular units. Sixteen students, some from neighboring school

This chapter was supported in part by Grants H023R20018 and H086V40007 from the U.S. Department of Education, Office of Special Education and Rehabilitative Services.

districts, attend this school, which is staffed by two teachers and four teaching assistants.

Most teachers at Heritage High are organized into departments based on the subject area they teach (e.g., English, foreign languages, math, science, social studies, practical arts, fine arts, computer science). Each teacher has a classroom (although foreign language teachers rove), and there are offices for some of the department chairs. Teachers' rooms are located throughout the building. Curriculum planning is done on a departmental basis. None of the national professional organizations' standards (e.g., National Council of Teachers of Mathematics, National Council of Teachers of English) have been adopted; but curriculum committees are using the state curriculum frameworks to realign their curriculum, primarily in response to Heritage students' poor performance on the statewide tenth-grade assessment test.

One of the most exciting developments at Heritage High School is a result of the national school-to-work initiative. A local school-to-work council composed of students, teachers, and community members has developed community-based learning experiences for students at Heritage to better prepare them for the world of work after graduation.

Special education teachers at Heritage High have their own departmental office and teachers' lounge. There are four self-contained classrooms: one for students with emotional disabilities, one for students labeled trainably mentally retarded, one for students labeled educably mentally retarded, and one for students with language-learning disabilities. Students in these classes go outside of their classroom for physical education, music, lunch, and one or two lower-level mainstream classes; but most of their instruction is provided by special education teachers in their self-contained classrooms. There are two resource rooms in the building where English and math classes are taught throughout the day for students who are primarily enrolled in the general education track. In addition, many students come to the resource room for one-to-one tutorial or homework assistance.

Students with disabilities are included in mainstream classes in two different ways. First, some students with mild disabilities attend class unaccompanied because they are ready to handle the curriculum without any particular support or modification. The classroom teacher usually finds out that these students have an individualized education program (IEP) when they get their class roster at the beginning of the year. Teachers receive each student's modification sheet (describing seating preferences, the student's preferred learning style, and testing accommodations); but if they wish to see the student's IEP, they must sign it out of the special education office. Meetings between the classroom teacher and special education teacher are held on an as-needed basis, and the classroom teacher is responsible for grading the student.

The second manner in which students are included is through support from a teaching assistant. These students (from the trainable or educable classes) usually have more significant disabilities than students with mild disabilities in mainstream classes and may attend classes in music, art, or science. Support is provided by a teaching assistant who is responsible for sitting with the student in the class, adapting tasks on the spot, and working with the student outside of class to complete an occasional homework assignment or project. The special education teacher who coordinates these students' programs meets with the classroom teacher once at the beginning of the year to tell the teacher about the goals of the students' participation and then once per month to see how things are going. At the end of each term, the special education teacher works with the classroom teacher to determine the students' grades. Pass/fail grading is often used; but if a student is assigned a letter grade, it is followed by an asterisk on the report card, signifying that modifications were made to expectations or instruction.

When staff development workshops are held, teachers usually attend sessions that deal with their own subject area—math teachers go to the math workshops, and English teachers go to the English workshops. Special education teachers and staff have their own workshops dealing with issues such as behavior management, writing IEPs, and transition after graduation.

As a result of parent advocacy and technical assistance from outside consultants, three students with severe disabilities are included in general education classes for most of their school day, although determining the academic level in which these students will be enrolled is a constant struggle. Although the smaller class size and teaching style of many honors classes might provide an accommodating learning environment, the norm is for the students to be included in business math, alternative English, and applied life sciences classes, where instruction is teacher directed and workbook based.

Assessing the Quality of Education at Heritage

If Heritage High School teachers and administrators were to critically examine their student outcomes and educational practices, what might they find? Certainly, they would have much to be proud of. Each year the top 10 graduating seniors are accepted by prestigious universities.

The school is, by and large, a safe environment for learning, and students who are enrolled in extracurricular activities are proud of their school. Many students would report that they have teachers who take a personal interest in them and that they like going to school.

However, they might also discover that too few students take on the challenge of honors work or attempt the advanced placement (AP) examinations. In comparison with many other schools in their state, the percentage of students going on to higher education might be low. A follow-up study of students who were enrolled in special education at Heritage might find that most students labeled emotionally disabled are unemployed, the majority of students labeled mentally retarded live in segregated housing, and many students labeled learning disabled who go on to college drop out during their first year.

A close look at the curriculum for Heritage students might show that though there are some teachers who require students to show what they know by exhibition, most teachers evaluate students by using methods that measure rote learning or factual understanding, not evaluation or synthesis. Few interdisciplinary links between subject areas are made explicit for students.

Although the teaching staff are caring and committed to their students, the climate in the school is not characterized by enthusiasm and innovation. Many teachers might report that they would like to try different instructional techniques to increase student motivation and engagement, but they would probably feel constrained by the short class periods as well as by the lack of time for planning.

Undoubtedly, special education teachers would feel particularly disenfranchised. Their classrooms and offices are in a separate wing of the building, they have no opportunity for collaborative planning with their general education colleagues that might result in a more accommodating curriculum for students with disabilities, and they know that many of their students miss out on a positive high school experience because of their isolation within the school.

If Heritage teachers and administrators delved into the educational literature for some guidance about what they might change to improve teaching and learning, they would discover that three of their current practices stand in the way. Like many other high schools, Heritage needs to create a school schedule that provides longer blocks of instructional and collaborative team planning time; they must restructure the roles of general and special education teachers to reflect shared responsibility for all students; and they need to eliminate tracking and ability grouping to facilitate higher expectations and performance of all students within the mainstream of general education. The rationale for each of these changes is described in the remainder of this chapter and is illustrated by examples from schools engaged in unified school restructuring and inclusive education efforts.

CREATIVE USE OF TIME THROUGH IMPLEMENTATION OF INNOVATIVE SCHOOL SCHEDULES IS ESSENTIAL

The first organizational or structural barrier that impedes school reform efforts relative to equity and excellence is the daily schedule. Although data from one survey showed that 39% of high schools had changed to or were considering some form of block scheduling (Cawelti, 1994), students in most high schools are still "prisoners of time," according to a national study on school restructuring conducted by the National Education Commission on Time and Learning (1994).

Disadvantages of the Traditional High School Schedule

The traditional high school schedule, typified by Heritage's 7-period day with students going from subject to subject after 50-minute classes, results in fragmented instruction and learning; a lack of common planning time for teachers; and an impersonal, hectic school climate.

Day after day, short class periods are not conducive to teachers' use of instructional methods that result in high levels of student engagement, active learning, interaction, or authentic work. By the time students settle down at their desks and teachers do daily housekeeping tasks such as taking attendance or collecting homework, there are barely 45 minutes remaining. Science teachers often must spread laboratory experiments over several days, resulting in a lack of cohesiveness. Social studies teachers find it difficult to engage students in in-depth dialogue because of the short amount of class time. In an English class, teachers rarely have time for students to read, discuss, and write in one class period, so they resort to lectures. Even those teachers who would like to structure active, authentic learning experiences (e.g., sampling from a nearby pond and conducting experiments to determine pollution levels) are prevented from doing so by the structure of the day. This lack of instructional creativity is caused as much by the inadequacy of the organization (i.e., the school schedule) as by the shortcomings of its members (i.e., teachers) (Bonstingl, 1992).

For students with disabilities, short, fragmented classes are usually ineffective learning environments. Students who need a bit of extra time to locate their homework and focus their attention often miss large chunks of information because of the pace at which most teachers deliver information in an attempt to get through their material in the short period. Because of short class periods, teachers rarely utilize cooperative learning structures and students with disabilities miss out on valuable opportunities for social and academic interaction.

The typical high school structure also inhibits collaborative curriculum planning and teaching. General education teachers are isolated not only from their general education colleagues but also from special educators. Although most teachers have a period or two of preparation time every day, there is usually no attempt by administrators to schedule teachers' planning periods so that colleagues with whom they would like to collaborate are free at the same time. Even when colleagues *are* able to find a common planning period, 50 minutes is too short a time to fully develop an idea into a workable lesson or unit plan.

The third disadvantage of the traditional high school schedule is its contribution to a negative school climate. Walk through the halls of a large public high school that operates under a traditional schedule. Every 50 minutes, there is chaos in the halls as students rush from room to room with barely enough time to visit their lockers.

Block Scheduling Can Facilitate School Restructuring and Inclusion

The implementation of block scheduling is a tool that facilitates improved learning for all students and provides structural support for the inclusion of students with disabilities. It is a powerful albeit underutilized tool in achieving school reform (Canady & Rettig, 1995a).

Impact on Student Learning and Teaching Time

The creative use of time through restructuring of the typical high school schedule can lead to improvement in learning as well as more inclusive practices (Canady & Rettig, 1995b). The most commonly used block-scheduling format—the 4 × 4 plan—illustrates the advantages of most innovative schedules being used in the United States (Edwards, 1993). The school year is still divided into 2 semesters. Students enroll in four academic courses each semester that meet daily for approximately 90 minutes. Because twice as much instructional time is available each day, students complete a whole year's coursework in 1 semester. This block-scheduling plan acknowledges that the time required for learning varies greatly from student to student (Canady & Rettig, 1995b). Under this plan, both acceleration and relearning opportunities are possible for all students, without the stigma of makeup classes or pull-out services. Students who need more time to master course material are able to take the same course again during the second semester of the year. Instead of dropping out at midterm in a traditional school because they feel that they will never catch up before the end of the year, students know that they have another whole semester in which to demonstrate their proficiency and achieve a passing grade. Students who are able to complete most course requirements in 1 semester then have the opportunity to enroll in advanced high school– or college-level courses during their senior year.

Santana High School's schedule is representative of a school with a mixed block schedule, which is depicted below:

Block 1   7:30–8:30
Block 2   8:36–10:10
Block 3   10:30–12:04
Block 4   12:45–2:19
Block 5   2:25–3:25

Block 1 is a traditional semester-long course that is mainly used for elective classes such as student council, AP exam preparation, music, and yearbook. Blocks 2–4 are 9-week-long classes in which a traditional semester's worth of material is covered. Block 5 is a common planning period for teachers and is used as a tutorial period for students who need to use the library, see their counselor, or make up some work. Thus, the majority of students attend three 94-minute academic classes per day for 9 weeks. As a result, teachers interact with approximately 90 students per week rather than more than 175 (as is typical in a traditional high school) and have time each day to collaborate with colleagues. The impact of block scheduling on students with disabilities is summarized in Table 1.

Block Scheduling Creates Common Planning Time

A second benefit of a restructured school schedule based on blocks of time is the natural creation of common planning time. Because teachers teach fewer classes per day and the preparation periods that they have are longer, the free periods that they have are longer, too. With half as many classes per day to schedule, it is twice as easy for administrators to align common planning periods for teachers who wish to work together. When special education teachers take part in the design of curriculum, accommodation for students with disabilities can be incorporated into the lesson plan right from the start. (Inclusive lesson design is addressed in Chapter 5.)

At Souhegan High School, common planning time for ninth- and tenth-grade teachers was provided by instituting a teaming structure within a block schedule. For a 3-hour block of time in the morning

Table 1.   Characteristics of block schedules and impact on the inclusion of students with disabilities

Characteristics of block schedules	Impact on inclusion of students with disabilities
Each class period is longer.	There is more time for teachers to give individual attention to students.
	Teachers use more accommodating teaching strategies.
Teachers see fewer students every day.	Fewer students means more opportunity for teachers to get to know students personally.
Students can complete 1 year's coursework in less time.	Students can take a greater variety of courses or accelerate their education.
Teachers teach fewer classes each day.	There are fewer classes for special education teachers to support.
	Special education teachers need to become familiar with fewer content areas each semester.
Students take fewer classes per day.	Students with disabilities can register for a lighter course load.
Teachers have longer preparation periods.	More opportunities exist for meaningful collaborative planning with special education teachers.
Students pass classes fewer times each day.	There are fewer occasions for behavior problems to arise.
Students and teachers report feeling less rushed and more satisfied with school.	Teachers feel generally more positive about teaching.
	When teachers' basic classroom needs are met, they are more open to risk and innovation.
Students "encounter" less material in each class but master more (O'Neil, 1995).	With less material for students to master, it is easier to identify the most important learning goals for students with disabilities.

and a 1½-hour block of time in the afternoon, a team of four general education teachers, a special education teacher or teaching assistant, and approximately 100 students study English, math, social studies, and science. The use of each block of time is totally within the control of the teaching team. One week, the schedule may be adjusted so that students have a double period of each subject every other day. When interdisciplinary units are being taught, teachers can suspend the typical class schedule altogether and work with small groups of students throughout their wing of the building. If the math teacher needs extra time to introduce a new concept, then the science teacher might give up a period or two.

When students are off-team in their elective, arts, and modern language classes, the core academic teachers have daily common planning time. They are joined by the special education teacher who is a member of their team and, on 1 day each week, a guidance counselor. These common planning times also provide an opportunity for parents to meet with many of their children's teachers at one time. The typical ninth- or tenth-grade schedule at Souhegan is depicted next:

7:30–10:00	Academic Block
10:00–11:30	Electives, Arts, Languages (core teachers have planning time)
11:30–12:00	Lunch
12:00–12:30	Advisory
12:30–2:10	Academic Block

Even in schools that have not changed to a block schedule, common planning time can be found if it is a priority for staff and administration. The vignette that follows illustrates how time for planning can be provided for teachers within a school that utilizes a traditional schedule.

An Example of Common Planning Time within a Traditional Schedule

Even in districts that have not yet moved to a totally restructured school day, it is possible to create time for instructional planning to facilitate inclusion if the school community is ready for it. This was the situation in a school district in New Mexico. Of the 1,800 students in this rural district, approximately 69% were Latino, 15% were Native American, and 15% were Caucasian; the remaining 1% were African American or Asian American. The students with disabilities, who composed 17% of the total school population, had IEPs that addressed their needs within the context of general education classes. All of the teachers had received training, technical assistance, and support with regard to curricular adaptations, collaboration, and multilevel instruction (Collicott, 1991). Family members were involved in program development and had regular interaction with district administrators. School site-based decision-making teams had written action plans to revise their curriculum and instruction to include thematic and authentic units, cooperative groups, block scheduling, and essential questions. In addition, a number of community connections had been established with the local college, businesses, health services, a tribal council, and social services agencies.

Based on the research literature, it seemed that the schools in this district were implementing the components necessary for creating inclusive, restructuring schools. However, as one teacher sighed, "Every kid is included, the curriculum is becoming more integrated, and the teachers are more empowered than ever, but our next staff development day isn't for 6 weeks. When do we develop plans to teach?" Obviously, one component that had not been adequately addressed was time for curriculum planning and reflection on practice.

In an effort to create more team planning time, teachers from several schools brainstormed solutions that would not sacrifice total instructional time. The need for consistent planning time within the school day was clear, and it appeared that the idea had districtwide support. The superintendent's only stipulation was that consistency be maintained across schools within the district; that is, a situation could not be allowed to develop in which one school dismissed early on Tuesday and another dismissed early on Wednesday. After many hours of focus groups and asking community members their preferences, it was determined that a late start every other Thursday was a solution that the entire community could accept. This schedule change would not interfere with sports or other after-school events; it would not result in large numbers of teenagers unsupervised on the streets at noon; and parents with younger children in the school system could plan their schedules for their children across grades. In addition, by giving up half of the staff development days allocated under the old system, the total amount of instructional time was not reduced.

Teachers were able to plan integrated lessons with a range of students in mind. As a result, they had fewer curriculum adaptations to make after lessons had been created. In fact, as teachers met and discussed instructional units, it was common to hear them think through the lesson aloud, taking on different student perspectives.

Block Scheduling Creates a More Positive School Climate

The third effect of restructuring the school day is its positive impact on the school climate. At Heritage High School, students and teachers rush from class to class; each teacher instructs more than 120 students per day; and there is little opportunity for teachers to get to know students individually. When teachers have fewer students to teach, they are able to get to know each student more individually—a key to providing a supportive education to all students, including those with disabilities. When Santana High School converted to a block schedule, it experienced a dramatic reduction in disciplinary referrals during a year in which other schools within the same district saw increases (see Table 2).

GENERAL AND SPECIAL EDUCATION TEACHERS WITH NEW JOB DESCRIPTIONS THAT REFLECT SHARED RESPONSIBILITY FOR ALL STUDENTS MUST COLLABORATE TO DESIGN CURRICULUM, TEACH, AND EVALUATE STUDENTS

In traditional schools, general education and special education exist as two separate systems (Lipsky & Gartner, 1989). Curriculum and materials used in special education often do not parallel classroom materials, and the connection is weak between what occurs in the special education classroom and the general education classroom. Communication with parents is infrequent, and generally there is no collaboration between general education and special education teachers. Students leave the general education classroom or are permanently placed outside it to receive specialized instruction that is delivered in a manner different from typical classroom teaching. Responsibility for assessment of student progress is not clear, so parents sometimes receive a report card and a progress report that sometimes seem unrelated. The role of the special education service coordinator, though necessary to some extent, tends to absolve other faculty mem-

Table 2. Comparison of disciplinary referrals under block scheduling

	Number of referrals	
School	1993–1994	1994–1995
Grossmont	7,584	7,627
Helix	5,058	4,899
El Cajon Valley	6,994	9,293
Mount Miguel	8,423	9,059
El Capitan	8,286	9,830
Granite Hills	5,745	6,258
Monte Vista	9,875	10,612
Santana	**5,614**	**2,365**
Valhalla	4,338	5,253
West Hills	3,624	4,436

bers of their responsibilities for students who receive special education services. Communication between special and general education teachers occurs on the fly—during lunch, in the hallways, and before or after school.

According to Sarason (1982), schools tend to mirror the teacher preparation programs from which their teachers graduated. Thus, "is it any wonder that general and special education evolved as separate systems?" (Villa, Thousand, & Chappie, 1996, p. 43). Although there are some examples of college programs that communicate to teachers the expectation that they will educate all of the children in their classes, most are still organized according to categorical labels such as *learning disabilities, emotional and behavioral disabilities, severe disabilities, gifted and talented,* and *general education.*

As schools begin to include students with disabilities within the mainstream and at the same time change many of the traditional practices and structures within that general education environment, a closing of the great divide between special and general education is necessary (Stainback & Stainback, 1984), particularly with respect to teachers' roles. Teachers' roles and responsibilities should be based on a vision of inclusive education as a seamless system in which information is shared among special and general education teachers and parents, curriculum and materials are common, and all students receive the educational instruction and support they need in the same classroom. This new model will not only enhance education for students with disabilities but also benefit all students.

Until teacher education programs restructure their programs to reflect the demands on teachers in today's classrooms, local schools must take the lead in designing this new paradigm. A conversation about new roles for all teachers has been occurring at Souhegan High School since 1992. During the 1993–1994 school year, all faculty were surveyed regarding the roles and responsibilities of both general and special education teachers. After tabulating the results of the survey and talking with all faculty groups, it was clear that the majority of faculty saw a great deal of overlap in the two roles. Based on the survey results and taking Souhegan's mission statement into consideration, new job descriptions for special and general educators were written. Within the school's *Career Ladder* manual, which describes the roles and responsibilities of teachers, the use of teaching strategies for heterogeneous groups of students and collaboration with special education teachers were emphasized. A new special education job description for a learning specialist was also written (see Figure 1). The learning specialist job description reflects the collaborative nature of assessment, curriculum design, instruction, and communication

I. Job responsibilities relating to instruction
    1. Instruction is available to any student for whom the teaching team desires assistance.
    2. Identify and/or gather appropriate instructional materials.
    3. Assist in adapting materials and instruction.
    4. Provide small-group or individual instruction in or out of the classroom.
    5. Teach the whole class.
    6. Keep informed on and assist in utilizing strategies that promote inclusion.
    7. Supervise special education teaching assistants in the classroom.
    8. Monitor students' academic work.
    9. Develop and assist in implementation of behavior management plans.

II. Job responsibilities relating to assessment and evaluation
    1. Grade students' performance.
    2. Administer and interpret educational tests as necessary.
    3. Assist in developing appropriate exhibitions and demonstrations.
    4. Direct special education referrals through proper channels.
    5. Facilitate the prereferral process.

III. Job responsibilities relating to communication
    1. Attend team planning meetings.
    2. Communicate regularly with the parents of students for whom the learning specialist is case manager.
    3. Attend and facilitate update and problem-solving meetings. Keep all teachers informed of student needs and status. This includes elective and foreign language teachers, guidance counselors, and advisors.
    4. Provide support for additional personnel involved in meeting students' needs as specified in IEPs.
    5. Facilitate use of specialists from outside agencies.

IV. Job responsibilities relating to record keeping
    1. Develop and write IEPs with input from teaching teams.
    2. Keep necessary records: Annual Statement of Program, referrals, minutes of meetings, telephone logs.

Figure 1.   Job description of Souhegan High School learning specialist.

among general and special educators and parents. The implications are far reaching for what effective Souhegan special educators must know and be able to do. They must have an in-depth knowledge of curriculum because they will be expected to work with general education teachers as the curriculum is being developed. They must know how to assess what students know relative to that curriculum and how to provide materials and instructional support to help students reach the rigorous standards to which all students at Souhegan are held. Special education teachers must be able to work with individual students and small groups and be able to manage large-group instruction. To ensure collaboration with their general education colleagues in all of these functions, special educators must have strong interpersonal skills.

Although the job description of the learning specialist relates primarily to curriculum and teaching, the learning specialist must also be willing and able to participate with his or her colleagues in broader school conversations and committees that deal with academic standards, curriculum design, disciplinary policy, school climate, and continuous quality improvement. There are a few tasks that remain the primary responsibility of the special educator, such as knowledge of special education regulations and procedures and associated record keeping.

TRACKING HAS BEEN ELIMINATED, AND MOST CLASSES ARE HETEROGENEOUSLY GROUPED

The third and perhaps most emotionally charged innovation that can be proposed by a school is the elimination of tracking and other ability-grouping practices. When tracking is challenged, objections are raised not only from teachers concerned about heterogeneous grouping but also from the parents of students who are in the higher academic tracks (George, 1988). Their concerns echo a number of common though inaccurate beliefs about ability grouping, including the following:

- Ability grouping promotes achievement within all tracks because students can learn at their own rates with students who are similar to them.
- Teachers can tailor instruction better when their students are homogeneous with respect to ability, learning style, and rate of learning.
- Less capable students will get lost and their self-esteem will suffer if they are in heterogeneous classes.
- More able students will be held back by being in heterogeneous classes.
- It is easier for teachers to teach homogeneous classes.
- It is easy to determine in which track or group a student ought to be.
- If tracking and ability grouping are eliminated, then the curriculum as a whole will be watered down because teachers will lower their expectations (i.e., curriculum standards) and slow the pace of instruction to reach the most challenged learners in the classroom.

For students with disabilities, ability grouping and tracking have deleterious consequences. First, tracking within the general education mainstream legitimizes the existence of separate special education classes. In other words, if it is defensible to group students *without* disabilities by some perceived measure of potential or performance, then it is easy to argue that students *with* disabilities are also served well by being grouped with other students with disabilities. Second, when students with disabilities are mainstreamed or included in general education classes within a tracked school environment, teachers tend to place them in the lowest-track classes. They reason that putting students with disabilities in the mainstream will be difficult, so they ought to be placed in a class where they will face the least academic challenge. Even if the teaching style or the content of an upper-level class seems to be a better fit for a particular student with disabilities, placing him or her in a relatively higher track goes against the whole logic and organization of the tracking system. Thus, students with disabilities—who would benefit from the best teachers, the most interesting curriculum, and a more organized and focused classroom environment—are often mainstreamed into the roughest lower-track classes. Third, teachers of lower-level classes are understandably resistant to inclusion because they view students with disabilities as the "straw that breaks the camel's back"—that is, as very needy learners within a class of students who already pose learning and behavioral challenges.

Despite the emotional and political nature of the arguments surrounding tracking, there is a large body of research that is clear about the impact of tracking on student learning. Findings of this body of research, summarized in Table 3, indicate that tracking and ability grouping do not result in consistently higher academic achievement for most students, frequently lead to stigmatization of students in lower tracks, and have a negative impact on measures of student affect such as self-esteem and future aspirations. As long as schools track students without disabilities, inclusion for students with disabilities will be viewed as a challenge to the very foundations of educational philosophy and practice. Administrators will ask themselves, "If we include students with disabilities in higher-track classes, then how will I justify ability grouping to the parents of students in the lower tracks?" Teachers will ask, "If our school tracks the general education students, then how can it make sense to mainstream students whose abilities are so much lower than those of the typical students?" Teachers of lower-track classes will argue that their classes are already overloaded with students who have difficulty learning, so it would not be

Table 3. Summary of research on tracking and ability grouping

Research finding	Source
There is little evidence that ability grouping or tracking improves academic achievement, while there is overwhelming evidence that it retards the academic progress of students in low- and middle-ability groupings. A few studies have found that tracking the highest-achieving students increases their academic performance.	Cotton and Savard (1981) Featherstone (1987) Kulik and Kulik (1982) Oakes (1985) Rowan and Miracle (1983) Slavin (1987)
Expectations of students are higher and instructional practices more effective in higher-track classes.	Good and Brophy (1987) Oakes (1985) Rist (1970)
Ability grouping and tracking widens the achievement and knowledge gap between students.	Rist (1970) Weisendanger and Birlen (1981)
Ability grouping reduces expectations for students' future educational aspirations beyond high school.	Rosenbaum (1976) Schaefer and Olexa (1971)
Low-ability grouped students, including those in special education classes, have lower self-esteem and expectations as well as the social stigma of being less smart.	George (1988) Vanfossen, Jones, and Spade (1987)
Ability grouping and tracking have negative effects on student relationships.	Sorenson and Hallinan (1986)

fair to any of the students to mainstream students with disabilities; they would not get the attention they need, and their presence would detract from the needs of the other students in the class. We have even heard it argued that, if students with disabilities are included in lower-track classes, other students will be self-conscious in confronting "students who are in even worse shape than they are. They'll think that their class is just for students with disabilities, and they won't want to be identified that way."

Elimination of tracking requires a commitment to involving all stakeholders in the detracking process, the provision of time and support for teachers who are responsible for designing new course sequences, and a commitment to staff development to assist teachers with curriculum design and instruction that is effective for heterogeneous groups of students. Because it represents a change that has the potential to have a profound impact on the inclusion of students with disabilities, special educators must be involved in detracking discussions from the beginning. They have not only a vested interest in the success of the effort but also valuable skills and knowledge about learning styles, adaptive curriculum, and effective instruction for diverse learners.

A RESTRUCTURED, INCLUSIVE HIGH SCHOOL

If Heritage High School were to embrace the philosophy and practices described in the previous chapters, how would the school be different? Within every subject area, classes would be detracked. Table 4 illustrates how five levels of ninth-grade English can be reorganized into four heterogeneously grouped classes. When the 12 students from the old special education class are included within the four restructured heterogeneous classes, the special education teacher and teaching assistant are available to teach with their general education colleagues and to provide support to every student in those classes, not just those with identified disabilities.

The change to a block schedule has provided common planning time for general and special education teachers, who meet every day to design curriculum and discuss students with extraordinary learning challenges. Longer class periods result in a number of changes in curriculum and instruction. Teachers use a greater variety of teaching techniques. Within most classes, students are engaged in group work more frequently. Laboratory experiments are started and finished in the same day. In a 90-minute period, teachers find more time to confer with individual students. Science teachers are able to design field experiments because there is enough time to leave the building, get to the field site, do some observations or collections, and get students back to school for their next class. Students with disabilities find it easier to stay organized because they have fewer notebooks of which to keep track. Many students report that they get more out of each class because the teacher seems less hurried and there is more time for questions or individual help.

Table 4.   Conversion of tracked English classes to heterogeneously grouped classes

Old course title	Student enrollment	New course title	Student enrollment
Honors English (one teacher)	16	English 9	25
College prep English (one teacher)	24	English 9	25
General English (one teacher)	30	English 9	25
Tech-prep English (one teacher)	18	English 9	25
Special education English (one teacher and one paraprofessional)	12	N/A	N/A

When it is time to evaluate students' work, teachers assign more authentic tasks. They have not only half as many assignments to grade but also more in-class time for students to present their work and get feedback from their classmates or other observers. Classroom teachers feel more comfortable assigning a grade to the students with disabilities in their classes because they know them personally.

Finally, even though Heritage is a large high school, the atmosphere created by block scheduling would be calmer and quieter than the school experiences under its present schedule. With less movement of students in the hallways, disruptions would decrease and the overall behavioral climate of the school would improve.

CONCLUSIONS

Although the three structural changes described in this chapter provide opportunity and freedom for teachers to redesign curriculum and instruction for their newly diverse classrooms, a conceptual model and practical examples are needed to help teachers figure out, "What do I do Monday morning?" (Falvey, Givner, & Kimm, 1996, p. 117). The elements of an inclusive curriculum design model—the eighth and final practice that is essential for inclusive, restructuring schools—are presented in Chapter 5 and are followed by specific unit and lesson examples in Chapter 6.

Implementation Suggestions for Teachers

1. Compare your school's practices with those outlined in Chapters 3 and 4. Read the literature on innovative scheduling and tracking.
2. Identify one principle or practice that needs to be addressed and in which you would invest time and energy to change.
3. Find out which committee or planning group in your school addresses that issue. If you have a school safety and climate committee or a diversity committee, that is where social justice issues as they relate to students with disabilities should be discussed. Many schools have special education task forces composed of parents and teachers. Every member of that group should join a general education task force or committee.
4. After you identify an appropriate committee, join it! Even if you are the first special education teacher to become a member of that group, and even if the first reaction of people is "We don't deal with special ed issues in this committee," be willing to work on issues that affect the general school population.

5. Share chapters in this book (or other resources that make the connection between inclusion of students with disabilities and overall school improvement or reform) with the members of that group.
6. Ask the group to evaluate your school's practices in one particular area.
7. Gather reading materials to share with the group and propose that each member read one article or chapter and share its contents with the rest of the group at a future meeting.
8. Identify knowledgeable "outside" resource people (e.g., from another school, a nearby university or consulting firm, a professional association, your state department of education) and suggest that they attend a meeting of your group to present their viewpoints.
9. Enlist another teacher or two to work with you on addressing an issue you have targeted to change.

Leadership Suggestions for Administrators

1. Do some investigative work related to the participation and achievement of students with disabilities in your school.
2. Call your state department of education or a state-level professional association to find out the names of schools that are engaged in systemic reforms that include issues of diversity and disability. Talk to their administrators to find out how they have introduced innovative ideas and practices. Visit them and talk to teachers, students, and parents.
3. Locate some reference materials on the topic and share them with your administrative colleagues.
4. Bring up the topic of inclusion of students with disabilities at an administrative team meeting and propose that your school address the issue in a schoolwide, comprehensive manner.
5. If your school already has a school improvement team or some other group that addresses current educational issues, bring the issue of inclusion, tracking, or block scheduling to that group. If such a group does not exist, establish one with an inclusive mission such as investigating how your school makes all students feel a sense of belonging, evaluating achievement of students enrolled in low-track classes, or moving students with disabilities from separate classes into general education classes.
6. Identify a critical friend for your school—an outside person from a local university, a professional association, or your state department of education—whose role is not to evaluate your school but to be a reflective listener and a facilitator of change.

REFERENCES

Bonstingl, J. (1992). *Schools of quality: An introduction to total quality management in education.* Alexandria, VA: Association for Supervision and Curriculum Development.

Canady, R., & Rettig, M. (1995a). *Block scheduling: A catalyst for change in high schools.* Princeton, NJ: Eye on Education.

Canady, R., & Rettig, M. (1995b). The power of innovative scheduling. *Educational Leadership, 53*(3), 4–10.

Cawelti, G. (1994). *High school restructuring: A national study.* Arlington, VA: Educational Research Service.

Collicott, J. (1991). Implementing multi-level instruction: Strategies for classroom teachers. In G. Porter & D. Richler (Eds.), *Changing Canadian schools: Perspectives on disability and inclusion* (pp. 191–218). Downsview, Ontario, Canada: G. Allan Roeher Institute.

Cotton, K., & Savard, W. (1981). *Instructional grouping: Ability grouping* (Topic Summary Report, Research on School Effectiveness Project). Portland, OR: Northwest Regional Educational Laboratory.

Edwards, C. (1993). The four-period day: Restructuring to improve student performance. *NASSP Bulletin, 77*, 77–88.

Falvey, M., Givner, C., & Kimm, C. (1996). What do I do Monday morning? In S. Stainback & W. Stainback (Eds.), *Inclusion: A guide for educators* (pp. 117–139). Baltimore: Paul H. Brookes Publishing Co.

Featherstone, H. (1987). Organizing classes by ability. *Harvard Educational Letter, 3*(4), 1–4.

George, P. (1988). *What's the truth about tracking and ability grouping really???* (Handout). Available from University of Florida, Gainesville.

Good, T., & Brophy, J. (1987). *Looking in classrooms* (4th ed.). New York: Harper & Row.

Kulik, C., & Kulik, J. (1982). Effects of ability grouping on secondary school students: A meta-analysis of evaluation findings. *American Educational Research Journal, 19*(3), 415–428.

Lipsky, D.K., & Gartner, A. (Eds.). (1989). *Beyond separate education: Quality education for all.* Baltimore: Paul H. Brookes Publishing Co.

National Education Commission on Time and Learning. (1994). *Prisoners of time: Report of the National Education Commission on Time and Learning.* Washington, DC: U.S. Government Printing Office.

Oakes, J. (1985). *Keeping track: How schools structure inequality.* New Haven, CT: Yale University Press.

O'Neil, J. (1995). Finding time to learn. *Educational Leadership, 53*(3), 11–15.

Rist, R. (1970). Social class and teacher expectations: The self-fulfilling prophecy in ghetto education. *Harvard Education Review, 49*, 411–451.

Rosenbaum, J. (1976). *Making inequality: The hidden curriculum of high school tracking.* New York: John Wiley & Sons.

Rowan, B., & Miracle, A. (1983). Systems of ability grouping and the stratification of achievement in elementary schools. *Sociology of Education, 26*(3), 133–144.

Sarason, S. (1982). *The culture of the school and the problem of change.* Needham, MA: Allyn & Bacon.

Schaefer, W., & Olexa, C. (1971). *Tracking and opportunity: The locking out process and beyond.* Scranton, PA: Chandler Press.

Slavin, R. (1987). Ability grouping and student achievement in elementary grades: A best-evidence synthesis. *Review of Educational Research, 57*(3), 293–336.

Sorenson, A., & Hallinan, M. (1986). Effects of ability grouping on growth in academic achievement. *American Educational Research Journal, 23,* 519–542.

Stainback W., & Stainback, S. (1984). A rationale for the merger of special and regular education. *Exceptional Children, 51,* 102–111.

Vanfossen, B., Jones, J., & Spade, J. (1987). Curriculum tracking and status maintenance. *Sociology of Education, 60,* 104–122.

Villa, R.A., Thousand, J.S., & Chappie, J. (1996). Preparing teachers to support inclusion: Preservice and in-service programs. *Theory into Practice, 35*(1), 42–49.

Weisendanger, K., & Birlen, E. (1981). A critical look at the reading approaches and grouping currently used in the primary grades. *Reading Horizons, 22*(1), 54–58.

5

Unit and Lesson Planning in the Inclusive Classroom

Maximizing Learning Opportunities for All Students

Joseph J. Onosko and Cheryl M. Jorgensen

Sara

On the first day back from vacation, Sara, a ninth-grade social studies teacher, announced to her class that they would be reading *The Autobiography of Malcolm X* (X, 1962) to start off their study of Black History Month. A few students sat a little straighter in their seats because they were very interested in African American issues and had always wanted to read this book. Several students in the back row uttered a soft "Yes!" They had watched the movie six times in the last year, had seen an interview with Spike Lee about Malcolm X on MTV, and believed that they could ace the unit without opening the book. Four students had read it in eighth grade, but their ninth-grade teacher assured them that they would get something different out of the book this time. Beth, the special education teacher, leaning against the back wall, had a panic-stricken look on her face. She thought to herself, "The teacher didn't tell me. I'll have to get on the phone right now to locate an audiotape version of the book. If we're lucky, they'll get it to us by the beginning of next week. And what about Sam? Maybe if he watches the movie, he might get something out of it. What will he do during class time when they're reading the book?" Sara surveyed the class for some signs of enthusiasm and shook her head at the students' apparent disinterest in good literature.

What's wrong with this picture? *The Autobiography of Malcolm X* is a book of intense interest for an audience dealing with contemporary issues. How is a teacher to interest students in issues that will affect their lives and that have made America what it is today? What gets students interested enough in a subject that they will work to improve their abilities in the areas of reading, writing, speaking, and critical thinking?

Trish Walton, an English teacher in Concord, New Hampshire, experiences little difficulty engaging ninth graders in her heterogeneous English class. Every year she teaches a unit designed around the proposition "Tough Times Don't Last, Tough People Do." Students read a variety of young adult literature such as *I Will Call It Georgie's Blues* (Newton, 1983) and *Remembering the Good Times* (Peck, 1985). During the first half of the unit, each student carefully examines how a character from his or her book made it through tough times. To aid

This chapter was supported in part by Grant H023R20018 from the U.S. Department of Education, Office of Special Education and Rehabilitative Services.

The authors thank Trish Walton, an exceptional ninth-grade English teacher at Rundlett Junior High School in Concord, New Hampshire, for sharing the student performances described in this chapter and for her input during the planning stages of this chapter.

students in their analysis, they answer four questions about their chosen character: "Who is _____?" "What does he or she value?" "Where does he or she find strength and peace?" and "What are his or her support systems?"

The second half of the unit finds students answering the same four questions about themselves and then sharing their reflections in class using a variety of presentation formats. Trish gives students a number of presentation options that reflect an appreciation for students' varied talents, learning styles, preferred modes of communication, and need for ownership. In addition to their presentations, students submit a one-page reflection paper.

Each year a wide variety of projects are shared in Trish's classes. Chad, a student who struggled with school but was not formally identified as having learning disabilities, carved a totem pole out of wood that included a fish, a boat, a basketball, a baseball, and a catcher's mitt. He shared with the class that these objects represented what he valued most in his life. He related that he gained strength and peace from these pursuits and received support from his teammates in difficult times.

Marta, an academically capable student, created a 20-page book composed of original short essays, poems, illustrations, and photographs. Amanda, a student with reading and writing difficulties, made an audiocassette of contemporary songs and oldies that revealed her answers to the four questions. Songs included James Taylor's "You've Got a Friend" (1971), Bette Midler's "Wind Beneath My Wings" (1988), Dire Straits's "Walk of Life" (1985), and The Beatles' "With a Little Help from My Friends" (Lennon & McCartney, 1967).

Some of the culminating projects were collaborative efforts. Four girls wrote and videotaped vignettes showing two very different ways in which parents might tell their children they were divorcing. In the first, the parents simply announced the news to the children with little explanation and then left them to deal with their feelings in isolation. In the second, the parents told their children the news but then discussed with them the fears that the children might have about abandonment, the fact that each parent would still be an important part of their life, and where the kids might go for support when they were feeling sad or needed to talk (e.g., school guidance counselors, clergy, trusted relatives). Each member of the group then wrote a paper sharing the difficulties she experienced when her parents divorced. Each reflected on the coping strategies she used, the sources of peace and strength in her life, and where she received support.

The performances just described represent the kind of thoughtful, creative work that teachers would like to see from all of their students. These students not only acquired new information, ideas, and skills but also were able to relate what they learned to their own lives and the lives of others.

What enables some teachers to consistently generate high levels of engagement, commitment, and performance among so many of their students? Our own work as teachers, supervisors of practicing teachers, and school restructuring consultants commits us to the view that careful unit planning is essential to their success.[1]

Before sharing our ideas on unit planning for the inclusive classroom, we would like to highlight some core assumptions or beliefs about students, learning, and instruction that undergird our planning model and, we surmise, the work of many teachers who are able to engage all of their students. These core beliefs include the following:

1. A belief that all students have value and unique gifts to offer their school (rather than believing that some students are gifted, most are mediocre, and the others are somewhere below average)
2. A belief that all students can think and learn (rather than believing that thinking and learning can occur with only select students)
3. A belief that diversity within a school community is to be embraced and celebrated (rather than believing that diversity is to be tolerated or splintered through ability grouping, tracking, and other measures)
4. A belief that effective teaching methods for students with disabilities is actually good teaching for all students (rather than believing that those kids need separate instructional practices that are inappropriate for other students)
5. A belief that students learn best when studying interesting and challenging topics that they find personally meaningful (rather than being fed a steady diet of dull, recall-type questions that lack challenge and remain divorced from students' lives)
6. A belief that students learn best when they are actively and collaboratively building knowledge with their classmates and the teacher (rather than passively receiving through lectures and private readings the teacher's and text's constructed rendition of knowledge)
7. A belief that students differ in the ways in which they most effectively learn and express their understandings (rather than believing that students think and learn in similar ways)

The remainder of this chapter describes an approach to unit planning that reflects a commitment to these seven assumptions. Eight

[1]Other related factors are addressed in Chapters 3 and 4, such as common planning time, opportunities for teachers to engage in peer-mediated reflective inquiry, and an administrative vision that supports ongoing reform and growth.

Table 1.   Eight essential elements of inclusive unit design

1. A central unit issue or problem
2. An opening grabber or motivator
3. Lessons that are linked to the central issue or problem
4. Richly detailed source material
5. Culminating projects
6. Varied lesson formats
7. Multiple assessments
8. Varied modes of student expression

elements or features of effective unit planning for the inclusive classroom are described and justified, and numerous classroom examples of each element are provided.[2] This planning model can be used by middle and high school teachers working individually or in teams. Some of our examples reflect discipline-based study, whereas others are interdisciplinary in scope. The chapter concludes with a discussion of supports and accommodations that serve the needs of students with extraordinary learning challenges.

EIGHT ESSENTIAL ELEMENTS OF INCLUSIVE UNIT DESIGN

The eight essential elements of inclusive unit design are displayed in Table 1. A thorough description of each element, its relevance to the inclusive classroom, and associated examples are presented in the subsections that follow.

Element 1: A Central Unit Issue or Problem

Classroom research consistently describes students as passive receivers of fragmented and superficial bits of information and ideas requiring little thinking beyond recall and recitation (Brown, 1991; Cuban, 1984; Goodlad, 1984; Sirotnik, 1983). This is due, in part, to ineffective unit design. Too many units are structured around a laundry list of facts, names, concepts, events, and topics culled from a textbook. Each lesson then targets a certain number of items from the list, and the unit is concluded when all of the items have been addressed and the students have been tested. Not surprisingly, such an approach results in fragmented, superficial, and lower-order student understanding.

How can teachers in diverse, inclusive classrooms pursue cohesive, in-depth study and intellectual challenge with all of their students without being asked to perform the impossible task of designing separate lessons for each student or numerous groups of students?

---

[2]Several of the elements of unit planning were previously discussed in Jorgensen (1996), Onosko (1996), and Onosko and Swenson (1996).

Table 2.   Turning topics into central issues and problems

Topic	Issue or problem
The Gulf War	Ultimately, was the Gulf War a success or a failure for the United States?
The Four Seasons	Why are there seasons?
The Short Story	What makes a short story great?
Citizenship	What are your rights and responsibilities as a U.S. citizen?
Earthquakes	Should we fear an earthquake here?

The answer is an approach employing a central unit issue or problem (usually stated as a question) that challenges all students yet is tolerant of varied levels of student performance during and at the end of the unit.[3]

Structuring a unit of study around an issue or problem (rather than a wide-ranging topic or list) serves a number of important functions. It creates a distinct shape or backbone to the learning experience and provides direction and coherence across lessons. The central problem ensures intellectual challenge. Without a challenge, there is little motivation or need to think! The problem or issue also serves to narrow the topic, delimiting content coverage and reducing the likelihood of fragmented and superficial treatment of subject matter. Less coverage is absolutely necessary if students are ever to develop dispositions, skills, and understandings associated with higher-order thinking (Newmann, 1988; Onosko, 1991; Prawat, 1991; Wiggins, 1989). In addition, sustained study of important issues and problems is inherently more meaningful and motivating to students than learning a set of disconnected or loosely connected facts, ideas, and events. Finally, classroom pursuit of a common problem (rather than students' individually pursuing different, unrelated tasks) increases students' desire and ability to exchange ideas and collaborate with peers. Table 2 provides examples of how traditional curriculum topics can be transformed into issues and problems.

---

[3]Borrowing from Newmann (1990) and Schrag (1988), the authors define *problem* as any task that requires students to use thinking skills; dispositions of thoughtfulness; and prior knowledge to interpret, manipulate, and evaluate information and ideas because the students are not sure how to proceed. In the context of unit planning, any task that requires students to think in a sustained manner can be considered a problem. Some problems find experts in basic agreement on what counts as a correct answer (e.g., Why are there clouds? Did the New Deal or World War II end the Great Depression?), whereas other problems generate substantial disagreement (e.g., What is intelligence? How should nuclear waste be discarded?). Typically, *issue* or *controversial issue* refers to problems of this second type. Hence, all issues are problems, but not all problems are issues. Competence and success as an adult in public and private life require that students gain an ability to work through problems of both types.

Consider the potential for fragmented, superficial, and lower-order understanding in a unit designed around the topic The Revolutionary Period. As stated, the topic provides very little direction for teachers and students. All social, political, religious, geographic, and economic aspects of the period are appropriate for study. (History textbooks usually reflect this encompassing approach.) When a unit lacks focus, too often the teacher's content selection is diverse, lengthy, and fragmented. Worse yet, no selection at all occurs as the teacher indiscriminately attempts to cover everything. Bewildered students (and even some teachers) ask themselves the following at the conclusion of such units: "How does everything fit together?" "I'm confused—what does this have to do with what we did the other day?" "It seems that all we do is memorize all these events from the past." Lest the reader think that the authors exaggerate this problem, one of the authors' daughters (an eighth grader as this book was being written) had to memorize definitions of 121 people, places, and events surrounding the Civil War!

Compare the above topic-based approach to an issue- or problem-based approach framed around the question "Were the colonists justified in revolting from England?" Knowing that they must work throughout the unit to answer this challenging question, students are engaged from the start. Students must learn about the contentious relations between England and the colonies, assume the perspectives of both sides, consider the legitimacy of civil disobedience in this and possibly other contexts, and then decide whether they could support the actions of the revolutionaries. The central issue enables the teacher and students to identify (and narrow down) what content is needed for study (British and American actions that generated tension and the underlying rationales for these actions) and provides a purposeful and challenging reason for studying the period (to take a position on the central issue). An issue or problem can be framed as either a question (as found in the current example), as a provocative proposition (e.g., the colonists were not justified in revolting from England), or as a problematic task (e.g., as a class we are going to decide whether the colonists were really justified in revolting against England).

Cathy Fisher, a tenth-grade social studies teacher at Souhegan High School in Amherst, New Hampshire, begins the curriculum design process by writing a question to frame the unit—a question that all students can answer. She said,

> I was very nervous at first about having all students, students with severe disabilities and all students really—they're all different, in my room. How could I pick material that they all could understand and connect with? I've found out that creating questions that all students can answer is the key.

When I did a unit on slavery and the Civil War, we used the question "Can you be free if you aren't treated equally?" Some students in my class could answer that question using information from their Civil War reading and by thinking about the progress of civil rights in the United States. One or two students in my class had to approach this question first from their own personal perspectives. Amro knew that he was treated differently from his brothers because of his disability, and he has a strong opinion about that. If we start with his personal experience, it's a little bit easier for him to make a connection with the Civil War.

Teachers in the diverse, inclusive classroom want to ensure intellectual challenge and powerful learning for all of their students. Units designed around an issue or problem maximize opportunities for higher-order thinking, in-depth understanding, and cohesive (i.e., nonfragmented) learning. (Table 3 offers additional examples of central issues and problems and summarizes their important characteristics.) Ensuring participation among all students also requires some modification and personalization in student performance expectations. How this is to be done is explained in some of the other unit design elements that follow.

Element 2: An Opening Grabber or Motivator

Learning depends as much if not more on student interest and motivation as one's prior knowledge, reading and writing ability, and so forth (Gottfried, 1985; Shirey & Reynolds, 1988; Stipek, 1993). We must somehow help kids plug in and turn on their mental engines. With respect to unit design, this means that the opening lessons of a unit are the most critical. Introductory unit grabbers are activities that draw students into the material and motivate them to explore the

Table 3.   Characteristics and examples of central issues and problems

Characteristics
1. They require higher-order thinking of all students.
2. They place students in the roles of investigator and active learner.
3. They place teachers in the role of facilitator of student inquiry.
4. They offer a sense of adventure and are fun to explore and answer.
5. Students with varying levels of sophistication can pursue them.
6. They help teachers limit the breadth of content coverage.
7. They provide direction and coherence to daily lesson planning.

Examples
1. What makes a person wise?
2. Overall, has the United States made progress?
3. Is it ever ethical to lie?
4. The Fourth Amendment: When are search and seizure unreasonable?
5. Immigration: How do we decide who gets in?
6. What makes a persuasive essay persuasive?

unit's central question or issue. Failure to do so can easily result in students not paying attention or remaining marginally engaged for the remainder of the unit. Too many teachers expend their greatest effort at the end of a unit during "mop-up," "salvage the unit," and "info dumping" review sessions rather than at the beginning, when the crucial task of engaging minds must take place.

A grabber can last from 10 minutes to one or more lessons and might involve any one or more of the following: a short story, a film clip, a slide show, song and lyric analysis, a brainstorming session with students, a brief simulation, or a field trip. Classroom teachers know best what is likely to capture the interest and imagination of their students.

An introductory grabber might involve students in an overview of some of the perspectives or solutions that one might adopt regarding a problem or issue. Students might even be asked to take a preliminary stand themselves or predict a possible answer, or they might simply be exposed to a new topic from which the central problem would emerge in later lessons. Whatever the length or format, an effective unit grabber triggers student interest, reveals the teacher's enthusiasm for the upcoming unit, and introduces or foreshadows the central problem or issue to be explored.

It is important that the unit grabber or kick-off activity be accessible (i.e., understood) by all students; otherwise, the activity has failed its purpose! If the grabber involves difficult readings or requires students with learning disabilities to interact with materials or ideas beyond their understanding or intuitive grasp, then they may just give up and say to themselves, "This is too hard" or "I'm not interested in this." In short, the best grabbers invite and excite all students. Finally, the grabber can serve as a preliminary assessment tool and guide to future lesson planning, informing the teacher of students' current understanding of the material about to be studied.

Consider the following example of a unit grabber by John Laurent, an outstanding University of New Hampshire social studies intern. The teacher begins the unit of study by passing out information on 50 inventions familiar to most students, including some of the actual objects (e.g., an aspirin, a paper clip, a computer); a short video clip on inventions; and photographs, drawings, and a list. In pairs, students are then asked to identify what they consider to be the 10 most important and 10 least important inventions from the list and jot down reasons for each of their selections. The class reconvenes, and volunteers begin to share their thinking with the class. Very quickly, a lively discussion ensues as students advocate for their preferred inventions and question (and reflect on) the legitimacy of their classmates' alternative selections. Near the end of the allotted time, the teacher offers to the group the following central unit question for study, "What have been the most significant inventions of the 20th century?"

Element 3: Lessons that Are
Linked to the Central Issue or Problem

Although immensely helpful, structuring a unit around an issue or problem does not guarantee that individual lessons will add up to more than the sum of their parts. If lessons are to assume a purpose beyond their own internal coherence, they need to be sequenced in ways that advance students' understanding of and ability to answer the unit's central problem or issue. There is no one correct way to sequence lessons to achieve this purpose, primarily because there is no one correct way to think about most problems and issues. We do believe, however, that some general strategies exist that can help teachers link lessons more effectively so that students' thinking and learning remain on track.

One method is to identify the various positions or viewpoints that exist regarding the unit's central issue or problem. These viewpoints can be used to guide the design of daily lessons. For example, students in a psychology class might address the question, "Why do we dream?" Two or more lessons could be devoted to Freud's theory that dreams represent repressed ideas and experiences that the ego attempts to keep submerged in the unconscious. Next, students might spend 2 or more days exploring Jung's view that dreams are symbolic expressions, not repressions, that provide important opportunities for self-discovery, individuation, and wholeness. Other perspectives might include Adler's view that dreams provide insight into impending decisions (rather than reflect unresolved conflicts from the past), or Crick's dismissal of dreams as a series of meaningless images resulting from rapid eye movement (REM) and other brain-processing activities. Following exposure to a handful of theorists, students would begin to formulate their own position on the nature and purpose of dreams.

Another method to link lessons is to identify key concepts, events, people, and other understandings that students will need to effectively address the unit's central issue or problem. These items can then be used to organize and structure daily lessons. This is not the laundry list approach alluded to previously. Instead, identified items are only those that are clearly relevant to the exploration and understanding of the problem or issue. These items should not be taught as ends in themselves but rather should be explored in the context of students' growing understanding of the unit's central problem or issue. For example, in a unit exploring the question, "Were the colonists justified in revolting from England?" students must consider a series of British and American actions and reactions (e.g., Sugar Act, Stamp Act, Townshend Acts, Boston Tea Party, Boston Massacre) and also come to understand important concepts (e.g., virtual versus direct representation, social contract, civil disobedience) in order to answer the central issue. These events and ideas can provide direction for the sequencing and design of lessons.

A third approach to linking lessons is to identify important subquestions that need to be considered to intelligently address the problem or issue. The questions that are identified can then serve to structure the unit's set of lessons. For example, to address the policy issue of whether state X should adopt the death penalty, a number of related subissues emerge: Will the death penalty reduce a state's homicide rate (a factual issue)? When, if ever, is a state justified in taking a human life (an ethical issue)? By what legal means can an execution be stayed (a legal issue)? What is the difference between first- and second-degree murder (a definitional legal issue)? Each of these questions can become the basis for one or more lessons.

There are also a number of strategies to link lessons during the delivery of a unit. For example, by prominently displaying the central problem or issue on flipchart paper taped to a wall or on the chalkboard, students are reminded of the big picture and the need to link what they learn in a given lesson back to the unit's central issue or problem. Linkages can also be enhanced when the teacher explains or asks students to explain how daily lessons relate to the central issue or problem. A third technique is to ask students to explain at the end of a lesson how it contributed to their understanding of the central problem. Students should also be cognizant of how homework assignments are designed to help them address the unit problem. Finally, having students periodically determine areas where additional research is needed not only provides the teacher with direction for future lessons but also reveals to students how past lessons have helped them build their understanding.

For students with learning disabilities that involve difficulties with organization or memory, these linking strategies are especially helpful in preventing students from getting lost as the unit progresses. Graphic organizers can also be used to create a visual display of the knowledge-building process. For example, the grid format displayed in Figure 1 might be used near the end of the unit to help students synthesize material and ultimately to decide which reform efforts they would have supported during the early 20th century. Earlier in the

| | Central issue
Early 20th-century reform efforts: Which would you support? | | | |
Reform group	Causes pursued	Methods used	Degree of success	Would you support this group?
Knights of Labor				
American Federation of Labor				
Farmers' Alliance				
Populist Party				
Progressive Party				
Industrial Workers of the World				
W.E.B. DuBois				
Muckrakers				

Figure 1.   Graphic organizer to help students compare and assess 20th-century reform efforts.

unit, separate graphic organizers for each reform movement might have been created to help students develop their understanding.

Element 4: Richly Detailed Source Material

What is richly detailed source material? One way to describe these materials is in relation to the dominant resource: the traditional text-book. Textbooks typically exhibit a paucity of detail and are rarely framed around issues or problems. The presentation of material often lacks coherence or meaningful organization within and across chapters. Textbooks tend to make claims and offer conclusions with little empirical or logical support and, therefore, are of little help in designing lessons and units that promote students' thinking (Kahane, 1984). Concepts are presented but not defined, or they are defined but examples are not given. The writing is typically banal and devoid of controversy (Fitzgerald, 1979; Tyson-Bernstein, 1988), and, on rare occasions when issues are mentioned or problems are presented, competing perspectives and solutions are not explained. Too often the cumulative effect is a class of disengaged and dispirited students!

However, richly detailed source material, or *rich detail*, triggers student interest and promotes subject matter expertise. Students learn about competing viewpoints and the rationales and arguments that underlie these viewpoints. Important supporting facts are stated, and contested factual claims are explored. Concepts receive elaboration, including the presentation of examples, counterexamples, and analogies, all of which are critical to real conceptual understanding. Rich detail also promotes students' empathic entry into issues that might otherwise have remained remote to them. Rich detail includes lively readings, such as eyewitness accounts and other primary source materials, magazine articles, video clips from movies and documentaries, images and pictures that also provide visual text, short stories, biographies, and so forth. In short, rich detail helps students to become and remain interested in and to develop a perspective on the unit's central problem or issue. By working hard to find a variety of source material that presents rich detail, accommodation for students with disabilities is built into lessons and the unit. Students with varying learning styles—visual, auditory, or kinesthetic—can glean information from at least one source if many modes are used.

At Souhegan, tenth-grade teachers Jennifer Mueller (science) and Scott LaLiberte (English) designed a unit called "Lives of a Cell." In English, students read Lewis Thomas's (1974) book by the same name, and, in science, they examined the question, "How can you tell if something is living?" Jennifer wanted to be sensitive to the different reading and experience levels of the students in her class, so she created an in-class resource library on cells that included college texts, Time-Life series books, journal articles, videotapes of the Public Broadcasting System's *Nova* series, picture books, and an interactive computer program that explained meiosis and mitosis. She invited every student to use any and all of the materials and stressed that each had value because they showed different perspectives on the same subject material. In this way, she gave equal value to students' varied experience levels and acknowledged that learning through a different mode was okay.

Element 5: Culminating Projects

Culminating projects provide students with opportunities to share the fruits of their labor; that is, to synthesize information and offer their understanding of the unit's central issue or problem. Unlike traditional units of study, culminating projects do not include typical pen-and-paper tests, though one format could be a well-crafted essay or position paper that is shared with others. Culminating projects encourage group interaction and creativity, appeal to multiple learning styles, and almost always contain some type of public performance. Examples include a speech; a skit or play; a radio broadcast; a live or videotaped television newscast; a whole-class or small-group debate; a poster display; a newspaper publication; a metaphorical representation of an idea, person, or event; or a small-group presentation.

Regardless of format, culminating projects ask students to share their perspectives on the unit's central issue or problem, not that of the teacher or some other authority figure. Units can contain more than one culminating activity. For example, a class might spend a day or two discussing or formally debating the proposition "Hate speech should be regulated." A day or two later, small groups of students might present a poster board representation of the kinds of hate speech and expression that they believe should be regulated, if any. Both the debate and the poster board activity ask students to synthesize their understanding and share it with the class.

Why are culminating projects important for the inclusive classroom? Culminating projects tend to motivate all students as they realize that the end result is not just a written test privately read, graded, and returned by the teacher, but rather an opportunity for students to demonstrate understanding and intellectual prowess in front of their peers. These activities are also motivating because students prefer working on collaborative projects (Goodlad, 1984). In addition, research consistently shows that cooperative learning formats result in higher student achievement compared with competitive, individual formats (Qin, Johnson, & Johnson, 1995). Culminating projects also require active student learning and greatly increase the likelihood of students' gaining both in-depth and cohesive understanding. Finally, culminating projects are a powerful means to develop students' thinking, and not only because the unit contains a central issue or problem that needs to be addressed. Many students, regardless of their prior achievement, are insecure about specific ideas that they generate and their overall ability to think. Culminating projects, because of their public nature, invite students to share their ideas and expose students to the ideas of their classmates. This form of public discourse enables students to see the validity, or at least the reasonableness, of their thinking, something that does not happen when intellectual work (e.g., a test, some other submitted task) remains a private dialogue between the teacher and each student. Through dialogue and sharing, students gain confidence in their thinking and a greater willingness to contribute in the future.

Element 6: Varied Lesson Formats

No matter how accomplished a teacher becomes with a particular instructional format (e.g., whole-group discussions), persistent use will eventually render it ineffective with most students. The old maxim "variety is the spice of life" applies in the world of education—students' appetite for learning is aroused when activities are varied. Teachers must remember to include this important spice in any unit design recipe. The desire for variety seems to be true for all students and therefore is an important element of unit design for the inclusive classroom. Engaging instructional formats available to teachers are numerous (Bower, Lobdell, & Swenson, 1994; Harmin, 1994; Johnson & Johnson, 1989; Saphier & Gower, 1987) and include the following:

- Interactive slide lecture-discussions that can include student role playing
- Simulation activities that give students a "you are there" experience
- Cooperative/competitive small-group activities in which members of a group work together against the efforts of other groups
- Think-aloud paired problem solving in which two students share their thinking about an idea, issue, or event
- Whole-class or small-group debates
- Jigsaw activities in which small groups of students learn about different aspects of a question or problem and problem resolution requires input from all members of the groups
- Mediator activities in which the class explores an issue without taking sides and tries to uncover one or more compromises that might bring the disagreeing parties together

When Trish Walton plans a unit, she builds in a variety of instructional formats and structures but acknowledges students' need for order by having each day of the week follow a predictable schedule. During her "Tough Times Don't Last, Tough People Do" unit, Mondays are movie or video days, Tuesdays are reserved for library research or individual in-class reading, Wednesdays are cooperative group days, Thursdays are student–student or student–teacher conference days, and Fridays alternate between visitor days (e.g., a visit from a local author or person who exemplifies the "tough people last" maxim) and an in-class catch-up day. This variety keeps students engaged and interested but also gives them an idea of what to expect on most days.

Element 7: Multiple Assessments
To ensure powerful learning, teachers need to monitor and assess students' progress throughout the unit, not just at the end. Too many students become victims of neglect, scattered along the sequence of lessons if their progress is not monitored regularly. Teachers are unaware of the number of casualties or when they happened if assessment occurs only at the end of the unit. The greater diversity found in the inclusive classroom makes the need for periodic assessment all the more critical. It is for this reason that multiple assessment is in-

cluded as an important element of inclusive unit design. (Grading of students with learning disabilities is a particularly vexing issue for teachers and is discussed in the next section of this chapter.)

What is it that teachers, students, or other audiences should assess? If units are indeed designed around a central problem or issue, then presumably assessment will be designed to monitor the extent to which students are developing a more sophisticated understanding of that problem or issue. What are the important ideas, facts, events, and perspectives that students need to know? Beyond the specific problem or issue being pursued, a number of other objectives are likely to direct teachers' efforts, including the development of skills (e.g., public speaking, spelling and punctuation, persuasive writing, research) and the cultivation of attitudes and beliefs (e.g., pride and confidence in one's work, commitment to democratic values).

Assessment can take many forms: class discussion, oral question-and-answer quizzes, quick reviews at the beginning or end of a lesson, take-home assignments, in-class writing activities, culminating projects, and so forth. Efforts should be made to make these assessment activities as authentic as possible, especially by embedding them naturally in students' efforts to solve the unit's central problem.

For example, at the beginning or somewhere in the middle of a unit, the teacher might ask students to write on a piece of paper the two or three best reasons or pieces of evidence they have uncovered so far to support their position on the question "What caused the extinction of dinosaurs?" Students would then pass in their papers, and the teacher would facilitate a discussion in which students share and debate their ideas. The conversation is used to help identify areas of factual disagreement and where additional teaching or inquiry is needed. The next day is then devoted to researching these contentious areas during a visit to the library. This naturally embedded assessment is superior to a true-or-false pop quiz that gets collected, is not discussed, and is not connected to the remainder of the day's activities.

Element 8: Varied Modes of Student Expression
Consensus is emerging among cognitive scientists that intelligence involves a number of relatively distinct abilities (rather than a general capacity) that can be enhanced through educational and other social interventions (Sternberg, 1996; Weinberg, 1989). As Gardner (1983) and Sternberg (1985) pointed out, however, our educational system primarily emphasizes intellectual activity involving logical-mathematical and verbal-linguistic forms of expression. As a result, schools tend to reward only students with particular aptitudes along these dimensions of intelligence. Equally unfortunate, such a system limits the opportunities of all students to cultivate other aspects of

their intelligence. In addition to intelligence research, research on learning styles suggests the need to design educational activities that resonate with a larger percentage of the school population (Dunn, Beaudry, & Klavas, 1989). What are these alternative forms of expression that reflect an expanded conception of intelligence and learning, and how are they to be incorporated when designing units of study?

Visual learning is one form of expression that needs to be given greater emphasis in the classroom. Students could be asked to create a metaphor that represents a concept that they have learned (e.g., a beehive is like a medieval manor) or to determine which metaphor is more accurate (e.g., Does a beaver or a turtle best represent the concept of *persistence*?) Students might also be asked to draw or in some other way create a visual image of their metaphor. Alternatively, they might be asked to create a political cartoon that reflects their side of the debate on a topic of controversy (e.g., requiring school uniforms).

Kinesthetic, sensation-based learning has also been identified as an important but underemphasized form of human learning and expression in schools. Students might be asked to participate in a classroom simulation of an idea such as entangling alliances during World War I. Students might act as heads of state, unwittingly sign a number of alliances with other countries, and then, to their horror, find themselves at war as a result of their entangling commitments. Other forms of expression that could receive greater emphasis include musicality (e.g., representing number patterns using musical notation) and spatial aptitude (e.g., constructing models of ideas or events).

Teachers ought to support students' development and refinement of the areas of intelligence or modes of expression in which they have the greatest interest and talent and to encourage students to explore and use other ways of knowing that are riskier for them. A strategy for managing such a growth process is, for every major unit, to allow students to produce one culminating project in the mode with which they are most comfortable and another in a new mode. Over the course of a semester, students might be required to try out three or four new modes. The evaluation of any project could be weighted more heavily on the product that used their strongest talent (e.g., for a linguistically talented student, 80% on an oral presentation) and a smaller percentage of the grade on a product that uses their less comfortable mode of presentation (e.g., 20% of a grade from an oral presentation by a student who is very shy or insecure). The ever-shifting balance among different modes could be negotiated between teacher and student over the course of the semester or year.

Ninth graders on Team 9A at Souhegan High School studied 20th-century conflicts in a unit based on Billy Joel's (1989) song "We Didn't Start the Fire." After they researched the people, places, and events mentioned in the lyrics, they were given great freedom in the mode by which they answered the unit's essential questions, "Who started the fire?" and "Are any fires still burning?" They produced final projects as varied as computer programs, videotapes, sculptures, slide shows, research papers, and comic strips. (A complete description of this unit is presented in Chapter 6.)

PUTTING THE ELEMENTS TOGETHER

Our systemic presentation of the eight elements of unit planning in no way reflects the messy, unsystematic process of actually developing a unit. On occasion, the teacher or team of teachers may start with an issue or problem, but just as often the catalyst for planning may be the discovery of an outstanding reading (rich detail), the creation of an idea for a student performance (a culminating activity), the awareness that a film excerpt has motivating power (an opening grabber), an unanticipated current event, or one of the district's many required topics of study. The actual process of unit planning defies reduction to a single, mechanistic step-by-step sequence or procedure. Regardless of the initial point of entry or general approach used, it is essential that each element of inclusive unit design be considered at some point during the planning process to maximize opportunities for all students to think and learn.

Supports and Accommodations for Students with Extraordinary Learning Challenges

The elements of inclusive unit design just described effectively accommodate most students with unique learning styles and minor learning difficulties. Additional supports and accommodations must sometimes be made, however, to ensure that students who experience significant learning, behavioral, and physical disabilities are active participants in the academic life of the school. They may need assistive technology to help them move because of orthopedic disabilities. Some students may experience significant communication difficulties, relying on electronic communication devices to express their thoughts, needs, and intentions, whereas others with multiple sensory disabilities such as blindness and deafness may need a variety of supports to gain access to information and ideas. The purpose of thinking about students' individualized needs is not to determine whether they should be in general classes but rather to determine what accommodations and supports are necessary so that they can participate and learn effectively. Even if their participation involves mastery of part of a lesson, being included in the mainstream of high school life has other important benefits (Baumgart et al., 1982; see also Chapter 1). The remaining portion of this chapter discusses these supports and accommodations.

We have identified five types of supports and accommodations that need to be considered when doing inclusive unit planning:

1. People support from classmates or adults
2. Modified materials or provision of technology
3. Individualized performance standards and expectations
4. Personalized instruction
5. Uniquely designed evaluation and grading plans (Tashie et al., 1993)

Each type of support is described next, and several examples of each are provided in the accompanying tables.

Support 1: People Support from Classmates or Adults

Some students may not be able to participate in classroom activities independently but can participate with support from classmates or an adult. Although some believe that the provision of people supports is preferable to making adaptations to materials or performance expectations, care must be taken not to develop an overreliance on others. Positive virtues of interdependence and cooperation need to be balanced with the development of self-reliance and independence. The role of aides or teaching assistants also needs careful consideration. Although their presence can be very helpful if they provide assistance to every student in a class, assigning them solely to a student with disabilities can interfere with the development of relationships between that student and his or her classmates. (A thorough discussion of community-based learning is presented in Chapter 9.) Examples of people support provided by classmates are presented in Table 4.

Table 4.   Examples of supports provided by classmates

- Katherine read to Don, who is blind.
- Mike rephrased questions for Rob, who has difficulty understanding a newspaper article.
- Trisha helped Sara move her arms and legs during warm-ups in gym class.
- Kelly guided Janna's hand to adjust the focus on the microscope.
- Katie and Lee conferred while writing a short story.
- Bill interpreted Shelly's signs to a new student in the class.
- Phil and Bob studied together for quizzes.
- Brooke made instructional materials for Jake, such as an audiotape of their group reading a book aloud and an outline of a reading on Native American religions.
- Megan wrote as Jessica dictated her story.

Support 2: Modified Materials or Provision of Technology
When a variety of materials rich in detail and using different media forms, as described in the first part of this chapter, are available to all students in a class, the need for extensive modification is reduced. For some students, however, rich detail is not enough; modification of these materials is needed for their full participation. There are at least five general ways to modify materials:

1. Use the same materials but have students interact with only part of them (e.g., completing half of the problems in a science assignment).
2. Change the format of existing materials but retain the same level of information (e.g., change the requirement from an essay to a multiple-choice test).
3. Supplement class materials (e.g., provide written instructions to supplement oral ones, show a completed model as a guide).
4. Substitute different materials for those used by classmates (e.g., a taped book rather than one in print, a different vocabulary or spelling list).
5. Use technology to bypass a student's physical or sensory challenges (e.g., use an enlarger to make the print in a book readable).

Many examples of modified materials are presented in Table 5.

Support 3: Individualized Performance Standards and Expectations
Within diverse, nontracked general education classrooms, diversity in student performance ought to be encouraged and celebrated. Chris and Lisa are good examples of students whose learning goals and performance expectations are dramatically different from those of their classmates.

    Chris is representative of students who are able to master some of the academic content of the curriculum. He is 17 years old, 2 years older than most of the other students in the sophomore class because he was retained during elementary school. He comes from an impoverished background and has experienced much family instability throughout his life. He reads at a second-grade level and has mastered basic addition and subtraction. His knowledge of the world is very limited, and at present he is unable to grasp complex concepts in science, social studies, math, and English. Although he is enrolled in a vocational education program for part of the school day, he also takes several general education humanities and science classes. In order for Chris to participate fully and learn optimally, different expectations must be established on a unit-by-unit basis through collaborative team planning. Within each unit, Chris is expected to

Table 5. Examples of modified materials

- Arthur completed a multiple-choice test by pointing to the letter *a, b, c,* or *d* written in four quadrants of a portable white board. A teaching assistant read him the question and the answer choices and then wrote Arthur's response on the answer sheet.
- Gene watched a *Nova* special about cells rather than reading about it in a science textbook.
- Facts about the Civil War were made into a matching quiz for Allison, who could not write an essay.
- Jessica's lines in theater class were tape recorded by a classmate. During the class performance, she leaned her head against a pressure switch connected to the tape player to read her lines at the appropriate time.
- Bernie used adapted scissors to cut out pictures for a collage in home economics class.
- Anne pointed to organs on a model of the human body instead of filling in the blank on a worksheet.
- Peter has very poor fine motor skills, so he used the microwave in home economics class rather than using pots, pans, and a stovetop.
- During a soccer game in gym class, Lisa pressed a switch connected to a buzzer to signal the end of the period.
- Nathan used an instant camera to take pictures of the steps of his group's science experiment. The photos were pasted into their lab notebook alongside his classmates' written observations.
- David's social studies textbook was scanned into a computer. Wearing headphones during study hall, he followed along as the computer read the chapter to him. When he did not understand a word, David highlighted it and a definition was provided to him by audiotape.

demonstrate knowledge of two or three main concepts through a hands-on culminating project. For example, when his tenth-grade class was studying heredity, Chris was expected to learn that physical characteristics are transmitted from parents to children in predictable patterns, that the probability of a person contracting a particular disease can be calculated by studying the medical history of several generations of that person's family, and that parents can increase their chance of having healthy children by following some basic dietary and behavioral guidelines. (Chris was not expected to learn the complexities of deoxyribonucleic acid [DNA] molecule structure and biochemistry.)

For a midsemester assignment, Chris made a collage of foods and beverages that are healthy for a pregnant woman. For his final culminating project, Chris researched and illustrated a four-generation family pedigree and calculated his chances of experiencing male pattern baldness and of developing diabetes as an adult.

Unlike Chris, Lisa is an example of students whose priority learning goals do not include mastery of content associated with the academic disciplines. Instead, her educational goals focus on communication, socialization, cooperation, and movement. Lisa is unable to move her arms and legs and gets around school by having classmates push her wheelchair. She communicates primarily through the look in her eyes, her moods, and an occasional vocalization. The quality of her life and the focus of her IEP consist of four components:

1. Social connections and friendships with students who do not have disabilities
2. Active involvement in classroom activities through direct hand-over-hand physical guidance
3. Opportunities to make choices about all aspects of her daily routine and her life
4. Involvement in a wide variety of social and extracurricular activities

What benefits might Lisa derive from participation in a tenth-grade social studies class? Should she be expected to answer the central problem or issue that frames the unit? What might be an appropriate culminating activity? To answer these questions, Lisa's team considers the learning objectives that are intimately connected to her quality of life. During a planning meeting, the team determines when opportunities will occur for Lisa to connect with other students, interact with materials through hand-over-hand guidance, make choices, and participate in class activities throughout the unit.

Connections with other students might occur during cooperative group discussions, pair reading, and debates. Lisa can use her hands with physical guidance to select materials in the library, type on a computer, pass out assignments, or search for information on a map. She can choose where to sit, whom the teacher should call on next, and which group she would like to work with on a project. As a member of the social studies class, she might join a student chapter of Amnesty International, run for student council, or testify at a state senate hearing on an education funding bill. Some teachers find the use of an activity matrix helpful in making an organized plan for addressing the individualized learning objectives for students like Lisa (Thousand et al., 1986). Lisa's participation in a typical social studies class can be recorded on a graphic organizer, shown in Figure 2. The cells across the top of this matrix represent instructional structures and routines that are used by teachers regardless of the topic being studied.

Changing expectations for students—whether modifying how they demonstrate what they know, changing the quantity of work that they are assigned, or personalizing learning objectives within a particular lesson—causes some teachers great concern. Teachers are wor-

Classroom activity/ learning objective	Arrival and dismissal from classroom	Teacher lecture or whole class discussion	Library research	Small group discussion in class
1. Make connections with students without disabilities	Lisa could come into and leave class in the company of other students. When the teacher gives the assignment, another student could write it in Lisa's assignment notebook.	The teacher could involve Lisa in the discussion by asking her questions and demonstrating her value to other students. If Lisa's responses are not understandable, the teacher can ask her friends "What do you think Lisa would make of this situation?" or "How might this issue affect Lisa's life?"	Lisa could work with a group of classmates in the library. If she sees other kids she knows, she can be pushed over to say "Hi" to them in the library.	Involving Lisa in small group discussions is a great way to keep her connected to other students. It is important that Lisa be assigned to groups in the same manner as other students. If they have a choice, give her one too. If other students are randomly assigned by the teacher, assign Lisa the same way.
2. Participate actively in class with hand-over-hand assistance	When the teacher calls attendance, another student can help Lisa raise her hand.	When it looks like Lisa wants to say something in response to the discussion, another student can help her raise her hand. If the teacher is using a map, she might have Lisa sit beside her and help her point to the region that is being discussed.	Other students could guide Lisa to select a book from a shelf. They could use her wheelchair tray to carry books (with Lisa's permission). She could hand over the books to the person scanning them at the checkout counter. She could sit at a computer terminal and help find information using a CD-ROM.	If students are working on discussion guides, they might be placed in front of Lisa so that the action is centered in front of her. If students are required to write group members' names on their worksheets, Lisa can use an inked hand stamp to "write" her name.

(continued)

Figure 2. Matrix of learning objectives and social studies activities for Lisa.

93

Figure 2. (continued)

Classroom activity/ learning objective	Arrival and dismissal from classroom	Teacher lecture or whole class discussion	Library research	Small group discussion in class
3. Make choices throughout the day	Lisa could be asked where she wants to sit when there is no assigned seating.	The teacher could ask Lisa her opinion about the topic being discussed and read Lisa's eyes or posture as a clue to her answer.	Lisa could choose between two books or magazines. She could choose at which table her group works in the library.	Lisa could choose which group she wants to join.
4. Participate in extracurricular and social activities	N/A	When the teacher solicits students for after-school help, Lisa might volunteer. She might be nominated as the class's representative on student council. If the teacher is the advisor for an after-school club like Amnesty International, Lisa might join.	Lisa might volunteer during her free periods as a library aide and restock shelves or deliver audiovisual equipment to teachers' classrooms.	If Lisa is involved in all small group discussions, where at least half the time is spent talking about nonacademic topics, she will hear about after-school plans that are being made. She might issue invitations to come over to her house through preprinted cards or notes written by her parents.

ried that changing expectations for students like Chris will destroy the integrity of their course. They are concerned about fairness if standards are flexible. With respect to students like Lisa, teachers often wonder, "Why is this student in my class if she isn't going to learn social studies?"

Personalizing expectations for some students does not necessarily mean a reduction in the overall rigor of a course. In fact, flexible and individualized expectations can increase rigor by requiring more of some students. *Fairness* need not mean all students receive the same education; it can mean that students receive what they need and give back to their classmates what they can share.

Even if Chris is not expected to learn the mathematical formulas that describe the expression of dominant and recessive traits, it is still fair to expect this understanding of other students. Even if Lisa is not expected to acquire social studies knowledge, she can be held accountable for demonstrating other forms of knowledge and skill, with the social studies class providing a normalized context for learning. Some examples of modified expectations are presented in Table 6.

Support 4: Personalized Instruction
When effective teachers conduct whole-class discussions, sit with small groups, or speak to students one to one, they personalize instruction for each student. They ask different kinds of questions, use a variety of motivational techniques based on the student's personality, and push the student to think more critically.

Some students may simply need additional information or to have instructions clarified to proceed with their work. Teachers often do this as a matter of course, as classmates do for one another. "What did he say?" students often whisper to one another. "We have to read Chapter 5 and decide if the authors are biased," they answer in return.

Teachers also need to ask different questions of different students to maximize participation and ensure a proper level of intellectual challenge for all students (Collicott, 1991; Onosko & Newmann, 1994). A teacher might ask one student a factual question such as "When was the Declaration of Independence signed?" To another, she might pose a conceptual question, "What were three important freedoms guaranteed by the Declaration of Independence?" To a third, she might ask a conceptual question that also requires creative application, such as "Can you think of a situation when a person's individual rights must be given up for the rights of a group of people? Do you think that's fair, and, if so, why?" Any of these questions has the potential to challenge a given student, primarily because what counts as intellectually challenging is determined by the particular resources

Table 6.   Examples of modified expectations

* Amro used a calculator to solve addition and subtraction problems in a tenth-grade math class while the other students worked on two-step algebra equations.
* For their culminating project, Matt and several other students built picnic tables to be used during nice weather at their high school. He demonstrated his knowledge of mathematics by following a blueprint, using measuring and cutting tools accurately, and assembling the table in the correct pattern.
* For his culminating activity, Chris was expected to use 3 sources for his history research project, not 10 like other members of the class. Instead of a written paper in the usual narrative style, he was allowed to hand in his note cards, which reflected summaries of the information he read from his source books.
* Although Taryn participated fully in the same tenth-grade classes as every other student, her priority learning goals did not include the content of science, social studies, English, and math. In science, students categorized plants by species, kingdom, phylum, and order. The names of plants in the same species were mounted on red posterboard, same kingdom on green, same phylum on blue, and same order on yellow. Taryn's goals were to sort the plants by color. She had numerous opportunities to practice fine motor skills in this activity, although she sometimes needed to ask a tablemate for assistance if she could not reach a card. She worked on this task at the same time that her group was studying for a test on the plant classification system.
* As Jim and his lab partners took apart a model of the human body to study the different organ systems, Jim was responsible for identifying each part's number. With support from a classmate in his group, he wrote the numbers down the left-hand side of a piece of paper and other students filled in the name of the organ.
* Marty's group made a time line of prehistoric eras. Marty cut out and pasted pictures of the appropriate animals (e.g., dinosaurs, saber-tooth tigers, mammoths) near each hash mark.
* Abby took slide pictures of the effects of clear cutting in a nearby New Hampshire forest. For a final project, she showed the slides as a classmate narrated.
* Amro's friend whispered his lines to him one by one during their skit on homelessness. As Amro said each word, his friend repeated it aloud so that the class could understand it.
* Michelle completed a fill-in-the-blank test using a word bank of possible answers.
* Jesse served as the moderator during a test review modeled on *Jeopardy!* He selected a question from the category that the contestant chose and handed it to his assistant to read aloud.
* Instead of completing a written examination on the new U.S. Department of Agriculture food pyramid, Juanita prepared a food from each level, which the class sampled after they were finished taking the test.

(prior knowledge, skills, dispositions) of the learner (Schrag, 1988). Because higher-order thinking is a relative construct, it can occur in any class at any grade level with any student (Onosko & Newmann, 1994). Instructional support must respectfully begin with the student's current level of intellectual challenge and understanding. Table 7 describes examples of personalized instruction for students with significant disabilities.

Support 5: Uniquely Designed Evaluation and Grading Plans
Teachers comfortable making curricular and instructional accommodations for students with extraordinary learning challenges may none-

Table 7.   Examples of personalized instruction

- The teacher held up her hands and asked Siobhan, "If you want to work with the mural group, look here [indicating her right hand]; if you want to work on the survey, look here [indicating her left hand]."
- The English teacher asked Chris, "Pick a topic to write about that is something you are really interested in. What about doing your poem about race cars?"
- As the teacher lectured about the causes of the Civil War, a classmate whispered in Amro's ear, "They fought the war so that the slaves could be free. People from the South decided not to be part of the United States anymore. Do you remember what color skin the slaves had?"
- While students worked in groups to make tetrahedrons out of clay and toothpicks, the math teacher talked Brian through the steps of making a one-dimensional square.
- After posing the unit's central issue to the class, "Can you be free if you are not treated equally?" the teacher paused and rephrased it for Aaron. "Aaron, do you think it's fair if you can't do the same things that other kids can? That is the question that we will be studying this week."
- A teacher crouched next to Jim's desk and said, "OK, Jim. We've got 10 different steps to follow here. Let's start with these two—just cover up the rest for now."
- To one student who was really struggling, the teacher offered praise and encouragement. To another student who was goofing off, she set a higher expectation by saying, "OK, Jay, you've got 20 minutes left. I want to see three really great questions by the end of the period."
- When a student, confused about how to start a chapter summary, came up to his desk, the teacher coached him through the first couple of steps. "Zaid, if I were you, I'd start by making a list of each of the characters and whom they are related to. This would confuse anybody! Come on back up after you do that, and we'll see where to go next."
- To Lisa, who experiences difficulty in communicating, the teacher said, "Lisa, I know that you have been interested in environmental issues in the past. Why don't you work with the river pollution group for today. At the end of the period, I'll check back with you, and, if you want to change groups, you'll need to tell me then."
- Using rudimentary sign language and some gentle physical guidance, the teacher asked Daniel, "Dan, please stand up [sign and a hand under the elbow], go get your book from your locker [sign and a gesture to the door], and then come to my desk [point to desk]."

theless express concern or frustration when it is time to evaluate and grade those students' work. The following comments and questions from teachers who attended a workshop on inclusive curriculum planning reflect concern for fairness and integrity in the evaluation process:

How do I figure out what this student knows when she has such a difficult time communicating?

It doesn't seem fair to evaluate them based on the same criteria as the rest of my students because they are learning such different material.

I think we just have to accept the fact that some students will always live in the "world of the C." All throughout their lives, they will be compared with other people and they might as well get used to it now.

If he surpasses what we all expected him to do, I think he deserves an A or a B.

With our district's emphasis on raising graduation standards and increased accountability, I'm worried that I'll be criticized for giving these students grades that some people think they haven't really earned. I can hear parents now if one of these students displaces their son or daughter in class rank.

The reality is that these students will never perform as well as their classmates without disabilities. To pretend that they are by giving them regular grades is doing them a disservice and makes a mockery of the work of other students. This does nothing to improve people's opinions about inclusive education.

The first step in resolving teachers' concerns and developing a fair system of assessment is to clarify that evaluation and grading are distinct processes with very different purposes. The purpose of evaluation is to assess what students know and can do. Evaluation as defined here should be based on multiple pieces of evidence examined by multiple observers, including the student. Grading, however, is one step removed from evaluation. It is the assigning of a shorthand symbol to represent the quality of student work. That symbol can be a numerical score or a percentage, a letter, a number on a rubric, or a label such as *novice, basic, proficient,* or *mastery* (New Hampshire Educational Improvement and Assessment Program, 1995).

How is evaluation to be conducted? Gersten, Vaughn, and Brengelman (1996) described a classroom teacher's system for evaluating (not grading) the progress of students with disabilities. This teacher designed IEPs for evaluation, taking into consideration students' learning styles, personalities, and the curricular modifications that were established. Her system consisted of

1. Test accommodations (e.g., administering tests orally, changing test format from essay to multiple choice)
2. Homework accommodations (e.g., shortening the assignment, grading them as complete or incomplete)
3. Evaluation of class participation, behavior, and effort (e.g., giving points for being prepared for class and for following classroom rules)
4. A discretionary category (e.g., giving extra credit for doing extra projects)

Effective and accurate evaluation of student work needs to occur continuously and include conversations with students about what characterizes high-quality work. In addition, most students are better able to visualize what teachers mean by *high quality* when they are exposed to actual examples, whether it is a piece of creative writing, the solution to a mathematical equation, a research project, a long jump, a five-course meal, or a speech. Effective evaluation also involves telling students what is needed to improve their work and providing them with resources to act on that feedback (Fuchs, Fuchs, & Hamlett, 1994).

How is grading different from evaluation? As previously stated, grading is the act of assigning a symbol, a shorthand notation that is intended to represent the quality of a student's work. Although the intent is to efficiently communicate evaluation information to students, parents, the larger school community, and others distant from the school (e.g., prospective employer, college admissions officer), grading usually fails miserably. Regardless of how elaborate the process or formula used to arrive at a grade for the student, there is often little relationship between grading and student performance (Grolnick & Ryan, 1987; Kage, 1991) or between grading and intrinsic motivation to learn (Butler & Nissan, 1986). In short, grading is not an informative or reliable method for evaluating and communicating what students know and can do (Kohn, 1994).

Grading serves the primary purpose of ranking students, of indicating how well each student performed compared with other students. Often this information is then used for educationally and ethically questionable purposes; that is, grades are used to assign students to particular academic tracks by perceived achievement or ability, to award honors and public recognition, and to predict future achievement (Oakes, 1985; Wheelock, 1992). Grades and class ranks are also used to screen students for college admission and job placement. For students with extraordinary learning challenges, these practices have led to the perpetuation of segregated classrooms, the denial of public recognition for personal best achievements, exclusion from postsecondary education, and restricted employment opportunities.

Both evaluation and grading profoundly affect students' lives and therefore must be undertaken with the utmost care and humility. We propose that teachers or teams of teachers use the guidelines described next to help them design reasonably fair and effective evaluation and grading methods for students with extraordinary learning challenges. Because of the time demands involved, we recommend that the development of truly personalized evaluations be limited to major units of study. (For purposes of communication and documentation, a written evaluation and grading plan can be developed for each student facing extraordinary challenges.)

GUIDELINES FOR
EVALUATING AND GRADING STUDENTS
WITH EXTRAORDINARY LEARNING CHALLENGES

Evaluation
- Involve the whole team in the design of evaluation methods and the criteria to be used.
- Ensure that the student always has one or more effective ways to communicate what he or she knows and is able to do.
- Make appropriate modifications in expectations, materials, and instruction that reflect the student's talents, interests, learning styles, and priority learning objectives. (Refer to the IEP for guidance.)
- Be sure to communicate evaluation information to students in a mode that they can understand.
- For each unit of study, specify the kinds of student products that will be evaluated, including homework, tests, and culminating projects.
- Communicate to the student (by telling, showing, demonstrating) the expectations you have for performance on homework, tests, and culminating projects.
- Use the student's IEP to identify short-term objectives that are appropriate to assess within each major curriculum unit.
- Specify the kinds of learning habits and behaviors that will be evaluated, such as attendance, preparedness for class, neatness, adherence to deadlines, asking questions, and seeking assistance from other students.
- When possible, use the same formats for evaluation that are used with typical students (e.g., conferences, written comments, evaluation panels, self-evaluations).
- Evaluate each student's work relative to a predetermined standard or the student's previous efforts rather than to other students' work.

Grading
- If possible, do not grade. Important information is lost when evaluation information is translated to a shorthand symbol.
- If grading is necessary, then grade according to a prearranged teacher–student contract or by evaluating how closely the student's work matched the teacher's expectations.

- Analyze grading patterns over time to discover whether students with disabilities are clustered in the lower-grade designations. If the system of assigning grades is fair, then this should not happen.
- If academic honors are given, then include a personal best category of recognition and be sure that all deserving students are eligible and considered.
- Give students with extraordinary learning challenges the same report cards or progress reports as typical students.
- Do not mark report cards with asterisks or special education codes. Record on the student's transcript the modifications that were used and advocate for a portfolio approach to documenting student learning over time.

Finally, as advocates for all students, including those with extraordinary learning challenges, educators ought to push for a critical examination of both the purpose and the process of evaluation and grading. Evaluation in an inclusive, restructured school is used to identify the kinds of supports that students need to learn effectively. Its purpose is not to sort or separate students or to represent by a single letter or number students' varied efforts and achievements spanning numerous tasks over time (Kohn, 1994).

CONCLUSIONS

The authors hope that this unit planning model helps teachers maximize learning opportunities for all of their students. Although numerous reasons have been given throughout the chapter to support the value of this model, the authors would like to close by highlighting a few of them:

- The model emphasizes students' intellectual growth through the sustained study of problems and issues past and present.
- The model promotes students' social development, including their sense of initiative, empowerment, and capacity to work with others toward common goals through active, collaborative inquiry.
- The model's commitment to excellence and equity for all students helps counter social trends toward increased inequities between the haves and have-nots.
- The model enhances student engagement and commitment to learning by structuring opportunities for creative, personalized forms of student expression.

In Chapter 6, examples of inclusive curricula from several subject areas are discussed. The examples reflect the core beliefs presented at the beginning of this chapter and the eight essential elements of inclusive unit design that followed.

Implementation Suggestions for Teachers

1. Identify a topic that you plan to teach next month.
2. Redesign the topic according to the elements presented in this chapter.
3. Ask a small group of colleagues to fine-tune your plan before you try it with students.
4. Make revisions based on your colleagues' suggestions.
5. Tell your students that you are going to teach an upcoming unit in a new way and ask for their feedback afterward.
6. When the unit is over, share students' work with your colleagues and ask them to evaluate the works' quality and rigor. Examine a variety of student work (e.g., projects from high-achieving students, from students who are unmotivated and disinterested in school, from students with identified disabilities, from typical students).
7. Establish a timetable for revising other units (e.g., one every other month, one each semester).
8. Put a copy of your unit outline in some colleagues' mailboxes. Talk about your revised plans in the teacher's room.

Leadership Suggestions for Administrators

1. Identify teachers in your building who are ready for change and are willing to take risks.
2. Share Chapters 5 and 6 (or other inclusive curriculum design resources) with these teachers and offer administrative support (e.g., release time) to enable them to revise one of their units according to this model.
3. Encourage these general education teachers to invite special education teachers to collaborate on the unit design.
4. Provide substitutes so that teachers have time away from school to redesign a unit.
5. Encourage your colleagues to be reflective about the unit after its completion.
6. Involve other teachers in a conversation about inclusive unit planning by allocating time during departmental or faculty meetings.

REFERENCES

Baumgart, D., Brown, L., Pumpian, I., Nisbet, J., Ford, A., Sweet, M., Messina, R., & Schroeder, J. (1982). The principle of partial participation and individualized adaptations in educational programs for severely handicapped students. *Journal of The Association for Persons with Severe Handicaps, 7*(2), 17–27.

Bower, B., Lobdell, J., & Swenson, L. (1994). *History alive!* Reading, MA: Addison-Wesley.

Brown, R. (1991). *Schools of thought.* San Francisco: Jossey-Bass.

Butler, R., & Nissan, M. (1986). Effects of no feedback, task-related comments, and grades on intrinsic motivation and performance. *Journal of Educational Psychology, 78,* 210–216.

Collicott, J. (1991). Implementing multi-level instruction: Strategies for classroom teachers. In G.L. Porter & D. Richler (Eds.), *Changing Canadian schools: Perspectives on disability and inclusion* (pp. 191–218). Downsview, Ontario, Canada: G. Allan Roeher Institute.

Cuban, L. (1984). *How teachers taught: Constancy and change in American classrooms 1890–1980.* New York: Longman.

Dire Straits. (1985). Walk of life. *Brothers in arms* [Recording]. Los Angeles: Warner Brothers.

Dunn, R., Beaudry, J., & Klavas, A. (1989). Survey of research on learning styles. *Educational Leadership, 46*(6), 50–58.

Fitzgerald, F. (1979). *America revised.* New York: Vintage Books.

Fuchs, L.S., Fuchs, D., & Hamlett, C. (1994). Strengthening the connection between assessment and instructional planning with expert systems. *Exceptional Children, 61*(2), 138–146.

Gardner, H. (1983). *Frames of mind: The theory of multiple intelligences.* New York: Basic Books.

Gersten, R., Vaughn, S., & Brengelman, S. (1996). Grading and academic feedback for special education students and students with learning difficulties. In T.R. Guskey (Ed.), *Communicating student learning, ASCD Yearbook* (pp. 47–57). Alexandria, VA: Association for Supervision and Curriculum Development.

Goodlad, J. (1984). *A place called school: Prospects for the future.* New York: McGraw-Hill.

Gottfried, A. (1985). Academic intrinsic motivation in elementary and junior high school students. *Journal of Educational Psychology, 77,* 631–645.

Grolnick, W., & Ryan, R. (1987). Autonomy in children's learning: An experimental and individual difference investigation. *Journal of Personality and Social Psychology, 52,* 890–898.

Harmin, M. (1994). *Inspiring active learning: A handbook for teachers.* Alexandria, VA: Association for Supervision and Curriculum Development.

Joel, B. (1989). We didn't start the fire. *Storm front* [Recording]. New York: CBS Records.

Johnson, D., & Johnson, R. (1989). *Cooperation and competition: Theory and research.* Edina, MN: Interaction Book Co.

Jorgensen, C.M. (1996). Developing inclusive curriculum right from the start: Practical strategies and examples from the high school classroom. In S. Stainback & W. Stainback (Eds.), *Inclusion: A guide for educators* (pp. 221–236). Baltimore: Paul H. Brookes Publishing Co.

Kage, M. (1991). *The effects of evaluation on intrinsic motivation.* Paper presented at the meeting of the Japan Association of Educational Psychology, Joetsu, Japan.

Kahane, H. (1984). *Logic and contemporary rhetoric: The use of reason in everyday life.* Belmont, CA: Wadsworth.

Kohn, A. (1994). Grading: The issue is not how but why. *Educational Leadership,* 52(2), 38–41.

Lennon, J., & McCartney, P. (1967). With a little help from my friends. *Sgt. Pepper's lonely hearts club band* [Recording]. New York: Capitol Records.

Midler, B. (1988). Wind beneath my wings. *Beaches* [Recording]. Hollywood, CA: Atlantic Music Co.

New Hampshire Educational Improvement and Assessment Program. (1995). *Educational assessment report.* Concord: State of New Hampshire, Department of Education.

Newmann, F. (1988). Can depth replace coverage in the high school curriculum? *Phi Delta Kappan, 68*(5), 345–348.

Newmann, F. (1990). Higher-order thinking in social studies: A rationale for the assessment of classroom thoughtfulness. *Journal of Curriculum Studies,* 22(1), 41–56.

Newton, S. (1983). *I will call it Georgie's Blues.* New York: Viking Press.

Oakes, J. (1985). *Keeping track: How schools structure inequality.* New Haven, CT: Yale University Press.

Onosko, J. (1991). Barriers to the promotion of higher-order thinking. *Theory and Research in Social Education, 19*(4), 341–366.

Onosko, J. (1996). Exploring issues with students despite the barriers. *Social Education, 60*(1), 22–27.

Onosko, J., & Newmann, F. (1994). Creating more thoughtful learning environments in secondary classrooms and schools. In C. Collins & J. Maugieri (Eds.), *Creating more powerful thinkers in teachers and students.* New York: Harcourt Brace Jovanovich.

Onosko, J., & Swenson, L. (1996). Designing issue-based unit plans. In R. Evans & D. Saxe (Eds.), *The handbook on teaching social issues* (pp. 89–98). Washington, DC: NCSS.

Peck, R. (1985). *Remembering the good times.* New York: Delacorte Press.

Prawat, R. (1991). The value of ideas: The immersion approach to the development of thinking. *Educational Researcher, 20*(2), 3–10, 30.

Qin, Z., Johnson, D., & Johnson, R. (1995). Cooperative versus competitive efforts and problem solving. *Review of Educational Research, 65*(2), 129–143.

Saphier, J., & Gower, R. (1987). *The skillful teacher: Building your teaching skills.* Carlisle, MA: Research for Better Teaching.

Schrag, F. (1988). *Thinking in school and society.* New York: Routledge.

Shirey, L., & Reynolds, R. (1988). Effect of interest on attention and learning. *Journal of Educational Psychology, 80,* 159–166.

Sirotnik, K. (1983). What you see is what you get—constancy, persistency, and mediocrity in classrooms. *Harvard Educational Review, 53*(1), 16–31.

Sternberg, R. (1985). *Beyond IQ: A triarchic theory of human intelligence.* Cambridge, England: Cambridge University Press.

Sternberg, R. (1996). Myths, countermyths, and truths about intelligence. *Educational Researcher, 25*(2), 11–16.

Stipek, D. (1993). *Motivation to learn: From theory to practice* (2nd ed.). Needham, MA: Allyn & Bacon.

Tashie, C., Shapiro-Barnard, S., Schuh, M., Jorgensen, C., Dillon, A., Dixon, B., & Nisbet, J. (1993). *From special to regular: From ordinary to extraordinary.* Durham: University of New Hampshire, Institute on Disability.

Taylor, J. (1971). You've got a friend. *Sweet baby James* [Recording]. Los Angeles: Warner Brothers.

Thomas, L. (1974). *The lives of a cell: Notes of a biology watcher.* New York: Viking Press.

Thousand, J., Fox, T., Reid, R., Godek, J., Williams, W., & Fox, W. (1986). *The homecoming model: Educating students who present intensive educational challenges within regular education environments* (Monograph 7-1). Burlington: University of Vermont, Center for Developmental Disabilities.

Tyson-Bernstein, H. (1988). *A conspiracy of good intentions: America's textbook fiasco.* Washington, DC: Council for Basic Education.

Weinberg, R. (1989). Intelligence and IQ: Landmark issues and great debates. *American Psychologist, 44*(2), 98–104.

Wheelock, A. (1992). *Crossing the tracks: How "untracking" can save America's schools.* New York: Free Press.

Wiggins, G. (1989). The futility of trying to teach everything of importance. *Educational Leadership, 47,* 44–48.

X, M. (1962). *The autobiography of Malcolm X.* New York: Grove Press.

6

Examples of Inclusive
Curriculum Units and Lessons

Cheryl M. Jorgensen

In Chapter 5, a model was presented for developing inclusive curriculum units and lessons. Although the author does not support the idea of a cookbook of inclusive lessons, this chapter does give a number of examples of curriculum units and activities that have worked for teachers. Perhaps these ideas will germinate the seeds of creativity that are present in all teachers. Even when a curriculum is designed to be inclusive from the bottom up, it is essential that teachers always be open to making modifications and adaptations for students who present extraordinary learning or support needs. In addition to descriptions of many naturally inclusive units and lessons, some examples of modifications for students with significant disabilities are presented.

    This chapter was supported in part by Grant H023R20018 from the U.S. Department of Education, Office of Special Education and Rehabilitative Services.

We Didn't Start the Fire

The lyrics of "We Didn't Start the Fire" (Joel, 1989) list many of the people, places, and cultural and political events of the mid-20th century, including Presidents Truman and Eisenhower, Senator Joseph McCarthy, the Korean conflict, *South Pacific* (Logan, 1958), and the advent of the television era. At the end of seventh period on a wintry Friday afternoon, Joel's recording was played for 89 ninth-grade students in their team-block classes in English, social studies, science, and math. During a whole-class community meeting on the following Monday morning, when the following essential questions were posed to the students, they knew that something would be different about the upcoming week. What is the fire? Who started the fire? Have any fires been put out? Are any fires still burning?

The English, social studies, science, and math teachers on the team had simple goals for this unit. They wanted to work on a project that would cross subject boundaries and teach students research and cooperative learning skills. Kim Carter, Souhegan's Information Center Director, suggested this song as a vehicle for accomplishing these goals. Based on Manchester's *The Glory and the Dream* (1974), the lyrics offer an encapsulated look at the second half of the 20th century.

As the week's activities were planned, opportunities were provided for students to choose work partners, engage in research, share knowledge with their peers, and have a good time. It turned out, however, to be more important as a learning experience for both students and teachers. They saw overwhelming evidence that, when careful attention is paid to students' individual learning styles and talents, all students can not only succeed but thrive in a rigorous academic environment.

By the end of Monday, each ninth-grade student was a member of a self-selected four- to six-student working group assigned to research one line of the song's lyrics. Team classes were canceled for the week, and students were encouraged to use all available school resources. Each student maintained a learning log, a research record, a self-evaluation, and a group evaluation. For their final exhibition, students were told to "wow" their teachers with a 5- to 15-minute presentation that would address at least two of the essential questions,

---

The "We Didn't Start the Fire" unit plan was created and contributed by Peggy Silva, Souhegan High School, Amherst, New Hampshire.

Teachers involved in the "We Didn't Start the Fire" unit described in this chapter were Gary Schnakenberg (social studies), Kris Gallo (math), Jessica Forbush (social studies intern), Bruce Shotland (science), Sally Houghton (special education support teacher), Jack Mattke (audiovisual specialist), Kim Carter (information specialist), Lynn Mauro (information assistant), and Peggy Silva (English).

explain a portion of the lyrics, and educate and entertain their peers. Each group submitted a project proposal outlining plans for the exhibition. Student work was assessed in 11 different categories ranging from "demonstration of preparation time" to "effective use of selected medium." The grading scale included the designations "distinctive," "effective," "acceptable," and "ineffective." Teachers reserved some grading points for the "wow" factor.

Students discovered laser disk technology as they viewed newsreel footage of historical events, explored CD-ROMs, and mastered video technology by dubbing in soundtracks and voice-overs. Some students watched *Ben-Hur* (Zimbalist & Wyler, 1959), *South Pacific* (Logan, 1958), and the Army–McCarthy Senate hearings (Schrecker, 1994). They laughed when they discovered that, although they were surrounded by sophisticated audiovisual equipment, they could not find a record player in the building!

Final exhibitions ranged from a *Saturday Night Live* (Michaels, 1975) skit in which students portraying Davy Crockett and Albert Einstein visited "Wayne's World" to a demonstration of a cycle theory model in which every person or event was identified as a problem, an inspiration, or a solution. One group re-created the explosion of the bridge over the River Kwai, and students watched Nasser's funeral while listening to the music of Prokofiev. One group of students performed a powerful theater piece incorporating the tensions of the 1960s from birth control to the Vietnam War. They learned about Joseph Stalin, Sputnik, Juan Perón, the Bay of Pigs, Princess Grace, the Suez Canal, James Dean, Dien Bien Phu, Sonny Liston, and Syngman Rhee. They watched live and videotaped skits, listened to lectures and music, and played *Wheel of Fortune* (Griffin, 1975). They learned together and had fun together.

Student evaluations and a debriefing demonstrated that students had mastered both content and process. They were able to reflect on what they had learned and how they had learned it. They outlined frustrations and suggested refinements for future activities. Above all, they "wowed" everyone with their commitment to their learning and to the assigned task.

In the teacher's words,

> We learned again that the old terminology doesn't work. We need to develop a new language to describe students—LD [learning disabilities], coded kids, SPED [special education], most abled, least abled, most challenged—these terms do not fit our everyday experience when we design [a] curriculum based on real-world solutions to real-world situations. Although 20% of our team population is labeled as *learning disabled*, visitors to our classroom cannot identify those students "most labeled." We acknowledge the need for special services; each of our 89 students requires special services at some point. Some need to learn to work with others;

others need to learn to demonstrate learning without a pen or a chapter test. Some of our students need help to write with clarity, to comprehend reading, to become better organized, or to present work creatively. Our students represent great diversity of skill, ability, and interest; but the balance shifts according to the nature of the tasks. Every time we grapple with essential questions that require active student participation, we hear students testify that they have learned more in 1 week than they could have learned in a month in a lecture-oriented classroom. With such powerful testimony, how can we ever return to those old methods?

Brandon

Brandon, who uses a letterboard to communicate, could participate in all aspects of the "We Didn't Start the Fire" unit. On the first day of the unit, when groups were being formed and students were selecting which stanza they wanted to work on, Brandon could use his letterboard to choose his group by spelling the names of the classmates with whom he wanted to work. If his group developed a play, Brandon could spell out his lines when it was his turn to speak and a classmate could say them aloud. If he needed to produce a written product, he could write a report on the computer and hand it in just like the other members of his group.

When Will We Ever Use This Stuff? An Interdisciplinary Student Performance in English, Math, and Science

The Situation: You work for an important state government agency. Your job involves researching and writing papers and making proposals concerning various projects. You are skilled in research, writing, and presenting information to various audiences. You are also often asked to work collaboratively with co-workers on various projects.

The Problem: Your supervisor has come to you with the following information: It will soon be "take our children to work" day. The local department of social services would like to place students who do not have a workplace to visit. The department would like to know of professionals who would be interested in hosting a student for a day, and all of the students they wish to place are interested in careers in math and science.

Your Task: You are expected to research a career for which knowledge of math and science is required on a daily basis. You are then to contact a professional working in this field and interview him or her about the career. Your interview must include a range of questions about the career and specifically ask how the person uses math and science in his or her field. You will then prepare a presentation based on the data you have collected. It is very important that you specifically address and give detailed examples of the identified math and science applications that the professional uses. Your presentation will be made to the local department of social services review board and may take the form of a written feature story with illustrations or an oral presentation with visual aids.

Learning Standards

This unit addresses many math, science, and English learning standards as identified by national, state, and local school groups. For example, the National Council of Teachers of Mathematics' Standard 4 states that students will be able to make logical connections between mathematics and other subject areas and show their ability to use math to solve problems in other areas (Thompson & Rathmell, 1988). The New York State Standards for Mathematics, Science, and Technology also require that students be able to apply math, science, and technology techniques to solve real-life problems (New York State Ed-

---

The "When Will We Ever Use This Stuff? An Interdisciplinary Student Performance in English, Math, and Science" unit plan was created and contributed by Jim Ludington, Mark Pellegrino, Sandy Hamilton, and Renae Roehrs, Gananda Central Senior High School, Walworth, New York.

ucation Department, 1996). The Gananda Central Senior High School English Department has identified an English standard as "[Students will] plan, produce, and deliver oral presentations, then evaluate using specific rubrics."

Guidelines for Students

1. In class, write a statement of purpose (i.e., what you are doing and why you are doing it) that can be used when contacting a person to be interviewed. This purpose statement will include your name, grade, school, and an explanation of the project.

2. Choose a profession that interests you and then research information about it. This research will help you formulate interview questions and is also an essential component of your presentation.

3. You will be expected to make a detailed outline of your research notes with a bibliography. Suggested topics for your outline include a description of the career, the education and training necessary for that career path, the duties and responsibilities it entails, use of math and science in the career, and contributions of the profession to society. A rubric is used to evaluate this part of the assignment.

4. Brainstorm effective interview questions. Your questions should be short, clear, interesting, and direct. Avoid obvious questions and questions that generate yes or no answers. Instead, prompt the person to give more lengthy and detailed comments.

5. Schedule an appointment to conduct your interview. Be sure the interviewee understands the purpose of the interview and that you will be using the information in a presentation. Use the rubric as a guide to prepare yourself for the interview.

6. Before you conduct your presentation, you should turn in a copy of your interview in the form of a written script and photograph showing how you will be dressed for the interview, an audiotape and photograph, or a videotape.

7. You may choose an original format for a final presentation, provided that you receive your instructor's approval, or you may choose one of the following formats: a feature story, 3–5 pages in length double-spaced with illustrations, or an oral presentation 5–7 minutes in length with visual aids such as charts, photographs, and graphs.

All formats must show detailed examples of at least two math and two science concepts and their applications as used by the individual in his or her work. Solved examples of formulas, as well as tables, charts, and graphs, would be acceptable.

Evaluation Rubric

Superior: The written, visual, and oral presentations are free of any math or science errors. The description of how the math and science concepts are applied is logical and thorough. The complexity of the applications being described exceeds the level to which they have been taught in school.

Proficient: Mathematical and science errors are inconsequential; they are not even worthy of being questioned. The descriptions are logical and thorough enough to be understandable to an expert. The complexity of the examples are no more than 1 year below grade level.

Acceptable: Some major mathematical and scientific errors may be present, but they are corrected upon questioning. The descriptions are incomplete or illogical enough to be confusing to experts but are corrected upon questioning. The complexity of the examples is not challenging as shown by being 2 or more years below grade level.

Not Yet: Major math and science flaws or errors exist. The descriptions are incomplete or illogical and are not corrected upon questioning. Applications do not go beyond common knowledge.

Rob

Rob is a tenth grader who experienced a traumatic brain injury following a serious car accident. Although he has regained a great deal of his physical and cognitive functioning, he experiences residual learning problems. Although his decoding skills are very good and have nearly returned to his preaccident levels, his comprehension is poor and he has difficulty retaining what he learns over time. Multistep problems or projects are overwhelming for Rob, and he often "doesn't know where to start." This unit, though multifaceted and complex, could be adapted easily for Rob because it has concrete aspects (e.g., interviewing a real person at a jobsite), includes time at the beginning of the unit for students to organize their thoughts and interview questions, and offers choices in how students will demonstrate what they have learned. As a result of his long stay at a rehabilitation center, Rob has developed an interest in medicine. Rob might focus on the use of math and physics by physical therapists during the rehabilitation process. Because Rob has difficulty writing, the option of doing a videotape interview and an oral presentation to his class would allow Rob to bypass some of his learning challenges and utilize his strengths.

Can You Be Free if You Are Not Treated Equally?

In Ken Burns's *Civil War* series (1989), historian Barbara Fields commented, "The Civil War is not over, and it can still be lost." She is referring to inequalities that still exist in the United States that keep some people from having the same degree of freedom as other Americans. For several weeks, tenth graders at Souhegan High School considered the essential question, "Can you be free if you are not treated equally?" by studying the period in U.S. history from Reconstruction to the present, focusing on the civil rights activities of the 1950s and 1960s. All students were expected to do a final exhibition at the conclusion of the unit chosen from the following options:

1. Write a letter to a student of history in 2028. Explain to the student some of the changes that have occurred because of the civil rights movement. Describe the present condition of civil rights in the United States. Use specific events to illustrate your points.
2. Research an event that illustrates how people have challenged the laws that restrict their freedom, for example, a case like *Brown v. Board of Education* (1954) or an action such as the Montgomery bus boycott. Describe the event. Explain specifically what these people did and why you think they chose that form of action. In your opinion, was it successful?
3. You have been a civil rights advocate since the 1950s. You have been asked to speak at a local college on your experiences in the movement and your opinion about whether people are free if they are not treated equally. Prepare and deliver a speech for this event.
4. Respond to the following Martin Luther King, Jr. (1964) quotation: "We know through painful experience that freedom is never voluntarily given by the oppressor; it must be demanded by the oppressed." Do you agree with this statement? Use specific examples from the civil rights movement that support your views.

The kickoff activity for this unit was a powerful in-class simulation of a slave ship voyage from Africa to the United States. Partitions between three adjoining classrooms were opened, and students from two classes played the slaves. Cathy outlined the actual dimensions of a slave ship on the classroom floor, and the students were packed tightly into this space. With the lights off, Cathy read from a ship captain's log, describing the characteristics of the human "cargo," the prices paid for them, the meager food rations given to the slaves, an

---

The "Can You Be Free if You Are Not Treated Equally?" unit plan was created and contributed by Cathy Fisher, Souhegan High School, Amherst, New Hampshire.

incident in which a slave attempting to escape was shot, and so forth. Following this activity, Cathy and her teaching partner, English teacher Scott LaLiberte, facilitated a lengthy discussion period.

Amro

Amro Diab, a tenth grader at Souhegan and member of Cathy and Scott's team, communicates by spelling on a letterboard and is labeled as having mental retardation. Amro's learning objectives for this unit are summarized on the form presented in Figure 1.

Summary of Learning Goals and Supports

Student: Amro Diab   **Subject:** American Studies

Class: Block C   **Unit:** Civil Rights

Lesson/Unit goals

1. Locate dates of the Civil War on a time line.
2. Describe African American perspective on slavery.
3. Tell one reason why the Civil War was fought.
4. Complete a modified exhibition at the conclusion of the unit that reflects personal perspective on the essential question.

IEP goals

1. Spelling correctly, use three new content-specific vocabulary words in class discussions or assignments.
2. Consistently use letterboard to communicate with classmates and teacher.
3. Volunteer one answer during each class period.
4. With support from classmates, compose three complete sentences to answer comprehension questions about the Civil War.

Supports and modifications

1. Must have letterboard and laptop for every class period.
2. Should be in a group with Ryan or Joe.
3. Should complete one out-of-class assignment per week.
4. Final exhibition should be modified to reflect Amro's interests and goals.

Figure 1.   Summary of learning goals and supports.

Superman and Odysseus: Heroes in Action

In ninth grade at Santana High School, all students in English are required to read Homer's *The Odyssey* (1919) and study Greek mythology. Unfortunately, many students do not have a natural passion for the world's first poet. They find this unit boring and cannot see its relevance to the 20th century. Comparing Odysseus to a modern superhero makes the unit come alive for them.

The movie *Superman* (Donner, 1978) provides an excellent beginning for a study of epic heroes and adventures. The film integrates universal heroic traits and unique cultural values. Clark Kent and his alter ego, Superman, embody characteristics of many heroes: mysterious origins, a sense of mission and the heroic journey, courage, physical prowess, intelligence, self-control, and areas of vulnerability. With his commitment to "truth, justice, and the American way," Superman is distinctly a product of the United States.

After viewing the film and answering a set of questions, students complete a comparison chart of the heroic traits of Superman and Odysseus. Students learn that heroes from the 8th century B.C.E. share many characteristics with today's heroes. The concept of *hero* and what a hero represents to society is almost universal. The students realize that our role models and mentors have not changed in more than 3,000 years.

Next, students create their own original hero. Individually or in groups, students design a hero that possesses some of the same universal traits. Students are guided by an original hero chart and a list of heroic traits. Then the students name and draw a picture of their hero. At the end of the unit, students write a two- to five-page story starring their hero. The story must contain at least four characteristics of an epic and remain consistent with Homer's poetic technique. At the end of the unit, students take turns reading their original episode to the class and sharing their illustrations. Through all of these activities, students are required to define *hero* and demonstrate an understanding of specific trademarks of an epic and an epic hero.

The unit is easy to adapt for students with various learning styles and talents. Some students can demonstrate understanding by cutting out pictures from a magazine. Others draw pictures or use computer programs to design their hero. Most students enjoy the movie and do not have any trouble making the connection between Superman and Odysseus. This project can also be adapted by using a variety of comic books in addition to the *Superman* movie.

The "Superman and Odysseus: Heroes in Action" unit plan was created and contributed by Kari Mumford, Santana High School, Santee, California.

David

David, a student who has autism, points to symbols generated by an augmentative communication software program to indicate his understanding of curriculum. Although constructing a fictional hero might be difficult for him, his assignment might be to sequence symbols to recall the events and characters from the *Superman* movie (Donner, 1978). Although this project would be different from that required of the other students in the class, David would still learn many of the same concepts about the characteristics of heroes, and the assignment would be challenging for him.

The Story of the Stick

This unit is a nearly perfect kickoff activity designed to get all students involved in an environmental science unit. First, students are organized into groups of 10. Each group is given a partially decomposed tree branch that measures about 1 inch in diameter and 4 feet in length. The teacher then sets up the activity by telling the following story:

> For the next several weeks, we are going to try to answer the question, "Are the New Hampshire forests healthy?" You are probably wondering what this stick has to do with that question. Can anyone think of a situation in science where we study a small thing in order to understand a larger thing? [Three students are called on to respond to this question and will probably give examples such as "We study atoms to understand matter," "We study cells in order to understand the workings of the human body," and "We study individual planets in order to understand the universe."] We are going to study these sticks to try to understand something about the forests that they came from. For the next few minutes, I would like you to work in your small groups to describe the stick. You should elect someone to record your observations. We'll be sharing them in about 7 minutes. The only rule of this activity is that everyone in your group must participate. Any questions? Go!

As the groups work, the teacher should encourage each student's participation but should not interfere in the process. A 1-minute warning is given, and groups are then asked to share their observations. Let each group share three to five observations in round-robin fashion. The observations can be noted on an overhead projector, flipchart, or blackboard. Common observations include furrowed, part of a whole, patterned, dead, splintered, made of wood, decayed, barkless, feels like a soft wood, and smells or tastes musty.

The second part of the exercise is to give the groups about 10 minutes to "tell the story of the stick." Tell students again that everyone must participate and that each group will be asked to perform or share their story. Elect a recorder and encourage both literary and scientific stories. Typical stories begin like this:

> One hundred years ago, a Native American girl was walking through the forest when she noticed a fallen tree on the forest floor. She broke off a limb and used it for a walking stick. Before returning to her village, she threw the stick into the river, where it floated to the other side. When the river dried up, bugs made the stick their home and gradually ate through the center, making furrows and tracks along its length.

Many groups add songs and movements to their stories, with each student playing the role of the various human and animal characters.

The "Story of the Stick" unit plan was created and contributed by Dan Bisaccio, Souhegan High School, Amherst, New Hampshire.

After each group has performed its story, the teacher should ask students how they might test whether their stories (or their hypotheses) are correct. Typical responses include the following:

> Go to where it fell and see if there are other, similar branches lying around. Look at dead branches that are still on trees, peel bark, and compare. Put a piece of unmunched wood in a case with some insects. See if the branch comes out looking like this one. Determine what it *isn't* first, then narrow down to a couple of possibilities. Find out what kinds of beetles eat different kinds of trees.

This activity is a natural way to involve all students. Students with no prior knowledge of botany or environmental issues can contribute important observations. In fact, the more diverse the observational descriptions, the better. Students who see the world from a linguistic perspective give right answers, and students whose talents are mathematical or logical also have valuable observations. The fun aspect of the activity motivates all students to participate. Unlike most introductory lessons ("Turn to Chapter 4 in your book and let's preview the chapter headings"), students who have difficulty in reading are not asked to do the very thing that makes them most discouraged. From the beginning of the unit, they see that they can be successful because their talents are as important as reading and writing.

Lisa

Lisa has multiple disabilities, uses a wheelchair, needs hand-over-hand physical assistance to manipulate objects, and has functional skills as short-term learning objectives on her individualized education program (IEP). The Story of the Stick kickoff and the research activities that follow it would present many learning opportunities for Lisa. First, if Lisa were included in the unit right from the start, then her right to belong would be evident not only to Lisa but also to her classmates. Lisa would need to reach and grasp the stick as it was passed to her by a classmate and then pass it on to the next person in her group. If Lisa's communication system has vocabulary categories such as colors, textures, and shapes, then she can offer her opinion of the stick's description during the first part of the activity. Even if Lisa were unable to use vocabulary like this to describe the stick, her classmates might translate her facial expressions or body language into words as they help her feel the stick.

Acquired Immunodeficiency Syndrome

In this unit, developed by English teacher Trish Walton, students practice their English skills while learning about a timely and important topic for adolescents, acquired immunodeficiency syndrome (AIDS). Although Trish believes strongly that almost every student can and should learn how to write well, there are many performance options built into this unit so that students who have difficulty writing can show what they know by other means.

Requirements
1. An entry in a reading journal on the topic of AIDS
2. Active participation in group discussions
3. One newspaper article, magazine story, or summary of a television program or news report about AIDS
4. A two-page summary of an article off the classroom AIDS bulletin board (First page should be a factual summary; second page should be opinion of or reaction to the major issues presented in the article.)
5. A position paper
6. A project about some aspect of AIDS

Possibilities for a project about AIDS include the following:

- Research an aspect of AIDS (e.g., history of the disease, use of drugs or alternative treatments, chronicle of the life of someone with AIDS). Use the research to write a traditional research paper or for a creative writing piece.
- Interview someone who works for an AIDS hotline.
- Interview someone who treats people with the human immunodeficiency virus (HIV) or AIDS.
- Interview someone who is an advocate for people living with HIV or AIDS.
- Create a survey to give to students and faculty. Administer the survey, compile the results, create graphics and charts based on the data collected, and summarize the findings.
- Prepare questions to ask people for a videotaped survey. Follow the steps given above for a survey.
- Read at least three AIDS books assigned in class or find others. Review them and determine what has been learned since the book was published.
- Write letters for a variety of audiences (e.g., a newspaper, congressional representatives, activist groups).

The "Acquired Immunodeficiency Syndrome" unit plan was created and contributed by Trish Walton, Rundlett Junior High School, Concord, New Hampshire.

- Create a book about AIDS for a younger audience.
- Write a book of poetry about AIDS issues.
- Create a photographic essay about AIDS.
- Draw or paint a number of pieces about AIDS.
- Design an individualized project.

Bernie

Even though Bernie is unable to read, he could participate in the AIDS unit with some low-tech modifications. Instead of reading one of the assigned books, Bernie could watch a movie version of *The Outsiders* (Coppola, 1983), which shows young people who feel as if they are discriminated against and as if they do not belong to mainstream society. Instead of requiring Bernie to write an essay about the movie, Trish might adapt the expectations for him and instead ask him to narrate his recollection of the story and offer a personal view of what it is like for teenagers who are part of the "in" group and those who are "outsiders."

Columbus Didn't Discover America!

In their third year of studying Spanish, students begin to read literature that has been written for a Hispanic audience. It is unabridged and deals with topics that are important to people who live in Spain and Latin America. In the fall of 1993, in honor of the quincentennial celebration of Columbus's voyage to the new world, Linda Kelley's Spanish III class studied the Native American view of the conquest and compared it with the European view. Students studied the events in Europe that led to Columbus's voyage, the response of various Native American groups to him and the other conquerors who explored the Americas, and the present-day views of European Americans and Native Americans with regard to their history.

Students compared excerpts from Cortes's diary (Cortes, 1908) and *The Broken Spears: The Aztec Account of the Conquest of Mexico* (Leon-Portilla, 1962). They also viewed the film *Columbus Didn't Discover Us* (Turning Tide Productions, 1992). They learned from these works that Native Americans and European Americans have radically different views about the relative advantages and disadvantages of the conquest for the inhabitants of the western hemisphere.

The final project for this unit was the task of writing a storybook for an 8-year-old Hispanic child. Students had to incorporate both viewpoints of the discovery in a way that would be appealing to a child of that age. Linda encouraged students to make liberal use of pictures, drawings, photographs, and cutouts from magazines. For the final exhibition, students read their books aloud to their classmates.

The variety of products acceptable for this assignment illustrated how it was adaptive for students with many different learning styles, talents, and challenges. Some students drew stick figures but used grammatically correct full-sentence prose. Other students drew elaborate pictures and captioned them with short phrases and sentences. Still others used computer-scanned photographs, drawings, and maps to illustrate Columbus's voyages and the reception he received from, and the reaction to him by, the Native Americans.

The directive to write a book for an 8-year-old child took the pressure off many students who would have been intimidated by the prospect of writing a book for an adult audience. On presentation day, all the students sat around in a circle and read their books to one another during storytime. Each book was graded on a number of criteria, including creativity, Spanish grammar, artwork, and faithfulness to the various points of view of the story.

The "Columbus Didn't Discover America!" unit plan was created and contributed by Linda Kelley, Winchester Thurston School, Pittsburgh, Pennsylvania.

Shawna

Shawna uses facilitated communication to participate in her high school classes. Because it takes her longer to express her ideas, page-length requirements are shortened and tests are sometimes modified from essays to multiple choice or matching questions so that she is able to complete her work in about the same time as other students. If she were a member of Linda Kelley's Spanish class, Linda might modify the length of the book writing assignment. Shawna might choose to write one short paragraph that summarizes her opinions about the topic and then choose computer-generated artwork to illustrate her writing.

Back-to-Back Drawing

Several Souhegan High School language teachers use this activity to reinforce vocabulary that has been taught in class. Students are paired with a partner and sit back to back. While looking at a picture or photograph, one partner describes the picture and the other partner tries to draw it.

Preparation
1. Choose four different pictures that relate to the specific vocabulary unit being taught.
2. Divide the class into four groups, giving each group one of the pictures. After electing a secretary, each group should generate a list of French, Spanish, or Japanese words that describe objects, feelings, or actions depicted in the picture. For each word, the group should also supply the English translation.
3. To prepare the students for the challenge of communicating the essence of the picture and clarifying misunderstandings, several target phrases are reviewed that they will need in order to work together to produce the new picture. These might include: "I don't understand," "Repeat that," "Excuse me," "Did you mean . . . ?"
4. The teacher should duplicate the vocabulary lists so that each pair of students has a picture and a vocabulary list for the next part of the activity.

In Class
1. Organize students in pairs. One partner should have the picture or photograph and the vocabulary list and another partner should have a blank piece of drawing paper.
2. Sitting back to back, one person then describes the picture and the other attempts to draw it.
3. When the artist feels as if he or she has drawn as much detail as possible and the describer has exhausted his or her instructions, they should compare pictures to see how closely the new picture matches the original.
4. When two pairs of students are finished, they exchange pictures, switch roles, and try another one.

Students love to share their drawings at the end of the class. Pictures can be labeled with the vocabulary words and displayed around the classroom.

The "Back-to-Back Drawing" unit plan was created and contributed by Eric Pohl, Souhegan High School, Amherst, New Hampshire.

Hilary

Because Hilary has significant movement difficulties, she might have the following short-term objective on her IEP: "During one-to-one instruction with her aide or the occupational therapist, Hilary will improve her tripod grasp by coloring within the lines of large bold drawings of familiar objects such as balloons, animals, and geometric shapes. She will make fewer than three marks outside the borders."

However, if Hilary were included in Eric Pohl's Spanish class, she would get plenty of practice on her fine motor skills in the back-to-back drawing activity, through daily practice in writing vocabulary words, and by using a computer to generate longer writing assignments. Her IEP might be written differently to reflect these fine motor learning opportunities that are present in the general education class (e.g., "Within a variety of general education classes, Hilary will practice her fine motor skills by using pencil or pen to complete short writing assignments, by participating in a creative art class, and by using the computer to complete longer writing assignments").

Whodunit?

Teachers, you know the feeling. You and your students return from April vacation wondering how you are going to make it through the next 6 weeks of school before the summer break. This same dilemma faced the teachers on Team 9A at Souhegan High School during the spring of 1995. They decided to brainstorm ideas for an interdisciplinary unit that would inject some energy into their students and themselves.

Math teacher Joanne McDeed was planning to teach logic for the next couple of weeks. English teacher Bethany Prunier wanted to do a journalism unit focusing on crime reporting and persuasive argument. Social studies teacher Jessica Forbush planned to introduce students to the Bill of Rights and related legal proceedings associated with the U.S. government's early days. Science teacher Chris Balch was planning a unit on evidence gathering and forensic science. What theme or topic might unite these different topics?

Of course—a murder mystery! Using the characters from Clue (Parker Brothers, 1986) as a foundation, the teachers presented a skit to their entire ninth-grade team of students and told them that they would be working together for the next 2 weeks to try to discover who murdered Bobby O'Sullivan, assistant director of student services. Each of the team teachers took the role of a Clue character.

During the first week of the project, experts from the legal and law enforcement communities came into the school to conduct topical workshops such as evidence collection, interviewing, arrest procedures, suspects' rights, courtroom procedures, and autopsy techniques. Students were divided into groups representing defense and prosecution teams, police officers, journalists, criminalists, and cryptologists.

Two identical trials were held so that all 95 students on the team had an opportunity to be actively involved in the project. Dean of Faculty Allison Rowe served as the judge for one trial, and a senior student who has excelled in mock trial competitions for Souhegan presided over the other trial.

This unit is another example of how rigorous academic learning can be embedded into an interdisciplinary unit of study that requires students to exhibit their knowledge through a realistic application. All different kinds of talents—verbal persuasion, tedious research, scientific investigation, logic, deductive reasoning, and courtroom theater—were required to solve the case, and every student found his or her special role in this project.

The "Whodunit?" unit plan was created and contributed by Jessica Forbush, Souhegan High School, Amherst, New Hampshire.

"Blooming" Worksheets

Is there any room for worksheets in a heterogeneous classroom that focuses on what students can do with knowledge rather than on rote memorization? Yes! Worksheets organized according to Bloom's taxonomy can provide a quick and easy way for teachers to assess whether students are mastering information as a unit progresses (Kagan, 1994). When designed to include questions at several levels of Bloom's taxonomy, the questions also test whether students are progressing past the point of identification and classification of information to more advanced levels of thinking about a particular topic. Here is an example of a worksheet in the area of geology.

Earth's Crust Worksheet
1. List four different ways in which minerals can be distinguished from one another.

1.	3.
2.	4.

2. Describe and compare the differences between igneous, sedimentary, and metamorphic rock.

Type/ Characteristics	Minerals	Placement of minerals	Contents of layers
Igneous			
Sedimentary			
Metamorphic			

3. If geologists found the fossils of older animals within layers of rock that were closer to the surface than the remains of younger animals, what might explain their findings?
4. Imagine that you are a geologist in 2500 and you are excavating the ruins of New York City. What clues would you look for to identify the evolution of transportation systems from the 18th through the 20th centuries?
5. One way to understand more about early Native American life is to excavate the bones found in Native American burial grounds. Make a persuasive argument for this practice from the view of a geologist. Make a persuasive argument against this practice from the view of a descendant of a Native American tribe.

South Africa: A Case Study of Cultures in Conflict

This interdisciplinary social studies and English unit for eleventh graders focused on the following essential question: "How does South Africa's past shape its present?" A number of interrelated events and themes in South Africa's history, including the unsettling of South Africa's indigenous people, the age of Colonization, and the inception and institutionalization of apartheid, showcase the clash of cultures in that African nation. The challenge to South Africans is to overcome their country's traumatic and contentious history of ethnic, racial, and tribal conflict to build an enduring democracy in which all South Africans are equal and secure.

In their English classes, students read *The Bride Price* (Emecheta, 1976) and *Things Fall Apart* (Achebe, 1959). For a final exhibition, students worked in small groups to design a time line of South African history or to blow up a frame (i.e., a specific event) from a film about South African history. Thus, all students in the class were able to see the big picture (in the time line) as well as learn about the role of specific events within the overall framework of the country's history (the blow-up).

The time line included a list of required items and a minimum of 10 choice items that significantly affected the history of South Africa. Each group's time line was evaluated according to the following criteria: 1) how well it was drawn to scale; 2) neatness, accuracy, and artistic style; 3) inclusion of required and choice items; 4) chosen items accompanied by written explanations of their significance; 5) visual appeal and readability from the back of the classroom; 6) an oral narration of the time line; and 7) a reference list.

The frame blow-up was an in-depth study of an event or other aspect of South African history such as the Great Trek, the Boer War, Steven Biko, Nelson Mandela, and petty apartheid. Evaluation of the blow-up was based on the following criteria: 1) 8- to 10-minute group oral presentation with all members participating; 2) use of visual aids to facilitate the acquisition of knowledge for all students; 3) explanation of the significance of the topic; 4) written outline of information; 5) reference list; and 6) a question that, if answered by classmates, would show comprehension of the topic.

The "South Africa: A Case Study of Cultures in Conflict" unit plan was created and contributed by Dick Miller and Christine Knapp, Souhegan High School, Amherst, New Hampshire.

The Endangered Species Board Game

The Situation: You work for the state department of environmental conservation. It is your job to educate the public about the plight of the state's endangered species. You are skilled in research, writing, and creatively presenting information to a variety of audiences, particularly when you must make a persuasive argument for them to take action. You are also often asked to work collaboratively with co-workers on various projects.

The Problem: Your supervisor has come to you with an idea for a new campaign. The department wishes to bring its message concerning endangered species to school-age children. They feel that the best way to do this is through the creation of educational board games.

Your Task: You must create an educational board game based on one of your state's endangered species. The game must be age appropriate and should be fun as well as educational for its intended audience. You will create a model of the game and then make a presentation about your game to the department's director. After refining your product, you will field-test the game with a group of teenagers, who will give you feedback so that you may further refine your product.

This unit addresses a number of national, state, and local school learning standards. The National Research Council's Science Education Standards emphasize student understanding of the diversity of organisms and their interdependence (National Academy of Sciences, 1996). Standard 7 from the New York State Framework for Mathematics, Science, and Technology requires that students demonstrate knowledge of science's contributions to the understanding of the natural world (New York State Department of Education, 1996). The Gananda Central Senior High School Graduation Outcomes requires students to produce original work that demonstrates creativity and artistic expression.

Materials: Standard-size gift or shirt box, index cards, markers, reference materials, and other materials to make game pieces.

Guidelines for Students
1. You will be assigned by your instructor to groups of three.
2. Briefly research organisms that are considered endangered species in New York State. The instructor and librarian will help you get started. At first, limit your search to endangered species that are native to New York State. You may choose other species only

---

The "Endangered Species Board Game" unit plan was created and contributed by Mark Pellegrino, Gananda Central Senior High School, Walworth, New York.

when all New York State native species are taken. Select one species that will be the focus of your project.

3. Using reference materials, answer the following questions about your species:
   a. What are the characteristics of the organism?
   b. What adaptations does it possess that enable it to be successful?
   c. What is its natural habitat?
   d. What environmental factors have led the species to become endangered?
   e. What caused the species environment to change?
   f. What recommendations can you make to aid in the continued existence of this species?

(Neatly write your answers to these questions and have your instructor check them before you continue.)

4. You are now ready to create your board game. You and your fellow group members must create and design everything: game pieces, tokens, cards, props, and the game board. Design your game to be played by two to four people ages 11–13. Remember to keep the emphasis of your game on the endangered species and its relationship to environmental factors and human influence.

5. Prepare an instruction sheet that clearly states the rules of the game.

6. Using a standard-size shirt box, create a nifty-looking cover that includes the title of your game. On the back of your box, write a description of the game and the instructions for play. It should also include relevant information concerning the endangered species, its environment, and defended predictions on and recommendations for assisting its continued existence.

7. You will then be required to give a 5- to 7-minute presentation that includes the answers to the questions you researched in Guideline 3 above and a description of your game.

8. All work will be graded according to a rubric.

9. After your presentation, the instructor and your classmates will give you suggestions for the improvement of your work. Use these suggestions to make any necessary changes to your game.

10. After your revisions are complete, place a survey form in your game box. Your game will be played and surveyed by members of the age group for which you designed it.

11. Look carefully at the suggestions given in the survey. Use these to further revise your game, and then turn the game in for a final evaluation.

Jessica

The endangered species board game offers a perfect opportunity for participation of students who are able to do part of an assignment rather than the whole project. Jessica experiences cerebral palsy and uses a Light Talker (manufactured by Prentke Romich) to produce written classwork. Although it would be difficult for Jessica to use her hands to actually construct the game board or make the game pieces, she could answer the background questions (e.g., Guideline 3), write the text for the inside cover of the game box, and construct questions that would go on the draw cards. The evaluation rubric for Jessica would need to take into account her inability to do the actual artwork and physical manipulation tasks but recognize her other contributions to the design of the game.

PANTS

This final exhibition required students to integrate several weeks' worth of study about countries on the African continent. Here is the setup: An international study by a blue-ribbon panel of experts has determined that one of the leading causes of Africa's slow pace of development is a poor system of transportation linkages. The International Monetary Fund, the Agency for International Development, the World Bank, the governments of each African nation, the European Community, Japan, and the United States have all pledged to make the creation of a transportation network a reality for Africa. Your task is to work with a design team to develop and present a possible design for this transportation network, the Pan African National Transportation System (PANTS). The network may include railroads, rivers, roads, lakes, and seas. Owing to their small size, the island nations of Sao Tome and Principe, Mauritius, Comoros, Seychelles, and Reunion need not be included. Madagascar and the Cape Verde Islands, however, should be. Of the 49 African nations included, 60% (i.e., 30) should be directly served by the system, with the stipulation that the remaining 19 nations must each border on at least 1 of the 30 directly connected nations. No dead ends are permissible.

Costs were figured at the following rates: railroads, $300,000 per mile; $300,000 for every 1,000 feet of elevation in mountainous terrain; tunnels, triple the cost per mile; $1 million per bridge; and $5 million for every port of embarkation and debarkation.

Each group was responsible for a presentation to the advisory boards of the organizations named above (i.e., the rest of the class) lasting 8–15 minutes. The presentations included total cost; a map; description and justification of the chosen route; and bid sheet, containing cost, and rationale.

Each student must indicate in a plan what he or she is going to do for this project. Each student is expected to contribute to the development of the project and presentation. A group grade was given on the final product (70 points), and an individual grade (30 points) was assigned to each group member based on evidence of the work plan being carried out.

Don

Don, a student who was unable to participate in the mathematical calculations involved in designing his group's PANTS plan,

---

The "PANTS" unit plan was created and contributed by Dick Miller, Souhegan High School, Amherst, New Hampshire.

was fully involved in the unit nevertheless. As his team members were identifying population centers, he matched the names of the cities and countries to flashcards developed by the team's teaching assistant. He was able to assist in drawing the map, which was coded to reflect the different legs of the system, such as roads, railroad tracks, bridges, and water routes for ships. He was responsible for taking his bid sheets to the teachers' room and making photocopies for every member of the class (i.e., the advisory board). Finally, he solidified his sense of belonging by sharing in the camaraderie of working on the project in a small group.

How Just Is Justice?

During their sophomore year of English at Santana High School, students are exposed to literature in which the issues of justice, racism, and prejudice are explored through a number of thematic units. Students begin the quarter by studying poems by Langston Hughes. Students are asked to respond to these poems in various ways, including cooperative group projects, oral presentations, and pictorial essays. These poems are used as a springboard for discussion prior to reading *To Kill a Mockingbird* (Lee, 1960) and *Of Mice and Men* (Steinbeck, 1937). A variety of learning activities are used to accommodate students' different learning styles and talents. One option is for students to create a newspaper of the time that includes interviews with the characters and editorials. A field trip to a local courthouse and meetings with lawyers and a judge help make the story settings real for the students. The culminating activity for the unit is the presentation of a mock trial of George's killing of Lennie. Each student takes on a specific role; a script is written, and the students, acting as members of the jury, learn about rules of evidence, logic, and other legal procedures. After the verdict is rendered, the class discusses whether it was a just outcome.

Throughout the unit, students are required to explore, clarify, and articulate their own values in relation to justice, racism, and prejudice. They observe the justice system at work and develop a new appreciation for the complexities of the trial process. This unit would offer a natural opportunity to discuss modern examples of people with labels of mental retardation who commit crimes, the insanity defense, and the controversy over determining competence. The discussion might begin with an exploration of the conduct and disciplinary policy within the students' own school and whether they feel that all students are subject to the same behavioral expectations and consequences. Balancing the rights of an individual with the collective safety and rights of all members of a community would emerge during the discussion.

The "How Just Is Justice?" unit plan was created and contributed by Eileen Bagg-Rizzo, Santana High School, Santee, California.

Natural Selection

The purpose of this unit was for students to study the process of natural selection by working with a hypothetical population of organisms in a hypothetical environment in the classroom.

Materials

Each team of four students was assigned a floor or table-top area and given a sheet of newspaper as well as many 1-inch squares each of newspaper, red paper, and white paper.

Team Setup and Roles

Students worked in teams of four. Each student on the team acted as a predator, removing individual species of prey through hunting. Teams then discussed and answered questions about natural selection theory that were demonstrated in this inquiry.

Experiment Description

In the first-generation hunt, each team of students spread out a piece of newspaper (i.e., the "environment") on the floor or table-top area. One student randomly scattered on the environment 10 newspaper squares, 10 red-paper squares, and 10 white-paper squares, representing individuals from three different species. Taking turns, each student on the team removed a prey by taking it off of the newspaper. The first hunt continued until each team member had removed five prey.

Survivor Count

At the end of the first round, teams counted the survivors according to type of species. Data were entered on a table and teams brainstormed responses to the following issues:

1. Does any population have more survivors than any other?
2. Write a hypothesis that might explain this difference.
3. Predict what you expect to happen to the population by the end of four generations of hunting.

Round 2 Hunt

Prior to Round 2, survivors were put back on the newspaper and were allowed to reproduce, adding one new member for each survivor. The total number of prey was again 30. Repeat the hunting, counting, and reproduction procedures three times. Then answer these questions:

1. Does it take a longer or shorter period of time to find one prey as you proceed through the generations? Why?

The "Natural Selection" unit plan was created and contributed by Carolyn Shields, Souhegan High School, Amherst, New Hampshire.

2. How does the appearance of the surviving individuals compare with the environment?
3. Do your hypothesis and prediction agree with your experience?
4. How well suited was each species for survival in this environment?
5. In the natural world, is appearance the only characteristic that determines whether an individual plant or animal is suited to its environment?
6. In your own words, what is natural selection?

Matt

Matt, a student who is unable to read or write using conventional spelling, participates in science labs by taking instant photographs of the different steps of the experiment. He pastes the photos into his group's lab notebook while the other members of his team write up their data analyses and discussion. His participation in the natural selection activity might consist of taking pictures of each step of the activity, sequencing them, and then giving a short presentation to the class as the photographs are displayed.

Lives of a Cell

Tenth-grade science teacher Jennifer Mueller and English teacher Scott LaLiberte designed this interdisciplinary unit focused on the essential questions "What is life?" "What are the characteristics that define life?" and "Why do we need to know if something is living?" In English class, students read Lewis Thomas's (1974) *The Lives of a Cell: Notes of a Biology Watcher,* in which life processes are presented through literary analogies and metaphors. In science class, students learned about cell structure and function. The final exhibition for the unit, which counted for both English and science, was the presentation of a one-act play or videotape about the life processes of single-cell organisms using metaphors and analogies.

Outcomes and Skills
1. Acquire and integrate critical information.
2. Interpret and synthesize information.
3. Express ideas clearly.
4. Effectively communicate through a variety of media.
5. Work cooperatively toward group goals.
6. Self-assess and monitor own behavior within a group.

Within a cooperative learning jigsaw structure, students were members of two groups. Students were first divided into six-member cell groups. On the first day of the unit, they worked in this group during the kickoff activity. The following is the scenario with which the cells groups were presented.

> You wake up and find yourself on an unexplored planet. As you are walking along, you come across something. Is it alive? What are the criteria and processes you will use to answer this question? Using your knowledge of the world around you, brainstorm ideas. Record everything! One student should act as timekeeper. You have 20 minutes for this activity. Another student should write down all of your ideas on flipchart paper. A third group member should facilitate everyone's involvement, and a fourth member will be responsible for presenting your group's ideas to the rest of the class. Go!

After each group shared their criteria and ideas, the whole class agreed on five or six life processes that they would research for the next few days. Each member of the base group was then assigned to work in a process group to conduct the research. Sources of information available to the groups included books (picture books, pop-up books, and textbooks, representing reading levels from primary to col-

---

The "Lives of a Cell" unit plan was created and contributed by Jennifer Mueller and Scott LaLiberte, Souhegan High School, Amherst, New Hampshire.

lege), CD-ROMs, videotapes and slide shows, and academic journals. At the conclusion of the research period, each process group was responsible for designing a learning activity for the whole class to teach about life processes. The learning activity needed to be composed of a reading assignment and summary questions answered by class members prior to the class activity, an oral lecture outlining content and providing students with notes, a lab or activity, and a journal outlining each group member's contribution to the presentation and an analysis of the effectiveness of the group's cooperative skills.

After the life process lessons, students returned to their cell groups to work on their play or videotape. Students were told that all of their group members needed to be included in the production and presentation of their final exhibition. Groups that chose the film option designed storyboards, wrote scripts, and learned how to use the videotape editing equipment. Groups that chose to write and perform a play wrote scripts, designed and built sets and props, and constructed costumes. Faculty coaches included the two major unit instructors, a media specialist, director of the information center (i.e., the library), the theater teacher, a special education teacher, and a teaching assistant. Two days prior to the presentations were dedicated solely to final preparation and rehearsal. All of the productions were presented on the same day during a double-period block.

Andrew

Andrew was a member of the team that completed the "Lives of a Cell" unit. Because he is very sensitive to being singled out for assistance during class, the modifications that Andrew needed were provided inconspicuously. During study hall, Andrew and several other students watched a movie that illustrated cell division and reproduction through magnification of a real cell and a computer graphics simulation. The special education teaching assistant worked with all of the groups throughout the project but devoted more time to Andrew's group. The teaching assistant made word–picture index cards for Andrew and used them to review and reinforce the facts presented in the movie and during class lectures. To prepare his lines for the final presentation, he first sequenced the index cards into sentences. With assistance from another student, he typed the words into the computer and printed out his script. A goal on Andrew's IEP is that he will learn three facts or concepts in every science unit. With modified materials and instructional support, he achieved this goal in the cell unit.

Moving Toward Empowerment

Barry Ehrlich and Edorah Frazer are teaching partners in Souhegan High School's senior seminar course. Senior seminar is a two-semester course that merges the study of current social studies issues and literature and guides students through the development of their required senior project. A unit that Barry and Edorah taught illustrates how rigorous learning outcomes can be assessed through a variety of student products, reflecting students' favorite learning styles and media. The unit was entitled "Moving Toward Empowerment" and followed several weeks of study about news and media bias, especially as they related to the portrayal of various stereotypes in U.S. society. Students worked individually or in pairs and picked a group of people in U.S. society who currently face discrimination. Students picked some of the traditionally discriminated against groups such as African Americans, gays and lesbians, and women; but they also chose to examine the discrimination against left-handers, smokers, and teenagers!

The essential questions that guided this unit were "What are the origins of discrimination?" "What is the nature of discrimination?" and "How does your focus group respond to discrimination?" At the end of the unit, students were responsible for demonstrating their knowledge and skills through one of five exhibitions. The requirements for each type of exhibition and a rubric for assessing students' progress toward the completion of their project are listed below. On Friday of each week, students had a brief conference with Edorah or Barry, and their progress was assessed. This strategy of assessing students' progress toward completion of their exhibition has helped students plan their time more effectively and has decreased the amount of last-minute cramming.

Oral Report
1. Minimum of five sources, including at least one book
2. Research notes on library forms
3. Annotated bibliography
4. Presentation outline
5. Three- to five-minute talk answering all of the essential questions
6. Required visual depiction of your report, which may be a computer slide show

For a grade of C, work on the slide show or visual has barely begun. Little information is shown. No presentation outline has been

The "Moving Toward Empowerment" unit plan was created and contributed by Barry Ehrlich and Edorah Frazer, Souhegan High School, Amherst, New Hampshire.

prepared. All essential questions are either not answered or insufficient. In a pair, the roles of each individual student are unclear. There is no evidence of equal effort.

For a grade of B, all of the squares on slide show are chosen, with at least some information in each. Work still remains. Presentation outline is complete. Answers to essential questions are clear and sufficient. Roles are chosen and clear. There is evidence of equal effort.

For a grade of A, all information is completed on the slide show. Finishing touches remain. Presentation outline is complete. All questions are answered and answers are sufficient. Pairs are practicing for oral presentation. There is evidence of equal work.

Research Paper
1, 2, and 3 from above

4. Rough draft turned in on Thursday 3/30/95
5. Six to eight pages
6. All essential questions answered

For a grade of C, there is no outline present or it is not detailed or complete. Specific sections are unclear. Pairs have no clearly defined roles. Research notes are still being obtained. Answers to essential questions are insufficient. There is no evidence of equal effort.

For a grade of B, the outline is present but not fully detailed. Essential questions can be clearly answered from information provided. Writing assignments are chosen and clear. There is evidence of equal effort. At least half of the pages are in rough-draft form.

For a grade of A, the detailed outline is complete. Essential questions can be clearly answered from information provided. There is evidence of equal effort. At least two thirds of the pages are in rough-draft form.

Time Line
1. Minimum of five sources, including at least one book
2. Twenty-five "hits" of information on the time line
3. Annotated bibliography
4. Illustrated with cutout or drawn pictures—at least half of the entries should be illustrated in some way
5. Two- to three-minute talk describing what you did and how it integrates the essential questions

For a grade of C, little information is transposed onto a time line. No illustrations. There are not enough hits on the time line to answer all three essential questions. Entries do not show sufficient depth to answer the essential questions. There is no evidence of equal effort.

For a grade of B, some information is on the time line and many of these entries are illustrated. Entries are detailed enough to clearly answer the essential questions. There is evidence of equal effort.

For an A, all information is on time line and many of the illustrations are complete. Entries are detailed enough to clearly answer the essential questions. There is evidence of equal effort.

Documentary
1. Minimum of five sources, including at least one book
2. Half-page summary of each article or source
3. Bibliography
4. Five to seven minutes of videotape
5. Script that is turned in as a rough draft and a final copy due on day of project sharing
6. Documentaries have either still shots of photographs or clips of the news, other documentaries, or actual events. You must include a still photograph and previously taped footage. For example, you may collect scenes from 10 movies and footage from five television shows that depict discrimination against war veterans and how veterans are trying to overcome discrimination. Then you might add a still of a veterans' memorial. You would then voice over how you answer all of the essential questions.

For a C, script is not completed. What exists does not answer all the essential questions. For pairs, there is no evidence of equal effort. Majority of editing is not completed. Not all requirements are met.

For a B, script is completed and answers all the essential questions. There is evidence of equal work. All requirements are met, but some editing work remains.

For an A, script is completed and answers all the essential questions. There is evidence of equal effort. All of the requirements are met, and finishing touches remain.

Art
1. Minimum of five sources, including at least one book
2. Research notes on library sheets
3. Annotated bibliography
4. Your art work could be one of several ideas (e.g., a mural showing the changes in the movement through time, a creation or re-creation of poster art, a series of paintings or drawings or sculpture that illustrate different eras of the movement)
5. Two- to three-page written description of what you are portraying and how it answers all of the essential questions

For a C, little work is complete. Paper does not exist in any form. Therefore, essential questions are not answered. In a pair, the roles are unclear. There is no evidence of equal effort.

For a B, the piece is in progress. Paper is in detailed outline form. Outline clearly shows how the piece answers all the essential questions. Roles for writing the paper are chosen and clear. There is evidence of equal effort.

For an A, art needs finishing touches. Paper is in rough-draft state but is presentable for review. Paper clearly shows how the piece answers all the essential questions. There is evidence of equal effort.

Sarah

For all students, particularly those with disabilities, the development of self-determination and self-advocacy skills is an essential developmental milestone that is related to their ability to make important life choices and experience a sense of control over their decisions. Sarah is a senior and will graduate next year. Throughout her life, her parents have steadfastly refused to let the label of Down syndrome dictate a separate education, limit her participation in a wide variety of typical community recreational activities, or restrict her dreams for the future. Although her parents' goal for Sarah during her last year in high school is graduation and acceptance into a technical college program, the most important goal in Sarah's mind is getting her driver's license! If Sarah were to participate in this unit, she might explore the issue of empowerment from the perspective of a young person with a disability. Although she has many interests and belongs to many groups that do not have a disability connection, Sarah might investigate her state's "People First" chapter and bring representatives in to talk to her senior seminar class. The development of a formal postgraduation plan for education and independent living might be a challenging and relevant final assignment for her in this unit.

In Chapter 7, the issue of friendships between students with and without disabilities is discussed. Although there are no cookbook recipes for friendships, there are a number of essential conditions that schools can put into place that create the environment in which meaningful social relationships can develop.

REFERENCES

Achebe, C. (1959). *Things fall apart*. New York: McDowell, Obolensky.

Brown v. Board of Education, 347 U.S. 483 (1954).

Burns, K.L. (1989). *The civil war* [Film]. Alexandria, VA: Forentine Films Production.

Coppola, F.F. (Director). (1983). *The outsiders* [Film]. Los Angeles: Zoetrope Studios.

Cortes, H. (1908). *Fernando Cortes: His five letters of relation to the Emperor Charles V* (F.A. McNutt, ed. & trans.). Cleveland, OH: A.H. Clark. (Original work published 1519–1526)

Donner, R. (Director). (1978). *Superman: The movie* [Film]. Los Angeles: Warner Brothers.

Emecheta, B. (1976). *The bride price*. New York: George Braziller.

Griffin, M. (Producer). (1975). *Wheel of fortune*. Los Angeles: King World.

Homer. (1919). *The odyssey* (A.T. Murray, ed. & trans.). Cambridge, MA: Harvard University Press.

Joel, B. (1989). We didn't start the fire. *Storm front* [Recording]. New York: CBS Records.

Kagan, S. (1994). *Cooperative learning*. San Juan Capistrano, CA: Resources for Teachers.

King, M.L., Jr. (1964). *Why we can't wait*. New York: Harper & Row.

Lee, H. (1960). *To kill a mockingbird*. Philadelphia: J.B. Lippincott.

Leon-Portilla, M. (1962). *The broken spears: The Aztec account of the conquest of Mexico*. Boston: Beacon Press.

Logan, J. (Director). (1958). *South Pacific* [Film]. Los Angeles: 20th Century Fox.

Manchester, W.R. (1974). *The glory and the dream: A narrative history of America, 1932–1972*. Boston: Little, Brown.

Michaels, L. (Producer). (1975). *Saturday night live*. New York: National Broadcasting Co.

National Academy of Sciences, National Research Council. (1996). *National science education standards*. Washington, DC: National Academy Press.

New York State Education Department. (1996). *Learning standards for mathematics, science, and technology*. Albany: New York State Department of Education, Office for Curriculum and Instruction.

Parker Brothers. (1986). *Clue* [Game]. Beverly, MA: Author.

Schrecker, E. (1994). *The age of McCarthyism: A brief history with documents*. New York: St. Martin's Press.

Steinbeck, J. (1937). *Of mice and men*. New York: Modern Library.

Thomas, L. (1974). *The lives of a cell: Notes of a biology watcher*. New York: Viking Press.

Thompson, C., & Rathmell, E. (1988). NCTM's standards for school mathematics K–12. *Mathematics Teacher, 81*(5), 348–351.

Turning Tide Productions. (1992). *Columbus didn't discover us.* [Film]. Wendell, MA: Author.

Zimbalist, S. (Producer), & Wyler, W. (Director). (1959). *Ben-hur* [Film]. Los Angeles: Loews, Inc.

7

The Promise of Friendship
for Students with Disabilities

Jill Martin, Cheryl M. Jorgensen, and Jay Klein

Amro

Amro Diab graduated from Souhegan High School in Amherst, New Hampshire, in June 1996. He marched across the stage to receive his diploma with friends and classmates. Amro was a 4-year member of the football team, a responsible employee at both the school store and a local grocery store, and an avid basketball player in the school's intramural league. Despite his inability to speak, his first-grade reading and writing skills, and his difficulty in learning, Amro had been fully included in general education classes and in after-school activities since ninth grade.

Amro will look back on his high school career with pride and accomplishment. For his senior project, Amro showed slides of his 4 years at Souhegan, concluding with his plans to continue working at a local supermarket stocking shelves and bagging groceries. In preparation for his presentation, he typed brief captions for each slide that became the text of his talk. As the slides were projected onto a screen at the front of the classroom, Amro painstakingly typed each caption again (copying each word letter-by-letter) using a computer projection system so that the audience could follow along during the slide show. He received a standing ovation from the audience members and a passing grade on his project. At the senior prom, Amro was voted king by a clear majority of his classmates. At senior awards night, he received the Souhegan Saber Prize, which honors the student in the graduating class who best exemplifies the school's mission statement, shown on page 35.

As is the case for many of his classmates, Amro's future plans are uncertain. When graduating seniors leave the predictability of their public school education and the security of their parents' homes, they go to work, enter the military, get married, or struggle through the first few months of college. Many students remain in touch with one another for years, whereas others will never attend a class reunion. When Amro and his classmates are asked to reflect on their best memories of high school, it is likely that they will focus less on memorable math and science classes and more on stories of victorious football seasons, summer jobs, parties, romances, the senior trip, and teachers who made an impact on their lives.

This chapter was supported in part by Grant H023R20018 from the U.S. Department of Education, Office of Special Education and Rehabilitative Services, and in part by a grant from the Administration on Developmental Disabilities.

What factors contributed to Amro's successful high school experience? Although he came to Souhegan with no effective means of communication, the introduction of a simple printed letterboard enabled him to communicate with teachers and classmates. His educational program was coordinated by an experienced inclusion facilitator who believed that Amro could benefit from being in the mainstream. A skilled teaching assistant provided effective support to Amro and was an active participant in team planning. Committed and creative teachers had access to staff development and consultation from a university inclusion expert. Curriculum and instruction were adapted to meet his academic goals. In addition, his parents provided a supportive home life and worked in partnership with the school.

Although each of these program components was necessary for a quality educational experience, it was the facilitation and support given to the development of social connections and friendships that made Amro's school experience truly exemplary. Unfortunately for many students with significant disabilities, their high school experiences are not as rich and their memories are not as positive as Amro's. Their lack of friendships and their narrow circle of social relationships are a source of frustration and loneliness, and they feel no joy and acceptance.

This chapter explores the conditions under which friendships develop and strategies for nurturing social relationships between students with and without disabilities. We address the barriers to developing relationships, the essential conditions and practices that can help a student overcome those barriers, and the appropriate role for adults in the process. Because our work is based on 11 years of experience in inclusive New Hampshire schools and on hundreds of conversations with students, the chapter offers a glimpse into the world of teenagers who are experiencing for the first time what it is like to go to school with classmates who need a great deal of support to learn, to communicate, and sometimes to move. These young people are teaching us how the culture of school, the complicated rules governing teenagers' social relationships, and the decisions that adults make about the educational experience of students with disabilities affects their social life in high school.

THE IMPORTANCE OF FRIENDSHIP FOR ALL STUDENTS

Jocelyn does give me friendship; she's there for me. When I need a smile, she gives me one. When I need someone to talk to, she listens. (A ninth-grade student)

Friendship plays an important role in everyone's life. For some people, friends are people without whom life would not be worth living. During the adolescent years, peer relationships and friendships become a significant source of influence and support. Csikszentmihalyi and Larson (1984) found that teenagers in the United States spend an average of 22 hours per week with their peers. "They report spending more time with their friends than they do with their families or by themselves, and the amount of time they spend in this way increases over the course of adolescence" (Cole & Cole, 1983, p. 584). As adolescents begin to seek distance from their parents and develop separate and unique opinions and personalities, "hanging out" with friends is a critical time for socializing and discussing serious issues with which they are confronted on a daily basis. Young adults depend on one another as confidants with whom to discuss their successes and failures, and they look to one another for approval and acceptance. For examples of how students at several New Hampshire high schools defined *friend*, see Table 1.

Although having individual friends is a basic need for teenagers, the need to belong to and be accepted by a group is also critical to their well-being and sense of worth (Kunc, 1992). Lichtenstein wrote,

> Peer groups are important in that they offer equal opportunity for participation to their members, which family or school do not provide to the same extent. Friendships and acquaintances allow adolescents a high degree of autonomy, spontaneity, creativity, and individuality, all traits considered important to personal development. Young people look to peers to validate their self-concept and to provide behavior models. Through interactions with friends, youth explore roles and learn social skills that help them make effective transitions to adult roles and responsibilities. (in press)

A tenth-grade student said, "If you are with a certain group of friends that you have been with for a long time, then that is considered 'your group.' There are a lot of people who don't like the word *different*, and they just try to fit into what everybody wants them to be."

Table 1.   Examples of how some New Hampshire high school students defined *friend*

Someone who is like family; someone I can't live without

Someone who is always there and really close

Someone who is around you and cares about you

Someone who is there to talk to, spend time with, laugh with, and have fun with

Someone I like to talk to, don't hate, enjoy spending time with—both in and out of school

Someone who I can talk to about personal issues, someone I trust and enjoy being with

Although it is tempting to put a negative value judgment on the importance of being "in" for teenagers, we must listen to the students who are telling us that belonging to a group is a necessary part of being successful in high school. Groups of teenagers established around students' common backgrounds or common interests are called *cliques.* Cliques have the power to decide who is included or excluded, thereby determining whether students feel a sense of belonging or of isolation. One tenth-grade student remarked, "In some schools, you have to prove yourself before you ever get into that clique or that group."

SOCIAL BELONGING AND STUDENTS WITH DISABILITIES

The need for friendships and a sense of belonging is the same for students with disabilities as for those without (G. Allan Roeher Institute, 1990; Wagner, 1991). However, young people with disabilities often encounter significant barriers to their social inclusion. An eleventh grader from an inclusive school observed, "It isn't really fair towards people with disabilities, because they are usually 'out'—they are never 'in' with anybody else. The attitude is, 'No way, I don't want to deal with it—if they are not like us, forget it.'"

Chang, author of *Adolescent Life and Ethos: An Ethnography of a U.S. High School,* found that, in high school,

> an individual's social status was often determined on the basis of clique affiliation, types and degrees of involvement in activities, appearance, and academic performance. . . . [P]opular cliques included . . . athletes, brains, pretty faces, and good bodies, who tended to be "high" class. Those classified as "unpopular" included smokers, [the tough kids], and special education students, who were often regarded as "low" class people. (1984, p. 169)

What explains students' attitudes toward their classmates with disabilities? Is it a lack of experience with people who have disabilities? Did their parents pass along their own prejudices? Is it typical for adolescents to seek out others whom they believe are the same and to reject those who seem different? Are there strategies that we can employ to change attitudes and the climate of the school to create opportunities for friendships to develop and thrive?

Essential Conditions

We have talked to students all over New Hampshire, analyzed the literature on friendships and social relationships, and spent countless hours among ourselves debating the problem of social relationships and friendships for students with disabilities. Although there will always be isolated examples of people with disabilities who develop real friendships in the absence of any of the factors that we think are predictive, it does seem that there are a number of variables that increase the likelihood that friendships will develop and stand the test of time. Referred to as *essential conditions,* these factors seem to be present in the lives of students who have the greatest number of friends and the most interesting lives.

A few years ago, it was in vogue to establish "circles of friends" for students with disabilities (Forest, Pearpoint, & O'Brien, 1996). Although we still think that those strategies can be useful in certain circumstances, we emphasize the importance of putting these essential conditions into place first. A word of caution: These conditions are not sure-fire ingredients in a "recipe for friendship" (i.e., put them all into place and—presto!—instant friendship!). Rather, they seem to establish the conditions and supports under which potential friendships can grow.

Do not look for magical solutions or brand-new strategies in the remainder of this chapter. In a sense, we believe that a return to the basics of inclusion is called for. Between the time in the mid-1980s, when the first elementary school–age students were included in general classes, and the late 1990s, when those students were entering high school, it seems as though we forgot some of the foundations of inclusion. The result is most evident in these students' empty social lives.

The seven essential conditions related to the development of an array of social connections and friendships for students with disabilities are

1. Full inclusion in all aspects of school, family, and community life
2. Access to a means of communication all the time and classmates who understand and know how to use the system
3. Provision of support in a way that promotes independence, interdependence, self-determination, and a reliance on natural supports
4. Student involvement in the inclusion process and in creative problem solving
5. Age-appropriate and respectful materials, language, expectations, and modifications
6. Involvement of family members and school personnel in facilitating and supporting friendships and social activities
7. Attention to the development of a schoolwide climate of acceptance and celebration of diversity

Essential Condition #1: Full Inclusion in
All Aspects of School, Family, and Community Life

The first essential condition for friendship is full inclusion. "When people with disabilities are kept apart from society—educated in separate classrooms or schools, employed in sheltered workshops, engaged in separate leisure activities—there are few opportunities for friendships to develop" (Tashie et al., 1993, p. 6).

If you hear terms like *part-time inclusion, inclusion program,* and *being included in some regular classes,* you can be pretty sure that it is not "real" inclusion. *Inclusion* is defined as the membership and full participation of a natural proportion of all students with disabilities in age-appropriate general education classes in the school that they would attend if they did not have a disability, with the provision of supports and services necessary for them to learn.

Because friendships do not simply materialize from thin air, there must be a logical first step—sharing time and space. Students have told us that it is only when they share academic classes or are involved in the same extracurricular activities that common bonds are discovered, such as family background, life experiences, shared acquaintances, and current interests and activities. Think about the opportunities that students without disabilities have to develop friendships. By the time they reach high school, they have been in contact with literally hundreds of other students who are potential friends—neighbors; kids with whom they took swimming lessons; members of their church, synagogue, or other place of worship; the students in their homeroom class each year; and so forth. Despite this large number of potential friends, most high school students have just three or four close friends. For students with disabilities, whose contacts may already have been limited by their membership in a self-contained classroom or by barriers to their participation in community recreation activities, full inclusion at the high school level is even more important if friendship is to be a reasonable goal.

Sometimes high school students are included part time or on a schedule of increasing participation in mainstream classes over a period of several semesters or years. When inclusion is handled in a piecemeal fashion like this (e.g., one class this semester, a second in the spring, a couple of periods reserved for resource help, check-in first thing in the morning in the special education room), the development of friendships is impeded. On the one hand, young people are told that students with disabilities have much to offer the school, are more alike than different from students without disabilities, and have the same rights and responsibilities as typical students. Yet, on the other hand, adults' behavior and what students see tell a different story. What is the message when students with disabilities ride a separate bus to school? When they enter and leave classes on a different schedule? When their lockers are clustered in one wing of the school? When they get progress reports instead of report cards? When they go to the special education office rather than to the nurse's office if they are sick?

The use of a special education–based language and rationale such as *appropriate, individualized,* and *least restrictive* is not a justification for separating students with disabilities from their typical classmates. It used to be appropriate for students with severe disabilities to live in institutions. Some students spend their whole day in the company of an adult outside of the mainstream in the name of individualized education. Why do we place students in programs that are called *least restrictive* instead of *most inclusive*? For it is in all of the common places in a school (e.g., the hallways, the school bus, the cafeteria, the smoking area, the locker rooms) where friendships develop and grow. A tenth-grade student said,

> We had a local band play at a school assembly for spirit week. She was out there with the rest of us, dancing up a storm. I never thought of the fact that we would like the same music. We've talked about going to a concert this summer!

Schools in which students are included full time (not just in "hands-on" classes or in "appropriate" activities or in "high-interest" subjects), where they follow the same schedule of classes and activities as typical students, are in an excellent position to support the development of friendships between students with and without disabilities. A ninth-grade student said,

> Before I got to know him, he would walk through gym class and I would ask him to play catch with us, and he would be a little bit hesitant. Now we are in the same earth science class, and we've both been staying after school to get help and I've gotten to know him and—like the other day, when I asked him to play catch with us, he got right in there and played. . . . We all had fun.

Essential Condition #2: Access to a Means of Communication All the Time and Classmates Who Understand and Know How to Use the System

The second essential condition for friendship is for students to have access to a means of communication all the time that their classmates understand and know how to use. Picture this scene: You are the inclusion facilitator for a student with disabilities who is entering ninth grade in her home high school. You are anxious for her to get off on the right foot and to make acquaintances quickly. You wheel her into her first-period class and up to the teacher's desk to hand over her late pass. The teacher glances at the pass and says, "Good morning, Crystal. Do you have a copy of your schedule for me to initial?" If Crystal does not answer, do you think the teacher will call on Crystal later in the class period?

As the students in the class gather around their laboratory tables, they talk among themselves. You introduce Crystal to the group by saying, "Girls, this is Crystal McMahon. It's her first year in this school." One of the girls says, "Hi. Where did you go to school last year?" If Crystal does not answer, even after repeated inquiries, do you think the girls will include her in their conversation? Do you think they will direct their questions to Crystal or to the adults around Crystal?

Students have told us that the issue of reciprocity in relationships is a key to their success. They expect their friends to "be there" for them by actively listening, reflecting their feelings, responding to questions, and so forth. They told us that unless someone has a way to communicate, the development of even a casual relationship is unlikely. The lack of an effective communication system for students with disabilities, then, can thwart both the initial exchanges that are essential at the start of a relationship as well as the kinds of interactions that sustain people's interest in one another as conversational partners and friends.

Amro Fits in

Amro, the young man introduced at the beginning of this chapter, entered high school without an effective means of communication. His classmates were told that he was shy and unable to speak. They were noticeably hesitant to interact with him, perhaps for fear that he would become nervous, that they would not know what to say to him, or that he would be in the awkward position of not being able to respond to their overtures. It was hard to tell what Amro was thinking, whether he understood what was being said to him, or what his opinions were.

After football practice one day, the school's inclusion consultant asked Amro and several of his teammates if they would attend a meeting to discuss a communication system for Amro. The consultant told Amro that she knew he had much to say, that he was frustrated about not being able to talk, and that she would help him spell out the words he wanted to say on a letterboard. Supporting him gently under his forearm, she asked,

"Who would you like to talk to, Amro?" On his letterboard, he spelled "KOCH" [i.e., *coach*]. At that moment, with just that one word, his football teammates knew that Amro was someone to whom they could relate, someone who understood what was going on around him, someone who had opinions and formed relationships—in short, a potential friend. He became someone who could interact with them just like all of their other friends.

Although students' access to and proficiency in using a communication system is an essential condition for friendship, another factor is equally important: The people with whom the student comes in contact must know how to interact with that student through the communication system.

Jennifer

Jennifer was a student at a large urban high school in New Hampshire. During tenth grade, she received approval from the school district for the purchase of an electronic communication device. Jennifer spent hours with the communication specialist learning to use the device, and eventually she was able to communicate complex answers to her teaching assistants when she took tests in class. As a result, teachers raised their academic expectations for Jennifer. However, none of Jennifer's classmates had been taught how to communicate with her when she used the device, and, for 2 months, she spoke only to adults. As soon as her classmates were taught how to support Jennifer when she used the device, as well as to program it themselves, Jennifer was able to sit with her friends and engage in conversation without the barrier of having an adult by her side. In addition, her friends were able to put up-to-date phrases and slang into her device's vocabulary, ensuring that Jennifer's vocabulary would sound like that of other 16-year-old girls.

Both Jennifer and Amro, although they had significant disabilities and were unable to speak audibly, were able to communicate using the same symbols (i.e., words) used by their peers. What does this mean for students who, despite attempts to provide them with word- or picture-based systems, use highly ambiguous means to communicate, such as gestures, facial expressions, or vocalizations? Bogdan and Taylor (1989), in their research with people who were closely related to individuals who had no formal system of communication, found that, if a close relationship existed between the two, then the person without disabilities believed that his or her friend was communicating, even if the intent of that communication was not obvious to other observers. They ascribed communication abilities and intents to their friend, whom others had labeled as unable to communicate.

Jocelyn

Jocelyn Curtin, an eleventh grader at Concord High School, is a young woman with Rett syndrome who has been included in general classes since early elementary school. Despite the fact that Jocelyn has no formal communication system, her friends speak of her as if they understand her moods, needs, and feelings toward them. In the videotape *Voices of Friendship* (Tashie & Martin, 1996), one of Jocelyn's friends described this phenomenon as follows:

> Jocelyn is a really good listener and you can sit and tell her any of your problems. One time we were at a school dance and one of our friends was sitting on the floor crying and Jocelyn reached out and put her arm on the girl's back. It just showed that she does understand how people feel, and she is there for you as a friend.

We know that unless friendships are mutual (i.e., unless both people feel that they are "getting something out of" the relationship), they often wither. Whereas you or I might not be able to tell what Jocelyn is communicating, the students who have become close to her have learned to read the nuances of her movements and behavior to tell what she feels or wants. Moreover, they say that they can see Jocelyn's intent in her eyes. Bogdan and Taylor (1989) also observed this ability of friends to read intent in another's eyes.

Essential Condition #3: Provision of Support in a Way that Promotes Independence, Interdependence, Self-Determination, and a Reliance on Natural Supports

The third essential condition for friendship is the provision of supports in a way that encourages the development of independence, interdependence, self-determination, and a reliance on natural supports. Many students with disabilities rely on assistance for education-related tasks such as writing, using the computer, engaging in sports activities, eating, attending to personal hygiene, and communicating. How and by whom this support is provided can either create barriers to friendship or promote the development of a variety of social relationships. Comments from high school students, presented in Table 2, illustrate their opinions regarding the effect on social relationships of the constant presence of an aide.

Although we know that having a teaching assistant constantly hovering over a student is not effective, it is impractical to always rely on other students to modify teachers' instructions, create on-the-spot adaptations to handouts, or help students complete homework assignments. A twelfth-grade student said,

> When her aide gets there, it is kind of like "C'mon, do this, do that," but when the aide is not around she really does have a mind of her own. Her aides and other teachers build a wall around her and no one gets in. She won't make any real friends if there is always a third party.

What might be the right balance of supports provided by students and adults? There are some resources available that describe strategies for answering this question, but few of them address the particular dilemmas encountered in high schools (Jorgensen, 1992). We propose the following strategies when planning for supports to high school students with disabilities:

1. Ask the student's opinion about support, and honor his or her wishes.
2. Discuss with all team members, including the general education teacher, the benefits of using natural supports as well as the potential costs to other students or teachers.
3. Make support decisions that provide more rather than fewer opportunities for students without disabilities to get to know and make connections with students with disabilities.
4. Put the most natural support into place first, and then, if necessary, add other supports later.
5. Change the nature of the activity or environment so that all students are working cooperatively and have to rely on one another for support.
6. Expand the responsibilities of paid staff to support typical students in the class so that they provide assistance not only to students with disabilities but to all other students as well.

Examples of Effective Support

Although the determination of effective and natural supports requires individualized consideration of students' needs relative to the demands of the school situation, experience has demonstrated that some generic types of support are common to many situations. The examples presented in Table 3 are not meant to provide an exhaustive menu of support options but instead may help readers think about support in a somewhat more systematic way—to provide a stepping-off point, so to speak, for thinking about what might work for a particular student in a particular situation.

Table 3 is organized first by the type of school activity (e.g., transitions [e.g., passing classes, arrival and dismissal], extracurricular activities [e.g., after-school clubs, school-sponsored social events], and a

Table 2.   Students' comments regarding teacher's aides

She's got a real strong attachment to the student, as if she were her own child.

Whenever you try to talk to her you can't because her aides are there and they just help her say what she is trying to say and you want to hear it from her. They do it for her, and then they say, "Is that right?" It's like you are having a three-way conversation and [the aide] is the interpreter and it is not right that way. . . . It just doesn't work.

She is always around the teacher, and they won't let her leave their sight.

She acts too much like an adult around teenagers because she's been around too many adults. If the school were able to put a teenager as her aide it would probably make her more happy, make her kind of like aware that she isn't an adult yet and that she has to live her life.

Her aides don't need to become pieces of her because she doesn't need them all the time.

She should grow up around people her own age and cause a little trouble.

I really feel her aides and other teachers are keeping her from making friends.

If an adult has to be there, [choose] someone who is mature and responsible to handle the situations if they need to be handled but someone who can also let loose and have a good time.

variety of classroom instructional structures such as teacher directed [e.g., lectures, note taking] and cooperative groups). Within each activity type, several scenarios are described using students about whom stories have been told throughout this chapter. For each scenario, an effective peer support strategy is suggested, together with an effective adult support strategy. Each strategy supports one or more of the guiding principles mentioned previously.

Four students are featured in the examples. Andrew is a knowledgeable, energetic student who communicates by typing on a handheld communicator. Andrew's greatest challenge is his short attention span. He especially likes physical activities and drama. Jocelyn is a young woman who is unable to purposefully use her hands and has no formal, symbolic means of communication. Her friends describe her as sensitive and caring. She works best in small, cooperative groups in which someone can give her lots of physical guidance and support. Jennifer uses an electronic communication device and powers her wheelchair using a one-finger control pad. She has high academic expectations for herself and has some difficulty with long-term memory and organization. Amro is a popular, easygoing student who reads at approximately the first-grade level, communicates by using a printed letterboard, and enjoys working with classmates on cooperative group projects.

A Cautionary Note About Peer Tutoring

Many high schools have invested a great deal of time and energy in the development of peer-tutoring programs (Villa & Thousand, 1996).

Table 3. Examples of effective peer and adult support in high school activities and environments

Scenario	Peer support	Adult support
Activity Type 1: Transitions When Andrew arrives at school, he needs assistance to go to his locker and then make it to his first-period class before the bell rings.	Have a student who rides on Andrew's bus walk into school with him. Situate Andrew's locker near a student who has the same first-period class as he does for the first semester of the year until the routine becomes familiar.	A hall monitor could walk Andrew from the front door to his locker.
Jocelyn often gets very agitated when she goes from class to class because of the noise and commotion in the hallways.	Two friends could walk Jocelyn from class to class, one pushing her wheelchair and one placing her hand gently on Jocelyn's shoulder.	Five minutes before the end of the period, a teaching assistant could talk softly to Jocelyn, letting her know that the bell is about to ring and reassuring her that she will not be alone in the halls.
After lunch, Jennifer must go all the way to the other side of the building to get the elevator to the ground floor, where her sixth-period class is. She is usually late and misses the first 5 minutes of class.	A classmate could give Jennifer a copy of the notes or announcements that she misses.	The teacher could make a photocopy of her notes and the daily assignment for Jennifer.
During the last 5 minutes of every class period, Amro points continuously at his watch, tries to get the teacher's attention, and frequently bolts out the door before the class is formally dismissed.	Amro could sit with his friends in classes, and they could remind Amro that the period is not over yet or that he as plenty of time to make it to his next-period class.	If Amro's hand raising becomes annoying, the teacher could talk to Amro about the importance of being patient and perhaps make a contract with him to encourage him to stop the behavior.
Activity Type 2: Classroom teacher directed For the first 20 minutes of class, Andrew's English teacher usually facilitates the whole class in a discussion of the previous night's reading.	Classmates sitting near Andrew could tell him to be quiet so that they can concentrate on the discussion.	A teaching assistant could assist Andrew in using his communicator to type out comments to add to the discussion. Andrew could then raise his hand and give the teacher the printed comment to share with the class.

In chemistry class, Jocelyn's teacher uses the overhead projector for 15 minutes each class period to teach calculations such as converting grams to moles and illustrating how bonds break and recombine in chemical reactions.

A teaching assistant could sit next to Jocelyn, rubbing her back when she becomes anxious and directing her to pay attention to the teacher.

In math class, Jennifer's teacher uses lots of different media and technology: an overhead projection system, a graphing calculator, a white board. It is very difficult for Jennifer to keep up with the pace of the class.

[Not appropriate in this activity]

This is a perfect opportunity for Jennifer to use the services of an upperclassperson peer tutor to review the math material during a free period.

The math teacher could make a photocopy of the overhead material to give to Jennifer at the end of the period or day.

During the last 10 minutes of senior seminar, Amro's teachers conduct whole-class discussions in which students react to one another's evolving research papers. Amro has great difficulty understanding the content of most of the students' work.

Students presenting summaries of their research should synthesize the information in terms that Amro understands, perhaps highlighting general concepts or making connections to real-world issues that concern Amro.

A teaching assistant might sit next to Amro and, speaking softly, interpret the students' reports in terms that Amro understands.

Activity Type 3: Classroom cooperative group activity

In science, Andrew works with three other students to complete a microscope laboratory activity.

A classmate could assist Andrew to take instant pictures of each step of the laboratory experiment. These pictures could be pasted into the group's laboratory notebook as illustrations.

A teaching assistant could rove the laboratory, assisting several groups, including Andrew's.

In English, Jocelyn's group is responsible for making a collage about the Vietnam War.

As they flip through magazines looking for words and images for the collage, Jocelyn's classmates should describe each picture and ask Jocelyn for input on where it might go in the collage. Empower the students to figure out a way for Jocelyn to contribute to the final product.

[Not necessary in this activity]

(continued)

Table 3. *(continued)*

Scenario	Peer support	Adult support
Jennifer is her group's leader as they survey the school grounds trying to locate examples of inefficient energy use for an environmental science class.	Jennifer could be the group's note taker, entering observations into her portable laptop. If the group encounters areas of the school that are inaccessible to Jennifer, then that information can be reported to the administration.	[Not necessary in this activity]
In social studies class, Amro and three other students put on a skit depicting a homeless person being turned away from a public shelter.	Let the students figure this one out. The only requirement for each group is that every member make a contribution to the final production.	[Not necessary in this activity]

Activity Type 4: Classroom individual seat work

Scenario	Peer support	Adult support
During a 50-minute study hall, students are expected to quietly work on their homework. Andrew has difficulty staying in his seat for more than 10 minutes.	On a rotating basis, all students might skip study hall to work on their community service project together with Andrew.	Andrew might volunteer to help a teacher during a free period in lieu of going to study hall. Andrew might join an extracurricular activity (e.g., chorus, band) that rehearses during study hall.
At the end of Jocelyn's math class, students take a 5-minute quiz to help the teacher gauge their understanding of the concept presented.	When students finish their quiz, they can hand in their papers to Jocelyn.	As students file out of the classroom, the teacher could provide hand-over-hand assistance to Jocelyn as she puts a date stamp on each paper to record when it was handed in.
Jennifer's computer system is not portable; it is located in the computer laboratory. However, she wants to remain in the same classroom as her peers when they are given some time at the end of the period to start on their homework.	[Not appropriate in this activity]	The math teacher might sit with Jennifer and clarify any questions that she has about the classwork or homework assignment.
During seat work time, Amro just sits at his desk organizing the contents of his knapsack while other students do their homework.	Amro needs to organize his knapsack several times per day so that he keeps his materials in order. Just let him! Amro should do his homework during study hall or an academic support period.	[Not applicable in this activity]

Activity Type 5: Free time

After lunch, students are allowed to sit outside and socialize. Andrew typically gets overstimulated and does not willingly come into the building when it is time to go to sixth-period class.	Andrew responds well to kidding around. Encourage Andrew's friendship with the class clowns, and he will willingly go wherever they do.	[Not appropriate here; any kind of adult support will turn into a power struggle]
When students have a free minute in class, they talk among themselves. Unless Jocelyn is involved in the conversation, she vocalizes loudly.	Jocelyn's classmates could be encouraged to speak with her honestly and tell her that she should not be so demanding of their attention.	The teacher might ask a group of students to brainstorm solutions to the problem. She might give Jocelyn a choice between a couple of the ideas. Jocelyn's communication specialist might also be asked to visit the class to try to figure out what Jocelyn is trying to communicate or whether she is just talking to herself.
Because it takes a long time for Jennifer to compose a sentence on her communication device, students tend not to engage her in conversation as they stand near their lockers during free moments.	Jennifer needs to take charge of figuring out a solution to this situation. She might ask the speech-language pathologist for some help in programming some short phrases into her communication device. Jennifer might approach one or two classmates and tell them how she feels about being left out of a conversation.	If Jennifer requests assistance, then the speech-language pathologist might program her communication device with brief phrases that respond to frequently discussed topics, ask questions of her peers, and so forth.
When Amro has a free period, he roams the school building trying to engage students and teachers who are involved in classroom activities.	Students and teachers alike should feel justified in asking Amro not to bother them while they are in class or are otherwise occupied in legitimate school work.	Amro's team might ask him if he would like to contribute some of his free time to help out in the library, the office, or the student activities office.

(continued)

Table 3. (*continued*)

Scenario	Peer support	Adult support
Activity Type 6: Personal hygiene routines		
Andrew needs assistance to go to the bathroom.	[Not appropriate in this situation] Issues of privacy and dignity are more important here than peer support. Some of Andrew's closer classmates might be told how to handle the situation should an emergency arise when the aide is not available. Only students who are completely comfortable in this role should be invited to provide this type of support.	Andrew must have a male available for assistance in the bathroom.
Twice each day, Jocelyn needs to be out of her wheelchair lying on her side to prevent skin ulcers.	It is important to give Jocelyn some choice about where this takes place. She may feel comfortable lying on a mat in the library or gym while other students are reading or doing warmup exercises.	If Jocelyn feels uncomfortable with either of these choices, then a teaching assistant and the school nurse could help Jocelyn out of her chair, and she could relax in the nurse's office by listening to music or taped books through headphones.
Jennifer needs assistance to comb her hair and put on her makeup.	Jennifer needs to feel in control of this situation. A friend might go to the girls' room with her and do touchups.	At Jennifer's request, a teaching assistant or other female assistant might help Jennifer comb her hair and put on her makeup.
After gym, Amro needs reminders to put on deodorant and comb his hair.	It is likely that with a few age-appropriate reminders ("Hey, 'Ro, do us a favor and use the Sure"), Amro will do what all the other guys do after gym.	The gym teacher could go into the locker room and give Amro a reminder and have a private talk with him about personal hygiene.

162

Activity Type 7: Physical education or sports activities

Andrew is unable to successfully participate in ball-related sports such as softball, volleyball, or tennis because of a lack of coordination.

Ask the other students to come up with a solution to this dilemma. They might say that Andrew could be the "tenth player" on a baseball team or the "sixth player" in a pickup basketball game.

If Andrew likes playing a particular ball sport, then he might take lessons during the summer at a town-sponsored recreation program or at a fitness club. The school's team coach might spend some time with him on a Saturday morning. Another role for the physical education teacher is to develop team sports that all students can play by adapting the rules or the equipment.

Because of her seizure disorder, there is no safe way for Jocelyn to participate in sports or games that have the potential for rough physical contact.

Students could be asked to brainstorm a role for Jocelyn during those physical education classes that are too rough for her.

The physical education teacher, together with the occupational or physical therapist, might develop an adapted game, taking into account safety issues for Jocelyn. When students rotate in and out of a game, they might assist Jocelyn to be the scorekeeper or just to sit with her and cheer on the other players.

Jennifer is on the student council, and they have challenged the faculty to a basketball game to raise money for a new trophy case in the school foyer.

Once again, asking Jennifer how she would like to be involved is the key to a respectful and inclusive solution to this situation. Jennifer might want to be scorekeeper and could do that independently by activating a switch connected to the scoring machine.

The adults involved might adapt the game to include Jennifer. Each team must include a player who uses a wheelchair, and that player must have momentary possession of the ball before a basket counts. Possession for Jennifer might be counted as it touches her hands.

Amro is frightened of heights, and a ropes course is part of the physical education curriculum.

Several students may be reticent about going up the high ropes. With guidance, reassurance, and support provided by students and the teacher, Amro might take a risk and feel proud of his new accomplishment.

A quality physical education program subscribes to the challenge by choice philosophy, and no student is forced to attempt skills that are beyond his or her capacity or comfort level.

(continued)

Table 3. *(continued)*

Scenario	Peer support	Adult support
Activity Type 8: Fine arts, music, technical education, home economics		
The tech ed teacher is wary of Andrew's being in the wood shop because of concerns about the power saws and other dangerous tools.	Have Andrew work on group projects with other students. They could operate the saws and other dangerous equipment, and Andrew could, for example, trace, measure, glue, or use a screwdriver or hammer.	The tech ed teacher or a teaching assistant could do the parts of a project that involve using dangerous equipment, and Andrew could do the remaining steps to complete the project.
Jocelyn is unable to move her hands well enough to manipulate a paint brush in art class.	Another student could work with Jocelyn hand-over-hand to fingerpaint.	Same support could be provided by a teaching assistant.
Most of the equipment in the cooking lab is not adapted so that Jennifer can use them independently.	Offer extra credit for students in technical education or computer courses to research and fabricate adaptations so that Jennifer could operate, for example, a microwave oven or a blender.	An important role for the occupational therapist is the adaptation of equipment and environments so that Jennifer can attend to independent living tasks. The time and technical support required to provide this service could be put into Jennifer's IEP.
Amro loves music and would like to play in the pep band, but the noise during football games is too loud for him.	[Not appropriate in this activity]	Amro could be provided with earplugs or headphones to screen out some of the noise.
Activity Type 9: Community service		
Andrew must keep a log documenting his community service hours and activities in order to get credit for graduation.	When other students are in the community service office entering their hours, they can sit with Andrew and help him make his entries in the computer log.	The community service advisor helps all students and can support Andrew as well.
Students who have their license drive their own cars to their community service locations. None of the students doing the same community service project at the local library as Jocelyn has a car in which her wheelchair will fit.	Other students could ride with Jocelyn in the accessible van.	An adult with a van operator's license could drive Jocelyn and her friends to their community service jobs.

Jennifer is determined to be involved in a community service project to make a local nature walk accessible to people who use wheelchairs and who are blind, but she cannot get out to the preserve because it is inaccessible.

Once again, ask the students participating in this project with Jennifer to brainstorm ideas. Other students could do a "video walk" through the preserve, documenting the barriers. Then they all could work on the plans to eliminate the barriers, and Jennifer could be the test engineer.

The students' community service advisor could help them get in touch with local companies that specialize in ensuring compliance with the Americans with Disabilities Act (ADA) of 1990 (PL 101-336) and environmental adaptations.

Amro is extremely shy and is unsure of how to approach a community organization to set up his community service project.

Surely other students are also inexperienced in communicating with business people. They could all work together to write letters to various businesses describing their community service project requirements. If Amro needed support during the interview process, then another student might come along for moral support.

The community service advisor holds tutorial sessions to teach students how to write letters of inquiry, place follow-up telephone contacts, and make a good impression in an interview. Amro's teaching assistant might sit with Amro and guide him through the process.

Activity Type 10: Extracurricular activities and after-school functions

Andrew loves to dance; but, in the past, some teachers have observed other students making fun of him when he is out on the dance floor.

Gather students together and tell them that Andrew refuses to go to future dances because of the teasing. Ask students what ideas they have. The purpose of the session is not to scold or lecture the students, but to enlist their help in solving the problem.

The role of adults in this situation is to create a forum for student discourse and to push them to expand their comfortable limits of tolerance.

Although Jocelyn loves hanging out with her friends on the weekends, her parents do not know how to get her invited along with the gang.

Another high school or college student might be hired to be Jocelyn's social director, that is, to serve as her voice to issue invitations of her own rather than always waiting to be invited by others.

Jocelyn's parents might invite several of her friends over to the house and talk with them about any issues that have to be considered when Jocelyn goes out with her friends. These might include eating, personal hygiene, transportation, cardiopulmonary resuscitation and other emergency procedures, and so forth. They need to communicate the level of risk with which they are comfortable.

(continued)

Table 3. *(continued)*

Scenario	Peer support	Adult support
Jennifer wants to participate in OM ("Odyssey of the Mind") competitions, but they are sometimes held at inaccessible schools.	Because the purpose of OM is to spark and nurture creativity and problem solving, give students the responsibility to figure this one out.	If students are having a tough time coming up with solutions, then the OM coaches might approach the competition coordinators and ask for their help. Some possible solutions might be bringing in portable ramps for the day, hiring sign language interpreters for deaf students, and, ultimately, scheduling future events at schools that are accessible.
Amro's parents are reluctant to let him go to parties or to drive around in cars at night with his friends because of concerns for his safety.	Amro's friends might talk to his parents and give them information about where they will be, assurances that they will not be drinking alcohol and driving, and the time that Amro will be expected home.	Amro's parents could discuss with his friends their concerns. Perhaps they would allow him to go out if certain friends were driving and if someone checked in periodically by telephone.

Although we believe that such programs, when open to all students as tutors and tutees, can be a beneficial learning experience, we have also heard about grossly inappropriate practices in this area. One high school with which we are familiar actually required peer tutors to spend time with students with disabilities outside of school, and points toward their grade were awarded for this service.

People with disabilities are surrounded for their whole lives by people who are paid to be with them. Although these paid staff may perform valuable functions, they cannot take the place of people who choose to associate with people with disabilities. Perske and Perske described the brochure of a fictitious "special friends" program at a human services agency: "Lonely? Need a Friend? Call Special Friends. Call now" (1988, p. 59). Starting this insidious practice when students are in school can prevent real friendships from developing. The use of peer tutors to provide academic support to students with disabilities in their general education classes can mask underlying problems, both with teaching and with students' social lives. In a sense, always having a peer tutor available takes the pressure off the system to accommodate diverse learners by varying instructional practices and implementing curriculum modification strategies. When students with disabilities are included in general education classes supported by other students enrolled in that class, an opportunity exists to discuss how all students can work together to learn. In cooperatively structured classrooms, students with disabilities are not always in the role of being helped. Furthermore, there is less confusion about whether students with disabilities actually have friends or are merely spending time with students who are, in a sense, being "compensated" (e.g., through academic or service credit) for being with them.

Essential Condition #4: Student Involvement in the Inclusion Process and in Creative Problem Solving

The fourth essential condition for friendship is the inclusion of students without disabilities in creative problem solving and decisions about inclusion. At high schools across the United States, students are welcoming their peers with disabilities into their classrooms but telling adults that they want to be included in the discussions and decisions concerning inclusion that will ultimately affect their everyday lives.

Introducing Students to Inclusive Education

In 1995, New Hampshire's Raymond High School made a commitment to return to their home high schools students with labels of significant disabilities who had previously been in out-of-district placements. With the intention of placing students full time in general education classes, the administration sponsored faculty and staff training prior to the opening of the school year to discuss support issues, curriculum modification, grading, and so forth. Students heard rumors indicating that a number of students with disabilities would be in their classes the following year, but the student body was not involved in the transition. Early in September, in a current issues class, a debate was held on inclusive education, and it was clear that the students felt that they deserved training similar to that given to teachers. When the students found out that their teachers had been given consultation by "experts" from the university, the students also requested workshops from the same experts!

In response to their request, the administration provided time for the entire student body to meet in small groups with a facilitator. The inclusion consultant was careful to structure the conversation around issues of diversity and social justice rather than telling students about the educational benefits of inclusion. In these sessions, students had an opportunity to ask questions regarding the systems change effort that their school was undertaking, and they were asked for their ideas relative to making the transition easier for students who had previously been in out-of-district programs. It was reassuring that the conversation focused more on the communication styles and support needs of the incoming students than on the question of whether the students belonged in their classes.

Student Involvement in Creative Problem Solving

Once students with significant disabilities are included in high school general education classes, ongoing problem solving is necessary in the areas of curriculum modification and, often, behavioral expectations and support. Particularly at the high school level, that problem solving ought to include students. Many schools with which we have worked have found that holding periodic brainstorming sessions has been a useful tool for understanding the culture of the school and how students with and without disabilities are faring. Some of these sessions have occurred spontaneously, for example, in the middle of an English class. Others have been held at a regularly scheduled time with a student or adult facilitator.

Only two rules govern these sessions. First, the students who attend are not being asked and are not expected to be friends with the student with a disability. To do that would imply the need for charity or benevolence on the part of the students without disabilities. The students are consulted as the real "experts" on surviving and thriving in high school, and they are asked to provide ideas and, if interested students come forward, to be part of a team that welcomes the students to the school and "show them the ropes." The second rule governing brainstorming sessions is that all contributions are valued and respected because this is a learning experience for both students and teachers.

Andrew

Andrew Dixon is a young man who has been in general classes in his neighborhood school since kindergarten. He is intelligent, charming, and active and has many disability labels. During lunch this past school year, Andrew was having a difficult time staying seated long enough to finish his meal. Some of the lunch attendants were becoming intolerant of his activity and were very close to asking that he no longer eat in the cafeteria with the other students.

To ward off this decision, his homeroom teacher, the district's inclusion facilitator, and Andrew's teaching assistant assembled a group of his classmates to ask for suggestions for making Andrew's lunchtime more efficient and manageable. The students' observations and suggestions included the following:

1. Andrew always sits with adults. Allow him to sit with other kids to prevent him from wandering from table to table.
2. Every student except Andrew is allowed to go outside 10 minutes before the next period begins. Allow Andrew the same privilege if he finishes his lunch on time and clears his place like all of the other students.
3. The person helping Andrew eat wears gloves, and several students said that that made Andrew look "contagious." Get rid of the gloves and maybe kids will not be so grossed out about sitting next to Andrew while he eats.

This particular brainstorming session ended with several beneficial suggestions as well as a plan to reconvene when there were issues bothering the teachers or students. Shortly after this meeting, several of the students requested a regular weekly meeting to talk about Andrew's membership in their class. Although the first few sessions focused on Andrew, subsequent meetings focused on issues involving other students in the group as well as on larger school issues such as racial divisiveness.

Essential Condition #5:
Age-Appropriate and Respectful
Materials, Language, Expectations, and Modifications

The fifth essential condition for friendship is the use of age-appropriate and respectful materials, language, expectations, and modifications. High school students with disabilities are often treated as though they are much younger than their chronological age, and this contributes to the perception that they are not "friendship material." In our experience, changing the attitudes and behavior of support personnel in this area is extremely difficult and requires a very direct approach from those individuals' supervisors or administrators. Among the most offensive examples of infantilizing students with disabilities are

- Talking to students in a higher-pitched voice as though one were speaking to an infant or a young child
- Talking about students in their presence without including them in the conversation
- Allowing students to wear clothing that is made for much younger students, such as cartoon character T-shirts, hairstyles that are outdated, bibs, ankle socks
- Allowing students to wear "easy-on, easy-off" clothing such as sweatpants when it is not absolutely necessary for hygienic reasons
- Permitting students to carry school supplies intended for younger students, such as lunchboxes, book bags, pencil cases, and so forth
- Using inappropriate behavior reinforcers such as stickers or smiley faces
- Using workbooks or other curricular materials that are primarily for younger learners when these are offered only to the student with a disability

In addition to using language and materials that are inappropriate for students' chronological age, there are several other mistakes that are often made with older students with disabilities that set them apart from their typical peers and can even perpetuate the very behaviors (e.g., immaturity, lack of behavioral control) that we want students to stop. These include the following:

- Students with disabilities are sometimes defined by their disability instead of being described with language that more clearly defines the characteristic that is important for the listener to know about. Table 4 displays some "old ways" in which students were labeled and some alternative descriptions that provide more useful infor-

Table 4. Comparison of traditional and affirming descriptions of students with disabilities

Instead of saying:	Try these words and phrases:
Becky has Down syndrome.	Becky is in tenth grade and is part of the Environmental Club. Becky likes making graphs and charts and has a flair for drawing. Becky has lots to say but has great difficulty enunciating clearly.
Josh is a nonverbal boy who has autism.	Josh is 12 years old and is in Mr. Kean's class. He sits next to Stephen and Will. Josh needs lots of different activities during the period to maintain his interest. Josh uses a letterboard to communicate.
He's one of our BD students.	Terrance did the "Walk for Hunger" last Saturday and finished the whole course. Terrance has great difficulty managing his anger. Terrance is a talented artist who needs adults to take a personal interest in him.

mation and that acknowledge students' assets rather than their shortcomings.

• More stringent behavioral expectations sometimes are held for students with disabilities than those in effect for typical students, such as requiring students to shake hands with strangers (e.g., "Brandon, can you shake hands with Mr. Johnson?"), asking students to recite their life history to school visitors (e.g., "Shawna, can you tell Ms. Phillips how you like it here at this school?"), or asking students to behave "correctly" when typical students' behavior is more the norm for the situation (e.g., telling students to settle down during free periods when typical students are also being loud and obnoxious).

• People sometimes make allowances for inappropriate behavior in students with disabilities that are significantly more lenient than the rules for typical students, such as allowing a student to interrupt a meeting or walk into the principal's office without permission

• People may stop students with disabilities in the hall to praise them or chat when that is not the way that other students are treated

There are several strategies for sensitizing both staff and students to issues of inappropriate language and age-inappropriate treatment.

The first step is to raise the issue of the importance of language in how we refer to students with disabilities. Talk to them about how people with disabilities were once categorized solely on the results of an IQ test. Ask people to imagine how frustrating it must have been for many people when they were given an IQ test and they had no means of communication for giving the answers.

Asking students with disabilities themselves to give an honest appraisal of how they are being treated is an important step. Another strategy is to ask a couple of typical students to shadow the student (along with his or her teaching assistant, if there is one) for part of a school day and to provide feedback about how the student is being treated. Typical students are quite good at spotting condescending treatment, and they can be very indignant about it on behalf of their classmate. Videotaping interactions between the student and his or her classmates or teachers can be illuminating for people who say, "But I don't think that I am talking in a higher-pitched voice." Although it may be difficult for a supervisor to criticize a staff member about his or her behavior in this area, continued use of inappropriate language or other disrespectful treatment must be stopped immediately.

Essential Condition #6: Involvement of Family Members and School Personnel in Facilitating and Supporting Friendships and Social Activities

The sixth essential condition for friendship is the involvement of school personnel and family members in supporting a student's social life. Although all students have different groups of friends—for example, school friends, sports friends, neighborhood friends, church friends—a common characteristic of students with a wide circle of friends is their family's involvement in and support of their social life, especially before they are able to drive. When students are in elementary school, parents of students with and without disabilities need to provide about the same level of support to enable their kids to get together. This support consists primarily of arranging get-togethers by telephone or direct conversation, hosting play dates or parties, and driving kids to activities at a community location or at a friend's house. Beginning in late elementary school, students without disabilities begin to manage their own social lives, relying on parents for permission and for transportation outside their immediate neighborhood.

By the time students without disabilities are in high school, they usually rely on friends or public transportation and parents are out of the loop except for permission giving and monitoring their children's whereabouts. The situation is much different, however, for some students with disabilities. Often students with disabilities have difficulty in communicating their wish to be included in after-school activities. Typical students wonder whether their classmates are allowed to cruise around town in a friend's car, hang out at the mall, or go to parties. For teens who use wheelchairs or have serious health problems (e.g., seizures, feeding tubes, difficulty in eating), the barriers seem insurmountable and everyone just gives up. There are a number of strategies, however, for overcoming these barriers and shifting some of the responsibility for a student's social life to him or her with the support of other teenagers (see Table 5).

Make friendship a priority on the individualized education program (IEP), and communicate that priority clearly to school staff. Parents need to make their child's social life a priority in his or her IEP. This can be accomplished by telling the student's team, including his or her guidance counselor, classroom teachers, and support staff, that friends and social connections are as much a priority as the student's academic work. Making this priority clear communicates to school staff that they can sometimes put friends and having fun ahead of getting work done for a class. All students sometimes put their social life ahead of their academic responsibilities, and so it should be for students with disabilities.

There are creative ways to include friendship and social connections as priority goals on a student's IEP. The most obvious is to include typical peers in the IEP development meeting, along with the student him- or herself. Students are the experts on the social opportunities available in a high school, and their presence at a meeting shifts the emphasis from adult-centered goals and concerns to those of students.

An IEP goal might be written as follows: "Jessica will increase the number of students with whom she engages in extracurricular and out-of-school activities." The short-term objectives relating to that goal

Table 5.   Strategies for facilitating social connections

1. Make friendship a priority on the IEP, and communicate that priority clearly to school staff.
2. Enlist typical students' help in brainstorming strategies for getting students more connected.
3. Support students to initiate out-of-school social activities with their classmates.
4. Make friendship facilitation a part of all support staff job descriptions.
5. Provide specific training for students in safety issues related to community outings.

might target skills such as asking other students for their telephone numbers, joining an after-school club, asking a friend for a ride home after school, or hosting a party at her house.

Enlist typical students' help in brainstorming strategies for getting students more connected. If typical students are involved in periodic brainstorming regarding issues of inclusion or student-specific support needs, the topic of friendship can be introduced and students can be asked to help figure out strategies for getting their classmate more involved in the social life of the school. It must be emphasized that the purpose of asking students to meet and talk about friendship issues is not to subtly recruit them into spending time with students who have disabilities. The purpose of these discussions is to raise all students' awareness about issues of belonging and exclusion and to support their natural sense of social justice and caring.

Support students to initiate out-of-school social activities with their classmates. What do students need to get themselves involved in after-school social activities? First, they need to know about those activities. Classroom teachers, support staff, and students need to inform students about sports events, dances, cultural activities, and fund-raising events so that students can be given choices about whether they want to attend. Second, students need a way to express their interest in a particular activity. The importance of a communication system that has vocabulary relating to these events cannot be overemphasized. Third, students need transportation to and from events. Until students are old enough to drive, this responsibility falls on parents. After students are able to drive, accessibility may be a barrier and the school's minivan may need to be made available to go to sporting events and other after-school activities. Fourth, students may need support once they get to the event. Use the rules of natural supports during after-school activities as well.

Make friendship facilitation a part of all support staff job descriptions. The involvement of school personnel and family members in helping students get and keep friends must be carefully balanced. If adults are too directive, then students without disabilities can become resentful, feeling as though they are being asked to be a friend of someone with whom they have not freely chosen to associate. The student with the disability learns helplessness and is disempowered when adults cross the line from supporting their social life to controlling it. An aide or communication specialist might rehearse with the student appropriate ways to ask other students for their telephone numbers. She might help the student get calling cards printed that list the student's telephone number and address. An aide might call parents or write them a note to let them know the names and telephone numbers of students with whom their son or daughter has classes or a common lunch period. Responsibility for facilitating social connections ought to be a formal part of all support staff job descriptions, and this role should be emphasized frequently.

Provide specific training for students in safety issues related to community outings. Sometimes students need direct instruction about issues like using a wheelchair, helping a student eat, sensitively assisting a friend in the bathroom, and so forth. Typical students respond best to information when it is provided directly and without a big deal being made about it. Adults need to be careful not to project their own feelings of discomfort about some of these issues onto teens who are able to deal with them in a matter-of-fact way.

Although all parents are concerned about their teens' safety, especially when cars are involved, parents of students with disabilities must learn to deal with the normal set of risks that come with increased freedom that teenagers have (Sauber, 1989). Teens accompanying a student with a disability into the community ought to be versed in reasonable safety precautions (e.g., carrying identification, traveling in pairs or groups, being cautious when dealing with strangers) and cardiopulmonary resuscitation (CPR).

Essential Condition #7: Attention to the Development of a Schoolwide Climate of Acceptance and Celebration of Diversity

The seventh essential condition for friendship is the creation of a school climate where differences are celebrated and honored. If schools truly believe that diversity strengthens their learning community, if they recognize that all students have unique gifts and shortcomings, and if public honoring of these gifts is part of the culture of the school, then all students will feel a sense of belonging and friendships will be commonplace. What if none of these "ifs" characterizes your school? What if intolerance is the norm and it is not only students with disabilities who are dishonored but also students of color, young women, students from poor families, and gay or lesbian students? What can one teacher do to make a difference for one student within an unaccepting culture?

First, identify students and other teachers who also share your sense of dismay about the culture of the school. Start a club or activity group that focuses on one or more social justice issues such as amnesty, the environment, sexual harassment, race relations, or homelessness. Students who participate in these groups probably have a fairly well-developed sense of fairness, and students with disabilities may be interested in joining these groups. If you teach an academic subject, then weave social justice issues and questions into your curriculum. (Examples of appropriate units from several different subject areas are included in Chapter 6.) Join your school's long-range planning committee and advocate for the development of a mission statement that recognizes the importance of diversity in a learning community. Work for the establishment of academic honors that recognize personal best achievements in many talent areas as well as comparative honors. Involve parents and community members in school-sponsored initiatives such as building housing for low-income families, sponsoring a food drive for a local shelter, and so forth. Support students with disabilities to advocate for themselves and their rights. Lessons in self-determination will last a lifetime and can benefit all students.

CONCLUSIONS

Brian

Brian's story illustrates both the possibilities for friendship and the disappointments that can occur when these principles and strategies are not followed. By most people's definition, Brian was among those students with the most severe disabilities. He does not speak, and print must be enlarged in order for him to see it. His records labeled him as untestable and concluded that he has mental retardation. His facial deformities make him unattractive by most conventional standards, and he is often physically abusive to himself and others. In short, Brian was a student for whom friendship seemed an elusive dream.

During Brian's first year of high school, he was included in a full array of general education classes, and a number of adults were identified to provide support to him throughout the day. A "bus aide" met him each day, and they sat together on the way to and from school. She accompanied Brian into the school building, where they were met by a teaching assistant. The assistant escorted Brian to his locker and helped him take off his coat and get organized for the first few periods of the day. In classes, the teaching assistant sat next to Brian and provided hand-over-hand assistance to him to enable him to manipulate classroom materials such as laboratory equipment, art supplies, cooking utensils, and so forth. When students assembled in the cafeteria, the teaching assistant took her break and a substitute aide sat with Brian while he had coffee and a snack.

At lunchtime, one of the cafeteria workers guided Brian through the lunch line, loaded his tray with the "Type A" lunch (without asking him what his preferences were), and brought the tray to a lunch table. The rest of the day consisted of more of the same—Brian was physically *in* general education classes but not truly *with* his classmates. Few students approached him to talk, because they were unsure what he understood or just how they were supposed to carry on a conversation with someone who does not speak. After school and on weekends, Brian spent time only with his family. He did not attend after-school functions and received no telephone calls from classmates.

Despite the lack of contact with typical students, Brian was learning a lot just by being in a typical environment. The aide assigned to Brian soon discovered that he did not need constant one-to-one guidance to successfully pass from one class to another. He seemed to know his schedule and where he was supposed to be every period of the day. He began to manage certain routines by himself—opening his locker, taking off his coat, carrying his backpack from class to class, and asking for coffee during his free time. He sat attentively in highly academic classes listening to discussions about Bosnia, *To Kill a Mockingbird* (Lee, 1960), and the Declaration of Independence. When teachers joked with Brian, he laughed a silent laugh at the appropriate times. By midyear, everyone on Brian's team questioned whether they really knew Brian, and they contacted a communication consultant to see if having a means of communication might uncover unrecognized abilities in him.

Although the method was and still is controversial, the team agreed that Brian would be a candidate for facilitated communication (Biklen, 1993). At the first session during which Brian was given an opportunity to use a letterboard to communicate, the consultant asked what Brian would like to do if he had a way to communicate. He spelled "WRITPEPLE" (i.e., *write people*). Over the course of the next several weeks, Brian's words came tumbling out through facilitation. Other students were taught to support him as he spelled, teachers raised their expectations for him in class, and more and more students began to speak to him in the halls and the cafeteria.

The pinnacle experience came, however, when Brian and two of his typical classmates accompanied several teachers to a national inclusion conference. Although the school's inclusion facilitator came along on the trip for support, Brian and his two friends roomed together in the hotel and were told that they had free run of the building. For the next 5 days, Brian changed right before their eyes. He no longer required the gloves that he usually wore to protect people from his scratching. He and his friends stayed up until all hours of the night ordering room service and watching in-room movies of questionable taste. At a workshop session where the boys talked about their school's move toward inclusive education, one of Brian's friends read a short speech that Brian had written earlier, in which he expressed the need for friends and asked to be accepted despite his disabilities.

Back at school after returning from the conference, Brian's circle of acquaintances expanded and students began advocating for significant changes in Brian's system of support. A neighborhood friend said he would sit with Brian on the bus and walk into the building with him at the start of the school day. The teaching assistant tried to back away from Brian whenever possible but continued to provide support to enable him to answer questions in class and converse with students during free time. Brian joined two after-school clubs and came to several school-sponsored activities. In terms of behavior control, Brian had more good days than bad. For the first time in his life, friends came over to his house to visit and drove him to and from school. Although his life was still far from being perfect or typical, both Brian and his parents sensed that Brian's future might hold opportunities that they had never before dared to imagine. Everything that is known about making inclusion work well was done. Natural supports were used to the greatest degree possible. Brian had a way to communicate. Friendship had become a priority for Brian and the members of his team. He was fully included.

Whereas most of the stories in this book have happy endings, Brian's does not. Midway through Brian's junior year, the school district had a crisis of confidence related to facilitated communication. They decided that the evidence supporting its efficacy was not strong enough to continue its use with Brian. They stopped facilitating with him and tried to teach him sign language. By the time he had graduated from high school, he consistently used the same three signs (EAT, COFFEE, and HOME) that he had used at the end of elementary school. Teachers stopped asking him questions in class. Students changed the way in which they spoke to Brian and confined their interactions to offhand comments and social niceties that they knew would not be reciprocated (e.g., "Hey, Brian, how's it going?"). Brian's behavior worsened, and a hands-off policy was instituted to protect the teaching assistant from being injured. So, Brian simply sat in classes and listened but did not participate.

The remainder of Brian's junior and senior years were marked by increasing uncertainty about whether Brian really belonged in general education classes. His transition plan was done halfheartedly, and responsibility for his program was merely transferred to an adult services agency. It is highly unlikely that Brian's classmates will stay in contact with him.

What went wrong? If we return to the list of essential conditions, we can see that many of them were simply not put into place or were not adequately supported. First, Brian's inclusion was poorly supported. Teachers were told that he was not expected to participate in their classes, that he was supposed to just sit and listen. Second, not only did Brian not have an effective means to communicate, but his only functional means of communication was actually taken away from him, with no substitute provided. Third, the teaching assistant provided all of Brian's support needs despite the fact that there were students eager to do so. Fourth, students were not involved in the infrequent planning meetings that Brian's team held. Fifth, Brian's family became disenchanted with Brian's education, and school officials considered them too needy to participate in making Brian's social life more complete. Finally, the commitment to Brian of individual teachers in the school was not strong enough to surmount the difficulties that arose in Brian's situation.

Those who know Brian, Jocelyn, Amro, Jennifer, Andrew, and other teenagers with disabilities have spent hours analyzing why some students' lives are filled with friends and activities and why others pass through high school unconnected. Brian's team failed to make the commitment to putting into place all of the essential conditions related to friendship development, not just those that were easiest or least controversial.

If the hope is to achieve the promise of friendship for students with disabilities, then a commitment must be made to create conditions that foster interdependence among all students within a school community that values everyone's gifts and talents.

A self-determination curriculum for students with disabilities has been recommended as a means by which to increase students' ability to advocate for their goals, needs, and preferences in all aspects of their lives. Chapter 8 describes how several schools have extended self-determination supports and instruction to all students, not just to those with disabilities.

Implementation Suggestions for Teachers
1. Gather a group of students together and ask them to talk about who is "in" at their school and who is "out." Ask them how stu-

dents with disabilities fare with regard to social connections and
participation.
2. For each student with significant disabilities at your school, assess
    his or her educational experience relative to the seven essential
    conditions presented in this chapter. Are students fully included?
    Does every student have a way to communicate, and do other
    students feel comfortable with the system? Are students with dis-
    abilities involved in a wide variety of extracurricular activities in
    the school? Is transportation a barrier to their involvement?
3. For each student, develop a plan to address those conditions that
    are not present.
4. Follow the suggestions presented in this chapter for overcoming
    the barriers to the development of social relationships and
    friendships.

Leadership Suggestions for Administrators
1. When reviewing students' IEPs, look for goals and objectives that
    target students' inclusion into typical extracurricular activities and
    general education classes. Do not accept objectives like "John will
    develop social skills by participating in a social skills group" or
    "Mary will name three characteristics of a good friend."
2. Make the facilitation of social relationships part of every staff
    member's job description, and evaluate the effectiveness of staff
    members by measuring how connected students are. Focus on out-
    comes, not on process!
3. Consider rearranging the work schedules of some staff members
    so that support is available during after-school activities. One
    group of aides could work from 7 A.M. until 1 P.M., and another
    group could work from 11 A.M. until 5 P.M.
4. Observe staff supporting students during nonacademic times, and
    redirect them if they are getting in the way of conversation be-
    tween students with disabilities and their classmates.
5. Provide training to staff on the correct way to facilitate natural
    supports.

REFERENCES

Biklen, D. (1993). *Communication unbound: How facilitated communication is chal-
    lenging traditional views of autism and ability/disability.* New York: Teachers
    College Press.
Bogdan, R., & Taylor, S. (1989). Relationships with severely disabled people:
    The social construction of humanness. *Social Problems, 36*(2), 135–146.
Chang, H. (1984). *Adolescent life and ethos: An ethnography of a U.S. high school.*
    London: Falmer Press.

Cole, M., & Cole, S. (1983). *The development of children* (2nd ed.). New York: Scientific American Books.

Csikszentmihalyi, M., & Larson, R. (1984). *Being adolescent: Conflict and growth in the teenage years.* New York: Basic Books.

Forest, M., Pearpoint, J., & O'Brien, J. (1996). MAPs, circles of friends, and PATH: Powerful tools to help building caring communities. In S. Stainback & W. Stainback (Eds.), *Inclusion: A guide for educators* (pp. 67–86). Baltimore: Paul H. Brookes Publishing Co.

G. Allan Roeher Institute. (1990). *Making friends: Developing relationships between people with a disability and other members of the community.* Downsview, Ontario, Canada: York University.

Jorgensen, C.M. (1992). Natural supports in inclusive schools: Curricular and teaching strategies. In J. Nisbet (Ed.), *Natural supports in school, at work, and in the community for people with severe disabilities* (pp. 179–215). Baltimore: Paul H. Brookes Publishing Co.

Kunc, N. (1992). The need to belong: Rediscovering Maslow's hierarchy of needs. In R.A. Villa, J.S. Thousand, W. Stainback, & S. Stainback (Eds.), *Restructuring for caring and effective education: An administrative guide to creating heterogeneous schools* (pp. 25–39). Baltimore: Paul H. Brookes Publishing Co.

Lee, H. (1960). *To kill a mockingbird.* Philadelphia: J.B. Lippincott.

Lichtenstein, S. (in press). Characteristics of youth and young adults. In F. Rusch & J. Chadsey-Rusch (Eds.), *Transition from school to work: New opportunities for adolescents.* Pacific Grove, CA: Brooks / Cole.

Perske, R., & Perske, M. (1988). *Circles of friends: People with disabilities and their friends enrich the lives of one another.* Nashville, TN: Abingdon Press.

Sauber, D. (1989). *Changing expectations/planning for the future: A parent advocacy manual.* Minneapolis, MN: Association for Retarded Citizens.

Tashie, C., & Martin, J. (1996). *Voices of friendship* [Videotape]. Durham: University of New Hampshire, Institute on Disability.

Tashie, C., Shapiro-Barnard, S., Schuh, M., Jorgensen, C., Dillon, A., Dixon, B., & Nisbet, J. (1993). *From special to regular: From ordinary to extraordinary.* Durham: University of New Hampshire, Institute on Disability.

Villa, R.A., & Thousand, J.S. (1996). Student collaboration: An essential for curriculum delivery in the 21st century. In S. Stainback & W. Stainback (Eds.), *Inclusion: A guide for educators* (pp. 171–191). Baltimore: Paul H. Brookes Publishing Co.

Wagner, M. (1991). Reflections. In M. Wagner, L. Newman, R. D'Amico, E. Jay, P. Butler-Nalin, C. Marder, & R. Cox (Eds.), *Youth with disabilities: How are they doing? The first comprehensive report for the national longitudinal transition study of special education students* (pp. 11.1–11.16). Menlo Park, CA: SRI International.

8

Empowering All Students Through Self-Determination

Thomas Michael Holub, Peg Lamb, and Myong-Ye Bang

Who Asked Miles?

Miles is a highly skilled twelfth-grade student with a significant learning disability. In the early years of his high school experience, he struggled with overall school success. Miles maintained average to above-average grades but was unsure of his future. Miles's parents were well-educated professionals who were active in the intellectual, cultural, and social circles of their community. One community member described them in this way: "There are few families who can note as many cultural and philanthropic contributions as the Browns. They are pillars in our community, husband and wife, role models for the rest of us."

Because of their commitment to Miles's education and the resources available to them, they had given Miles a laptop computer with an optical laser scanner. Miles's father's community connections provided him with opportunities to meet people who were willing to give him a job after graduation that had real career potential.

Miles attended the city's finest public school, which was known for its high ACT scores and a state-of-the-art educational facility. He was provided with intensive support from special education personnel. At his mother's insistence, Miles enrolled in Latin and received one-to-one tutoring to help him pass the difficult course.

So, what is the problem? The problem is not one of opportunity but one of autonomy. Miles was totally uninvolved in his own education. He had no interest in the foreign language tutorial, stating, "I always wondered why I was spending 3 hours a week on Latin tutorial. I didn't plan to speak the language. It was kind of my mom's thing, and I really didn't mind pleasing her in this way."

The jobs that Miles was offered by his dad's private sector colleagues were not in occupational areas in which he hoped to work. The courses in which he was enrolled were geared specifically to preparation for a 4-year college, a future path that Miles did not explicitly choose.

What are the implications of Miles's lack of involvement in the decisions that will affect his postgraduation life? Despite the strong web of supports that currently buoy Miles through the rough seas of

This chapter was supported in part by Grants H023R20010 and H023R20034 from the U.S. Department of Education, Office of Special Education and Rehabilitative Services.

high school, what will happen when they disappear after graduation? Will he sink or swim? Will he be able to develop a concrete plan for his life, based on his dreams and aspirations? When roadblocks cause him to stumble, will he have the resources necessary to build a support system around himself to carry him through tough times? What might a school system do to improve the chances that Miles and other students—those with and without identified disabilities—will be able to respond to the challenges of adult life?

Schools around the United States involved in broad-based school reform and in efforts to include students with disabilities in the mainstream of general education believe that the intentional teaching of self-determination skills is one of the critical factors related to the school and postgraduation success of all students. In this chapter, three schools that have made the teaching of self-determination skills a priority are profiled. Holt High School in Holt, Michigan, is a professional development school that has restructured many aspects of its organizational structure and curriculum, including the development of community learning experiences for all students. At Madison West High School in Madison, Wisconsin, students with and without disabilities can enroll in courses that teach self-determination. At James B. Conant High School in suburban Chicago, parents have taken an active role in helping their children develop self-determination skills that they need for school and for life.

Although each school focused first on the development of self-determination skills among students with disabilities, they all eventually expanded their efforts to include students without disabilities as well. Although the outcomes of self-determination instruction and supports for students with disabilities are heartening, the chapter concludes with a cautionary note about the necessity of also making changes in the school climate as a whole relative to its views of students with learning differences.

THE IMPORTANCE OF
SELF-DETERMINATION IN EDUCATIONAL PROGRAMS

The importance of self-determination as an educational goal for all students is presented in the following sections in a brief review of the literature.

Defining *Self-Determination*
Self-determination skills help youth realize their potential and advocate for themselves. *Self-determination* is an attitude expressed in determining one's goals and taking the initiative to meet those goals

(Ward, 1988). Self-determination gives youth a voice. It empowers them to make independent choices and express their own needs and interests. Self-determination enables youth to take risks and to learn from their experiences whether they fail or succeed. For youth with disabilities, self-determination gives them a chance to have typical life experiences and live with dignity and respect (Nirje, 1972).

The Importance of
Self-Determination for Youth with Disabilities

People with disabilities often have less control over their own fate than do people without disabilities. Perhaps this is because many people with disabilities are viewed as needing protection and others often make decisions for them. Removing the right to make choices takes away the right to seek what one desires, to learn how to make decisions, to anticipate the consequences of decisions, and to learn from mistakes (Hoffman & Field, 1995). Individuals must become the primary causal agents for their own actions without undue external influences (Wehmeyer, 1992). Causal agency implies that an individual makes or causes things to happen in his or her life and that these given actions are purposeful and lead to achieved ends (Ward, 1988).

Wagner (1990) documented the difficulties that young adults with disabilities experience after leaving high school by examining their residential living situations and social integration. Compared with 50% of youth generally, 75% of youth with mild disabilities continued to live with their parents 2 years after high school graduation. In addition, whereas 63% of similar-age youth without disabilities engaged in weekly social activities, only 38% of youth with mild disabilities did so.

This lack of autonomy and ownership has a detrimental effect on high school students' ability to plan for their futures while still in school. Many youth exit high school without a plan for the future or the ability to take control of their own lives. After graduation and during their final years in school, they often seem lost and confused about the decisions of adult life. Student involvement in transition at the secondary level has for the most part been either nonexistent or passive (Van Reusen, Bos, Schumaker, & Deshler, 1987). This situation is due in part to a lack of focus on teaching students specific self-determination skills that would enable them to make those future decisions and understand the consequences of them.

Self-Determination as a Valued Educational Outcome

These data and the frustration of school personnel and parents with the disappointing postschool outcomes for students with disabilities has led to a growing awareness that self-determination should be an educational outcome, balancing the risks and benefits involved in allowing students to make their own choices (Schloss, Alper, & Jayne, 1994; Wehmeyer, 1995). Many people suggest that, in fact, self-determination is education's ultimate goal for all students (Halloran, 1993). Federal legislation reinforces the importance of self-determination for students with disabilities. Both the Individuals with Disabilities Education Act (IDEA) of 1990 (PL 101-476) and the Rehabilitation Act Amendments of 1992 (PL 102-569) clearly support the development of self-determination skills.

The Relationship Between Self-Determination and Inclusion
Self-determination skills not only are essential to the development of effective postschool plans for all students but also can be a critical factor in the success of students' inclusion in the mainstream of general education while in school. The degree to which individuals with disabilities are truly part of their communities and their overall quality of life is closely related to their ability to choose from a range of life options (O'Brien & O'Brien, 1992). When they are included in the mainstream of school life, children and youth with disabilities must have the courage to test their own abilities and eagerly seek personal challenges (Ward, 1991). Self-determination provides youth with the attitude and the skills necessary to make and carry out important life choices and take risks. In summary, there are legislative, developmental, and educational rationale for making self-determination a part of every student's school program.

SELF-DETERMINATION: AN ESSENTIAL TOOL FOR RESTRUCTURING AT HOLT HIGH SCHOOL

Holt High School, a suburban school near Lansing, Michigan, has a population of 1,200 students in Grades 10–12, including 100 students with mild to severe disabilities. It is a professional development school that has been affiliated with Michigan State University since 1990. This partnership, supplemented by support from a U.S. Department of Education grant from the Office of Special Education and Rehabilitative Services, has assisted the faculty and administration with restructuring teaching and learning to better address the needs of all students. Like Madison West and Conant High Schools, Holt's experiences are depicted best through the voices of students.

Megan's Story

Megan began her transition into tenth grade at Holt High School as a very frustrated teen. After a dismal academic experience in the ninth grade, she was referred for a second special education evaluation to determine whether she had a learning disability. She was tested in elementary school because of her reading difficulties but did not qualify for special education services. Her learning difficulties continued and were compounded by a chorus of teachers over the years telling her that "she needs to try harder, she's just lazy, and anyone with half a brain ought to be able to remember kindergarten work." She responded by studying longer and trying harder, but, by the time she reached high school, the academic demand was too great for her without some accommodations.

Megan was an athlete and a real competitor. Each night after athletic practice, Megan began her self-imposed 4-hour study session trying to complete her classwork and studying for tests. She managed to complete most of her assignments successfully, but her low test scores were never representative of her efforts or abilities. Megan's frustration with school escalated as her cycle of anger and depression over her learning difficulties intensified. At her individualized education planning committee meeting, she said, "My brain cannot find the information that is there, and my hands don't always write exactly what my brain is thinking." This time the results of her evaluations indicated that she was eligible for special education services.

She faced the same dilemma that many students with disabilities in secondary schools encounter. She wanted and needed support to learn, but she stated that she did not want to be treated differently and risk the social stigma of being a special education student. She felt that her disability was her private business and that no one except her family needed to know. To relieve both her academic stress and her fear of social rejection, Megan agreed to participate in an independent study held in the library with a special education teacher and three other students with disabilities. Several of her classroom teachers arranged to work with her individually during this hour. This alternative offered her the academic support she needed in a setting that all high school students used for independent study time. She ended her sophomore year feeling more successful and emotionally stronger. However, her special education teacher, classroom teachers, and parents were concerned about the denial and shame Megan was exhibiting about her disability and how this would affect her in college and in the workplace. They had several questions:

- How do teachers and parents assist students like Megan to learn about their disability and develop the self-advocacy skills needed for success in adult life?

- How do teachers and parents help some students resolve the anger and shame they feel because they learn differently and teach them to accept responsibility for their own development?
- How do teachers and parents help all students develop the self-determination skills essential for them to make their own decisions and accept the consequences of their actions?

To answer these questions and in response to legislative mandates, two high school special education teachers, Peg Lamb (the Education Plus project director) and Jeanne Tomlinson designed and team-taught a pilot course in self-determination in January 1994 for 15 students with disabilities who were considered at risk of school failure. The school social worker, Arlene Brophy, collaborated with the teachers and facilitated weekly discussions focused on students' feelings about school. Megan enrolled in this class. The syllabus of the course is depicted in Figure 1.

The students learned about themselves through various lessons designed to actively engage them in thinking about their experiences throughout their school career and sharing these feelings in both small and large groups. One activity for processing their school experiences was to construct a large collage in a small group using magazine pictures and drawings with captions depicting how school felt to them and how they wanted school to be. This proved to be a very important activity for them. They were able to express their intense rage and frustration about their school experiences as well as create a vision of how school could be for them. Coming to terms with their feelings about school and their long history of frustrations with learning proved to be very difficult for the majority of the class, including Megan.

One teacher, Jeanne Tomlinson, commented on this phase of the class. "Neither Peg nor I was prepared for the intensity of rage and shame that the students expressed during the beginning weeks of the class." Megan became very hostile toward the teachers and the class and skipped classes on several occasions. She wrote in her weekly journals that "it's dumb to talk about the past" and that "no one needs to know about my disability; it was my secret." For most of the students, this was the first time that they had had a chance to delve into their feelings about their disability and their school experiences. The teachers of the class were the natural target for the students' anger and exas-

---

Syllabus of Holt High School Self-Determination Class

Purpose of the course

This class is designed to give students an opportunity to
• Learn about various disabilities
• Discover their learning strengths and challenges
• Explore feelings about their school experiences
• Examine situations depicting both internal and external loci of control
• Write a self-advocacy plan and share it with their teachers

Course objectives

• Students will learn about different learning styles and their characteristics.
• Students will become aware of their own unique learning styles by taking a learning style inventory, answering questionnaires concerning their reading and writing skills, and analyzing their own work samples.
• Based on their knowledge of their own learning styles, students will develop an individual self-advocacy plan to share with their parents and teachers.
• Students will begin to understand why exploring their learning styles and developing a self-advocacy plan are important to their education and employment interests.
• Students will develop a plan for keeping track of their daily assignments and monitoring their grades.
• Students and teachers will jointly develop and sponsor a forum for teachers and parents to share and discuss information about learning styles, self-advocacy, motivation, and self-esteem.
• Students will develop a presentation for eighth graders about different learning styles, accommodations, strategies, and skills that they will need to be successful at Holt High School.

Course requirements

• Develop an individual learning style profile
• Develop a self-advocacy plan
• Implement the self-advocacy plan in your classes
• Develop a system for keeping track of daily assignments
• Monitor your grades in all classes every 2 weeks (progress report)
• Participate in class discussions
• Write a reflective journal (minimum of one page) each week about what you are learning in this class
• Participate in the development of student, teacher, and parent forums
• Exhibit appropriate behavior and respect for peers and teachers
• Develop an individual class folder that includes your second-semester class schedule, student information card, information about your learning style, your self-advocacy plan, your progress reports, and your weekly reflective journal

Grades

• Course requirements (50%)
• Class participation (30%)
• Final exam (20%)

Figure 1.   Syllabus of Holt High School self-determination class.

peration because they symbolized the institution—school—that had misunderstood them for years. The social worker played a significant role in the first phase of the class by assisting the teachers with the facilitation of group discussions about these feelings. She met with Megan and several other students individually to help them address these issues.

Videotapes of famous people with disabilities, as well as former students and community members with disabilities, provided students with successful role models and a source of discussion and reflection about their own development. Classroom teachers participated regularly in class discussions regarding accommodations, alternative assessments, and the supports they offered to students when they were made aware of students' needs. These conversations helped students develop a rationale for advocating for themselves by developing a written plan to share with their teachers about their learning styles and the accommodations that they needed.

One major activity designed to assist students in synthesizing their newly acquired self-determination skills was to plan a presentation (including, e.g., skits, posters, poems) for middle school students. It helped them begin to understand their own learning strengths, challenges, and the need to self-advocate in school and in life. They were received very enthusiastically in the middle school classes and were very pleased about their ability to share what they had learned. One middle school student said, "I feel scared when I think about going to the high school, but now I know the teachers want to help me and am a little more ready to handle it."

The culminating activity of the class was a student forum for parents and teachers to describe their learning styles, challenges, and strengths, as well as the support that they needed at home and in school. This was a very emotional experience for both the students and the audience because it was the first time many students, including Megan, publicly shared their learning difficulties and described the support they needed from parents and teachers.

Impact of the Pilot Class

To investigate the impact of the pilot class, interviews were conducted with 11 students from the class and 7 classroom teachers who had these students in other academic classes. The students reported that they were more aware of their own learning styles, had a better sense of their needs as learners, and did better in their classes. Even though some students still struggled in school, they stated that, after taking the class, they knew what they could do to improve their performance in school. Before taking the self-determination course, when an interviewer asked them, "What is your strategy to deal with a failing situation at school?" their responses were "Get out of the class" or "Think that most students are not that smart." On the contrary, after taking the course, their new strategies for a failing situation were "Ask for help" or "Work through the problem again."

In her final journal, one student reflected on what she had learned about herself:

> I would never choose the weaknesses that I have, but without them I would not have the strengths that I have. Learning disabilities are with me for life. By acknowledging them and accessing the help others offer, I don't have to suffer by the title I have branded myself . . . "stupid." I can begin to trust that I am as talented as others.

Although Megan struggled with her feelings in the self-determination class, the experience proved to be worthwhile. During her senior year, she wrote an essay about her disability in which she stated that the self-determination class was the best class in the high school:

> As a student, I learned more about my disability personally, and I [now] understand more about how it is affecting my grades and my attitude. When I am aware of a disability, I become frustrated. But this class has helped me be more relaxed and comfortable. My grades over the last 3 years have continued to rise up the scale. When I look at my report card, I feel proud of what I have accomplished.

The seven classroom teachers who were interviewed agreed that it is very important for students to share with their teachers the accommodations that they need to be successful in school. Three themes dominated their responses:

1. The students in the self-determination class became more aware of their strengths and weaknesses as learners and more confident in sharing their needs and problems.
2. Classroom teachers were willing to provide the same accommodations to all learners in their classrooms.
3. All high school students need to become self-determined and learn how to self-advocate.

Incorporating Self-Determination into General Education Classes

The last two themes above cited by the teachers were the most significant in terms of the class in self-determination serving as a vehicle for further restructuring of teaching and learning at Holt High School to better meet the needs of all students. We feel strongly that changes must occur in the overall school climate with respect to honoring all students' learning styles; otherwise, the next generations of students with learning difficulties will reach high school feeling as badly about themselves as our current graduates do.

Based on classroom teachers' strong recommendations and the beliefs of the special educators that self-determination skills should be developed in all students, Holt High School was interested in finding ways to incorporate elements of the self-determination curriculum into general education classes. That opportunity was realized when the teachers involved in the tenth-grade MESH teaching team expressed a strong interest in developing these skills in all of their students during the 1995–1996 school year. (MESH is an acronym for math, English, science, and history.)

Each of the two MESH teams consisted of four academic teachers, a special education support teacher, and students, including a natural proportion of students with disabilities. The MESH special education teacher was responsible for collaborating with the four other teachers about accommodations for all students and did some team teaching in the classes. The teaching teams had a common planning hour three times per week, which they used to discuss student concerns, to incorporate self-determination skills into the curriculum, and to plan interdisciplinary units of study.

The MESH teams had three primary areas of emphasis. The first was to engage students in the core subjects in more meaningful ways by demonstrating relationships between subjects through cooperative projects that were related to the real world. The second emphasis was to foster a sense of belonging in a classroom community for students that evolved from consistently working and learning together with their peers and their team of teachers in a supportive environment. The third emphasis was to incorporate self-determination skills into the learning environment.

Students in MESH studied units on learning styles, teaching styles, and locus of control that were team-taught by the English and special education teachers. Based on their self-exploration in these units, all students wrote a self-advocacy plan detailing their learning styles, the teaching style that best matched their learning characteristics, their learning strengths and challenges, and their responsibilities for their own learning.

One of the most challenging and unresolved dilemmas was how to facilitate a personal sharing of each student's self-advocacy plan with all of the teachers. The logistics of 150 students sharing their plans with 8 teachers was overwhelming. The solution was to have each teacher read each student's plan, write a personal comment, and pass it on to the next teacher. This was difficult to manage, and several teachers found the time commitment for this task too demanding. Although the teachers opted for this method of reading the students' self-advocacy plans, the lack of the personal contact between the students and their teachers diminished the potency of the experience for both groups.

Student responses to these self-determination units were mixed. Most students reported that they liked learning about their learning styles and their strengths and challenges. They felt that this information helped them to be more successful in their classes. They reported that the MESH teachers tried to consider different learning styles and used auditory, visual, and kinesthetic methods to teach them.

However, a small segment of students resisted this self-study and thought it was "boring" and a "waste of time." They had a hard time internalizing what they learned about self-determination skills. Some students used their learning styles as an excuse not to try. Not surprisingly, these were the same students who struggled to connect with school and invest in academic work. The MESH teachers were frustrated by this group's reaction. However, this resistance should have been expected because, during adolescence, most students want more privileges without any additional responsibilities.

Melissa's Story

Melissa was a student in the tenth-grade MESH team. She is a friendly, outgoing, and caring young woman. She loves sports, is a member of the volleyball team, and is an avid skier. She has both a hearing impairment and a learning disability. She started tenth grade very anxious about her academic performance and ability to succeed in high school. In tenth grade, she enrolled in both the self-determination class and MESH. Her parents felt that she needed the more intense experience of the self-determination class to explore her disabilities and her strengths to help her gain more self-confidence in conjunction with an academic environment that would foster her self-advocacy skills and accommodate her learning needs. Her mother explained, "As Melissa's parents, we had been encouraging her to be more assertive about her needs and her beliefs. We felt that a class that would give her time to discuss and reflect on the importance of taking the lead for herself would be an important opportunity for Melissa." Like all of the students, Melissa wrote her self-advocacy plan.

Dear Teachers,
I have a severe hearing loss. I wear two hearing aids, but my hearing is not normal with them. Almost always I use lip reading. If I can't

see you, I probably won't understand what you are saying. Sometimes I hear the words but I don't know what the words mean. My vocabulary is around the fifth-grade level. The vocabulary words are usually the hardest part for me in learning. People need to face me and not cover their mouth when they talk. I can only lip read one person at a time. Large groups are hard for me. When people talk quickly, I miss everything they say.

I must have closed-captioned videos and TV because hearing-impaired persons can't lip read TV. If you write on the overhead during class, that really helps. The closer a person is to me, the easier it is for me to lip read, hear, and understand. If I work in small groups, I like my group to work in a quieter room or in hallways without distractions. Lip reading and trying to listen and understand takes a lot of concentration. Sometimes I get confused, and after a while I don't understand the topic.

Tests are difficult for me, especially essays. It's easier for me when I can tell the person the answer and he or she writes it down for me. I have a hard time putting my thoughts in writing. I seem to do better with multiple-choice tests because I usually recognize the answer. I have trouble memorizing. I also have trouble remembering things that I studied. I can learn something the night before a test, but I can have a hard time calling it back up for the test. I can't take notes, listen, and lip read a teacher at the same time. My teacher's aide helps me understand a lot of what I miss during the class. I do better on projects and reports than on written tests. I like to learn new things, and I'm looking forward to learning in your class. I'm a hard worker, and I try my best.

Sincerely,

Melissa Maksimowicz

After sharing her plan with her teachers, Melissa reported, "The teachers told me my plan was very helpful. It gave them a better idea of how to help me. It helped them to learn about hearing impairments." At the end of the year, Melissa summed up her sophomore experience this way: "All of my classes helped me to believe in myself and what I can do. They helped me to stick up for myself."

Melissa's parents played an active role in her educational experience. They wrote a letter to her teachers expressing their perspective on how they might think about their daughter's learning. An excerpt from their letter follows:

Melissa has a desire to learn. It seems that it would be helpful to use the metaphor of a race car driver and the pit crew. In this story, Melissa is the race car driver, and we are all the pit crew. Our race car driver is determined to make it around the track. How can we as the pit crew work together with the precision necessary to have our driver reach her goal and cross the finish line, not once, but over and over? Not so much to be the winner of the race, but to finish and finish with pride. The pride that comes with everyone knowing that they have done their best. The pit crew shares in the driver's victory by having provided every opportunity within reason to contribute to the driver's success.

In the fall of her junior year, Melissa was hired to monitor and maintain the women's locker room at a local athletic club. She was able to transfer her self-determination skills into the work setting. "When the members of the club mumbled and talked softly, I asked them to speak louder. The second time, I told them I had a hearing impairment and would they please speak up." After nearly a year's experience on the job, Melissa had a new goal:

> I really believe that in my job I can learn to work at the front desk. It will be hard because there are a lot of things happening—the phone, people at the desk, messages. I will need to have more training time than other people. The work on self-determination helped me to be strong enough to take on the challenge of learning new things. I am ready to try another job.

Brian's Story

Brian was a tenth-grade MESH student with a warm and engaging personality. He was liked by both his teachers and his friends. Even though Brian did not have a disability—he was considered a typical student—he also developed a self-advocacy plan at the end of the unit that clearly articulated his strengths, challenges, and responsibilities. In his reflective journal, he stated, "Writing my self-advocacy plan really helped me to think about my real strengths and what I need to take responsibility for." He wrote the following description of himself as a learner:

> The learning styles that I can learn and understand the best are visual and kinesthetic. Examples of visual learning [are] when the teacher uses overheads, videos, and the blackboard. Examples of kinesthetic learning are when we are going through a drill, practice, and experiments. I like working in groups and individually; it just depends on what the assignment is. One problem I have when working in groups is that I am always the one who has to do all of the work. I think I can express information the best orally. I give good presentations. The teaching styles that match my learning style best is when a teacher uses videos to teach. I cannot learn at all when a teacher stands in front of the class and lectures us.
>
> The strengths that I have are that I can work with people well and can get along with them. I also am very smart and creative. The most important thing is that I am willing to work hard to accomplish my goals. The things that I have problems doing are reading, spelling, and taking notes. My accommodations that I need when I am taking a test are a quiet place to do a test, longer time to take a test, and help in reading a test.
>
> My responsibilities that I have as a learner are that when I make a mistake, I can realize it and try to fix it. I need to take a responsibility whether the consequences of my decisions are good or bad. I ask for help from a teacher even after school.

Benefits of Incorporating Self-Determination in MESH

Interdisciplinary teaching teams, like MESH, are an ideal structure to incorporate the development of self-determination and self-advocacy skills. One characteristic of the structure was the development of an inclusive learning community in which all students work in teams and support one another's learning. Therefore, the learning environment was not competitive but collaborative. One student in a group discussion said,

> The whole MESH program is based on group projects and group presentations. I like it because if I do not know the answer, then the odds are pretty good that somebody else in my group will know it. Then I can get the whole thing done, and I think it works pretty good. The strengths and weaknesses of each of us are different. But everyone can contribute in some way.

A second characteristic of MESH that served to foster self-esteem, goal setting, and lifelong learning was that all people involved— teachers and students—were co-learners. The MESH teams viewed teaching and learning as a collaborative process among all people involved. The teachers served as coaches, facilitators, and sometimes experts. Teachers as role models demonstrated the attitudes and skills necessary to choose a desired goal, to plan actions to achieve the goal, and to experience the outcomes of a choice through natural opportunities. With the knowledge of the supports and accommodations that students needed as gleaned through their self-advocacy plans, teachers constructed lessons and materials allowing each student access to learning. They employed a variety of assessments, including oral tests and reports, group presentations, and visual representations of the concepts that they had learned.

A third characteristic of MESH was that the core subjects were team-taught with the support of a special education teacher. Students liked having two teachers in a classroom. One student mentioned, "It won't take forever to get help. When you need help, raise your hand. With two teachers you can get help right away."

The fourth characteristic of MESH was that students developed ownership of their learning. All students became more aware of their strengths and challenges as learners. They became better at articulating their needs and concerns. More students began to take responsibility for completing their class assignments, doing their homework, and monitoring their grades.

As a whole, the MESH teachers reported that most students improved their self-determination and self-advocacy skills through the units. They also believed that the development of these skills is very important for success in learning, developing self-esteem, developing a greater sense of empowerment, and improving motivation.

In a group debriefing session, MESH teachers shared that they sometimes struggled with trying to balance the time necessary to develop these skills with time for their academic content. In addition, they felt that they needed to have a better understanding of self-determination skills in order to more automatically incorporate them into their teaching. One of the MESH teachers stated,

> The lessons need to be infused more naturally, rather than introduced as chunks of indigestible pieces. You want the kids to use these skills naturally and become an integral part of themselves. We, as teachers, need to understand the skills involved in self-determination to such a degree that they automatically underpin our decisions in the classroom.

All of the teachers were unanimous that the development of self-determination skills needed to begin at the elementary level for all students. The development of self-determination skills was incorporated and supported to some extent across all subjects. In their interviews, the MESH teachers shared the following rationale for infusing self-determination skills into academic courses, rather than offering it as a separate course:

- Integrating self-determination with content subjects makes more sense.
- Concrete situations and materials are necessary to teach self-advocacy skills.
- It is easier to foster and maintain self-advocacy skills in the core subjects.
- Self-determination and self-advocacy skills become a normal part of the classroom routine, not a separate class just for students with disabilities.
- Most teachers already have some elements of self-determination in their classes, so it is a natural addition.

Promising Results, Persistent Dilemmas

Despite the successful and promising experience of infusing self-determination into the MESH curriculum, a number of concerns remain on the part of the classroom teachers, parents, and teachers of students with disabilities.

- If instruction in self-determination were completely infused into general education classes, then would students with disabilities have sufficient opportunity to fully explore their disability, come to terms with their intense feelings about their school experience, and practice developing and sharing their self-advocacy plans with their teachers?

- How might self-determination skills be taught to all students throughout their school careers?
- How might teachers balance the time that it takes to teach self-determination with the need to cover all of their course material?

Part of the solution to resolving these concerns is the infusion of self-determination values and instruction into the elementary schools. Perhaps if all students, including those with disabilities, began the process of learning about their strengths and challenges as young children, they would have a greater understanding of themselves as learners in high school.

A second strategy would be to begin including students with disabilities in the development of their own individualized education programs (IEPs) as a way of giving them practice in using their voice to articulate their goals and their concerns about the school experience. Through the continuous process of empowering students in elementary school and middle school, students might enter high school more accepting of themselves and much more enfranchised. The process of understanding oneself as a learner by developing individual educational goals is critical for all students, regardless of their learning characteristics. Third, the entire Holt community must continually renew their vision of a school in which all students are valued for their differences and in which curriculum and instruction reflect that diversity.

The Future of Self-Determination at Holt

Despite unresolved questions, Holt High School continues to inquire about new structural arrangements that will strengthen the development of self-determination skills for all students. In 1996, a large group of faculty, including MESH teachers, initiated a collaborative group with counselors and administrators to develop a strategic plan to foster student responsibility more consistently throughout the high school. The group is called the Three Rs, for rights, responsibilities, and rules. The intent is to develop ways for students to be held more accountable for their academic and social behaviors.

From modest beginnings as a pilot course just for students at risk of school failure and students with disabilities, self-determination has become part of the conversation about educational equity and excellence at Holt High School. Although there is much more to be accomplished, a majority of faculty are now talking about ways to restructure Holt High School to help all students develop more personal responsibility for their school experiences.

Megan's Story Revisited

Megan graduated from high school in 1995 with a plan in place to study at the local community college. At her exit individualized education planning committee, she was provided with a contact at Michigan Rehabilitation Services and the Student Support Services Center at the college. In early fall 1995, the counselor from Michigan Rehabilitation Services had received a letter from Megan describing her disability and sharing her goal to get an associate's degree. She requested help from their agency to purchase assistive technology to accommodate her reading and writing difficulties. The counselor was astounded at Megan's ability to self-advocate. The agency agreed to help her purchase the necessary equipment for her learning, and Megan enrolled in three classes. She wrote a letter to her former special education teacher, Peg Lamb, at the end of the first semester.

> Dear Mrs. Lamb,
>
> Self-determination has helped me develop strong self-esteem and become more aware of my learning differences. I've learned how to deal with the pressure of my classmates. Self-determination brought me out of my shell. I've opened up and become a more outgoing student and person. I really needed the boost in confidence from the class. The teachers have taught me how to talk one-to-one with my college professors and tell them what I need. I took a full-time job, and my job deals a lot with the public. Self-determination and the help of my teachers also taught me how to be assertive and speak into the eyes of my customers. Before, I didn't want to look at anyone eye-to-eye. I was scared, ashamed, and afraid of what people thought about me. After being able to identify my disability in learning comprehension, I felt real comfortable and confident with myself. I passed all my classes and have a 3.5 average.

Buoyed with confidence, Megan was now ready to move out on her own and assume full responsibility for herself, or so she thought. She took three more classes and started a part-time job in addition to her full-time job. By midsemester, she was really struggling. In the summer, she met Peg Lamb for coffee and told her that her second semester was a disaster. Peg listened with great concern as Megan told her the rest of her story:

Megan: Mrs. Lamb, the self-determination class helped me to see that I needed to do something. I put myself in a

Peg: position I couldn't handle, and, instead of sinking, I recognized my problems and tried to solve them one-by-one.

Peg: What did you do?

Megan: I talked to my teachers and told them my situation. They all helped me out, but I still couldn't pass. So . . . I moved back home. I now work one full-time job to pay for school and my transportation. My parents don't ask for rent, but I have to take care of responsibilities in the house.

Peg: How are you doing now?

Megan: Well, I've learned a lot about responsibility. What I wanted was to be an independent, responsible adult, but I need to take it one step at a time, not all at once. It crushed me to fail, but I didn't pick on myself. Instead, I made a new plan. I have an appointment next week with my college counselor, and I am going to school again this fall.

The conversation ended with Peg reassuring her that she was well on her way to becoming an independent, responsible adult. They both walked out of the café feeling a great deal of pride, Megan as a proud race car driver on her own course and Peg as a proud member of the pit crew. Megan knows that she has the capability to enter each race in her life with a plan and the skills necessary to regroup when she meets obstacles on the track.

SELF-DETERMINATION RELATED TO SUCCESS OF INCLUSION AT MADISON WEST HIGH SCHOOL

Madison West High School in Madison, Wisconsin, is an urban school with a socioeconomically and ethnically diverse population of 2,100 students. As a site for implementation of model secondary inclusion practice, many teachers were doubtful about the benefits of students with disabilities enrolling in challenging general education courses.

One general education teacher remarked, "It seemed highly unlikely to me that special needs kids could handle or benefit in any way from the rigorous courses I teach. We're talking precalculus and aeronautics as a mainstay, so I was a bit hesitant when we started talking inclusion."

The story of one young woman with significant learning difficulties, Natasha, illustrates how the adoption of a self-determination philosophy and the provision of special skills instruction was critical not only to her success in the mainstream but also to a change of heart among West's general education teachers.

Natasha's Story

As a ninth grader, Natasha had some anxiety relating to her high school experience but nevertheless arrived ready to learn. She enrolled in general education classes, where she received direct and consultative support from special education staff. At the end of the first semester, she received passing grades in five subjects and failed one. Her initial success was short-lived, however, and she fell far behind in the second semester.

"The classes were too hard for me and the teachers didn't understand me at all," she lamented. Her science teacher concluded, "Natasha doesn't seem to care about her education. She fails consistently yet never asks any questions, nor does she come in to talk to me. She doesn't belong in the course."

Natasha's difficulties were not an isolated situation. Many other students with disabilities experienced similar failures in the second semester, and the school's administration knew that their inclusion efforts were doomed unless they responded quickly and decisively. Under the leadership of West's principal, Elizabeth Burmaster, and the assistant principal for special needs, Jack Schleisman, a systematic plan was put into place to respond to the students' difficulties and the faculty's disillusionment.

First, inclusion of students with disabilities became a priority for schoolwide improvement. Staff development workshops were held for all teachers. The workshops consisted of training in instructional strategies as well as frequent opportunities for problem solving in individual students' situations. A self-determination component was added to many students' IEPs, and Natasha's experience is typical of the results of these interventions.

Natasha enrolled in a ninth-grade course in which a curriculum entitled Becoming Self-Determined (designed by Tom Holub, a school transition facilitator) was being used. Six thematic units were addressed in the course, including 1) self-awareness, 2) systematic development of aspirations, 3) planning for graduation and postschool life, 4) autonomy-building skills, 5) skills for seeking out and understanding support networks, and 6) methods and strategies for establishing social connections and relationships.

At the beginning of the course, Natasha expressed confusion and doubt about its relevance to her education:

> It wasn't easy for me to talk about my disability. The teachers and my mom had always whispered when they talked about it. It was like some dirty secret. Then all of a sudden my teacher wanted me to talk about it. They had me reading [my] IEPs. . . . To tell you the truth, I thought the whole idea [was bad].

Because of the academic success that she experienced shortly thereafter, however, her initial reservations diminished. She honed her self-determination skills by using them every day in her academic classes and in school-sponsored work experiences. By the time she graduated from high school, her views about herself and her abilities had changed dramatically.

> If a teacher ever told me to do extra credit work or anything on my own, I'd usually forget it. But once I did a couple of the activities [from the self-determination curriculum], I realized I wasn't doing them for a teacher. I was doing them for me. I liked owning my life. They kept saying, "Why did you decide to do this or that," and I kept thinking about what I heard. If I have any set of skills that matters to me, it's these. I know who I am, where I want to be, and how to get there.

At Madison West, the population of students electing the self-determination class continues to grow as a result of the natural advertising that occurs between students and increasing parent requests. Today fully included students with disabilities and many of their peers without disabilities have and take the opportunity to enroll in the course. A satisfied parent noted, "These kids have been given the right to become primary in their own lives. Surprisingly, they've taken their right and have moved gracefully through barriers and have become self-determined adults." A teacher's comments illustrate the impact on their attitudes that students' newly discovered sense of self-determination has had: "Three years ago I would have been shocked to find these kids successful as adults. Now I'd be comfortable to have them live next door to me. They are prepared for the future and they know that they own their futures!"

IMPORTANCE OF PARENTS
IN THE SELF-DETERMINATION PROCESS
ACKNOWLEDGED AT CONANT HIGH SCHOOL IN ILLINOIS

James B. Conant High School, a national blue ribbon school located in the northwest suburbs of Chicago, has a reputation for excellence that is acknowledged by educational professionals and parents alike. Although self-determination skills had been taught to students with learning and emotional difficulties for many years at Conant, school personnel were disappointed with the lack of follow-through by students' parents and generalization beyond the classroom.

In one teacher's words, "It seems like we are going way out of our way to teach skills and knowledge for self-determination, yet parents continue to give the kids anything they want and to do things for the kids rather than encouraging them to do things for themselves. It's contradictory to the process." Instead of blaming parents, Conant invited them to be partners with the school to develop a new approach. Ryan's story illustrates the effectiveness of the coordinated model of self-determination support and intervention, called triangulation (Holub, 1995).

Ryan's Story

Ryan, a student with identified learning and emotional disabilities, had a reputation that followed him throughout his school years. His service coordinator lamented, "I remember being at a meeting, discussing kids who would come to us from the junior high schools. When Ryan's name came up, everybody had a comment. Nobody wanted to case manage this kid. We all figured it was probably too late to have a positive effect on him anyway."

By the end of his sophomore year in high school, Ryan held the school record for suspensions. He dealt poorly with people in authority positions and fought with peers. He seemed out of control and at risk of dropping out. His mother, recently divorced and providing primary care and guidance, did not know where to turn.

She said, "I just cried. I blamed myself for the divorce, which seemed to fuel Ryan's problems. I sought out therapy for us all and took time off of work to always go to school when he got into trouble. Nothing seemed to help, and I felt hopeless."

Administration and staff noticed a similar theme in other students' lives. With assistance from a University of Wisconsin educational consultant who was part of the school's federal restructuring and inclusion project, a three-pronged system of education and support for self-determination was developed, with parents as key partners in the process.

Ryan's mother, together with other parents of students with and without disabilities, attended monthly support and informational meetings. At these meetings, parents were informed about the self-determination lessons their children were learning in school. Role-playing exercises helped them learn to deal with their children in positive ways that would promote rather than undermine their children's acceptance of responsibility. When their children came home from school every day, parents now knew what they had been learning in class and were able to reinforce those lessons.

Many parents found it extremely difficult to talk about their relationship with their children when they were feeling so vulnerable. "It was pure hell for me," admitted one father. "I was not anxious to openly discuss my parenting style with [the consultant]. I knew I'd been giving him anything he wanted to keep him out of my face. I recalled all the times I lied for him about cutting school so he could still wrestle."

Although the meetings were difficult for Ryan's mother as well, she continued to attend the meetings, eventually becoming a more effective supporter of Ryan's newly developing self-determination skills.

Ryan honestly described how he had changed as a result of the efforts of his teachers and his mother:

> You know, it was actually easier for me to mess up [when my mom used to save me]. I'd screw something up or get in a fight, and my mom would fix it. If there were times she wouldn't fix it, I'd call my dad. I never complained about it, but the more we talked about [skills and knowledge for self-determination], the more I realized how temporary things were.

Ryan's service coordinator elaborated. "Ryan used to see two worlds—school, where we were emphasizing self-determination skills for his future, and home, where he just kind of moved along like a floating log. When we finally merged the two, it was incredible. Ryan did things for himself and 'fessed up to his failures."

The triangulation model, based on a simultaneous, coordinated emphasis on a single competency or skill by students, staff, and parents, has been adopted by others at Conant High School, not just by teachers of students with learning difficulties. Other teachers at Conant have begun to use the model in their own classes. Conant's orchestra teacher related,

> I'm taking the same model and using it for increasing awareness relating to musical arts. I invite parents in to sample the menu I've prepared for their kids. I may have to give up a night away from my family, but the assurance I have for the school-to-home generalizability of what I teach is worth it.

Perhaps most important, the benefits of the model have accrued to other students throughout the system. Josh, a school football hero and potential valedictorian, said, "I actually wanted to talk about stuff with my parents. It wasn't like they were from some other planet. They had a general idea of what I was talking about."

Joann Hartmann, coordinator of Conant's school restructuring and inclusion project, summarized Conant's conviction. "Very simply, we were looking for a way to do what we knew we had to. We had the skilled staff, the administrative support, and kids with needs. We just needed to discover the methodology that would work."

CONCLUSIONS

This chapter has explored current educational strategies in self-determination and the impact that their implementation can have on the restructuring efforts of high schools to create assertive and self-determined youth. A word of caution is in order, however, about a potential danger in self-determination training. It is disturbing to hear students talk about the negative views they have of themselves that they attribute to their disability. Although giving these students self-determination skills is an appropriate strategy for helping them to make a smooth transition from childhood to responsible adulthood, the onus is also on teachers and school administrators to create school communities in which the construct of disability is replaced by a celebration of the differences that make each one of us a unique human being.

One of the most controversial practices in secondary education today is the provision of community-based instruction for students with disabilities that takes place outside the regular school building. In Chapter 9, this practice is criticized for both pedagogical and philosophical reasons, and strategies and alternatives are suggested for teaching all students important work and community living skills.

Implementation Suggestions for Teachers

1. Talk to adults with disabilities who are actively involved in making their own life choices. Visit settings in which adults with disabilities are separate from people without disabilities (e.g., day habilitation programs, sheltered workshops). Visit settings in which adults with disabilities are supported to have regular jobs and live in housing for people without disabilities. Think about what you want for your students when they graduate.
2. Bring parents of students with disabilities together to talk about their children's futures. Invite guest speakers (e.g., people with disabilities, professionals who support self-determination) to talk with parents and students.
3. Read books and articles about self-determination.

4. Visit an organization of people with disabilities who are engaged in personal self-advocacy, education, and lobbying, for example.
5. Establish collaborative relationships with school counselors who help students make postgraduation plans. Ask whether they would work with you to support students with disabilities to develop their postgraduation plans (formerly called *transition plans*).
6. Invite an outside critical friend to observe you as you work with a student to design his or her plan. Ask for constructive feedback, especially relating to how effectively you empower the student.

Leadership Suggestions for Administrators

1. Read the literature on self-determination. Invite guest speakers to address a group of teachers, students, parents, and professionals from the community who provide services to adults with disabilities.
2. Talk to other administrators about the need for all students to learn decision-making skills and to make thoughtful plans for their futures.
3. Consider starting a for-credit elective class for ninth or tenth graders that teaches them how to evaluate and understand their own talents and learning styles. Develop a learning profile on every student that he or she then shares with next year's teachers.
4. Revise IEP formats so that self-determination principles are evident in goals and objectives.
5. Monitor the way in which supports are delivered to students to ensure that teachers are encouraging the development of decision-making skills and allowing students to experience the consequences of their choices.

REFERENCES

Halloran, W. (1993). Transition services requirement: Issues, implications, challenges. In R.C. Eaves & P.J. McLaughlin (Eds.), *Recent advances in special education and rehabilitation* (pp. 210–224). Boston: Andover Medical Publishers.

Hoffman, A., & Field, S. (1995). Promoting self-determination through effective curriculum development. *Intervention, 30*(3), 134–141.

Holub, T. (1995). *Self-determination: An analysis of practice.* Madison: University of Wisconsin, Center on Education and Work.

Individuals with Disabilities Education Act (IDEA) of 1990, PL 101-476, 20 U.S.C. §§ 1400 *et seq.*

Nirje, B. (1972). The right to self-determination. In W. Wolfensberger (Ed.), *Normalization* (pp. 176–193). Toronto, Ontario, Canada: National Institute on Mental Retardation.

O'Brien, J., & O'Brien, C. (1992). Members of each other: Perspectives on social support for people with severe disabilities. In J. Nisbet (Ed.), *Natural sup-*

ports in school, at work, and in the community for people with severe disabilities* (pp. 17–64). Baltimore: Paul H. Brookes Publishing Co.

Rehabilitation Act Amendments of 1992, PL 102-569, 29 U.S.C. §§ 701 *et seq.*

Schloss, P., Alper, S., & Jayne, D. (1994). Self-determination for persons with disabilities: Choice, risk, and dignity. *Exceptional Children, 60,* 215–225.

Van Reusen, A.K., Bos, C.S., Schumaker, J.B., & Deshler, D.D. (1987). *The Education Planning Strategy.* Lawrence, KS: Edge Enterprises.

Wagner, M. (1990). *Highlights of the national longitudinal transition study of special education students.* Menlo Park, CA: SRI.

Ward, M. (1988). The many facets of self-determination. *Transition Issues, 5,* 2–3.

Ward, M.J. (1991). Self-determination revisited: Going beyond expectations. *Transition Summary: Options After High School for Persons with Disabilities, 7,* 2–7.

Wehmeyer, M.L. (1992). Self-determination: Critical skills for outcome-oriented transition services. *Journal for Vocational Special Needs Education, 15,* 3–9.

Wehmeyer, M.L. (1995). A career education approach: Self-determination for youth with mild cognitive disabilities. *Intervention, 30*(3), 157–163.

9

Community-Based
Learning for All Students

Mary C. Schuh, Carol Tashie,
Peg Lamb, Myong-Ye Bang, and Cheryl M. Jorgensen

Sean

Sean is a ninth-grade student who experiences significant disabilities. Since kindergarten, he has attended his neighborhood school and has been fully included in all general education classes and school events. This year, as Sean begins high school, his team recommends a different type of daily schedule. Although his typical classmates attend seven periods of classes per day from 7:30 A.M. until 2:00 P.M., Sean's team recommends that he enroll in only three classes in the morning and spend the remaining four periods of the day in the local community participating in independent living and vocational instruction. This instruction would include learning how to buy food in the grocery store, developing leisure skills at a local health club, ordering and eating lunch in a fast-food restaurant, and working three afternoons per week in a local business. Sean would travel to these community locations with other students who have disabilities and be accompanied by a special education teacher or teacher's aides. The team believes that this plan will help prepare Sean for life when his school career ends.

Is there anything wrong with this scenario? Is it necessary to forgo Sean's participation in academic classes and related school routines to adequately prepare him for adult life? What would he be missing if he left the school building for most of the day? However, if he does not participate in a community-based instruction program, will he acquire important work and community living skills?

To answer these questions requires that we examine critically the beliefs and practices related to both community-based instruction and inclusive education. The chapter begins with a brief history of the development of community-based functional curriculum. Second, the literature supporting inclusion is reviewed. The conflict between the arguments supporting community-based instruction and the benefits of full inclusion is obvious, and the remainder of the chapter focuses on opportunities that are available for students to learn functional skills within typical academic classes and school routines and on strategies for restructuring current programs and systems to provide inclusive work experiences for all students.

This chapter was supported in part by Grants H023R20010, H023R20018, H086J50014, and H158A1003 from the U.S. Department of Education, Office of Special Education and Rehabilitative Services.

The authors would like to thank Dr. Thomas Holub (Madison Metropolitan School District), Mr. Don Minor (Northwest Suburban Special Education Organization, Mount Prospect, Illinois), and Ms. Joann Hartman (James Conant High School, Hoffman Estates, Illinois) for their contributions to this chapter.

THE ORIGINS OF
COMMUNITY-BASED FUNCTIONAL CURRICULUM

In the mid-1970s, accepted educational practice for students with significant disabilities was based on developmental learning theory (Donder & York, 1984). This theory stated that curriculum and instruction for students with significant disabilities should reflect their current developmental age. So, for example, a student whose developmental age was measured at 6 months would be engaged in activities to build an understanding of object permanence, to encourage babbling sounds and mimicry, and to learn motor skills such as sitting independently and manipulating brightly colored objects. Then, as students mastered one skill, the next one in the sequence of typical developmental milestones would be taught. This model would apply to students with disabilities who were 6 months old, 6 years old, or 19 years old. Self-contained programs for students during this period resembled early childhood classrooms and enrolled students from a wide age range who were considered of similar developmental level (Calculator & Jorgensen, 1994).

A revolution of sorts occurred in the late 1970s with the publication of research conducted by Brown and colleagues at the University of Wisconsin–Madison (Brown et al., 1979). They suggested a radical shift from a developmental curriculum (because it failed to prepare students for the demands of adult life) to a functional skills curriculum, based on teaching students domestic, vocational, independent living, and leisure skills in the environments where students would need to exhibit those skills. Thus, a typical school day for students with significant disabilities might include learning to get dressed or make a bed in their own home, shopping for food at a grocery store, working in a community business, and learning leisure skills at a community recreational facility. Although students with significant disabilities spent the whole day in the company of other students who had significant disabilities, this model had significant advantages over the developmental approach. First, it was age appropriate—teenagers were no longer playing with building blocks and brightly colored beads. Second, generalization problems were minimized because students were learning in the environments where their skills would be used. Third, future employers and community members were getting to know students with severe disabilities as competent people who could fit in.

Evaluation of high school programs of this era found that students who had a variety of work experiences during high school and who actually left school with a job were more likely to be fully employed several years after graduation than those who had a classroom-based education (Hasazi, Gordon, & Roe, 1985). Widespread adoption of the community-based instruction model and a systematic process of helping students make the transition from school to work led to revisions in special education and rehabilitation law. The Individuals with Disabilities Education Act (IDEA) of 1990 (PL 101-476) and the Rehabilitation Act Amendments of 1992 (PL 102-569) codified the importance of planning for transition from school to adult life and mandated that schools develop written individualized transition plans for students with disabilities as part of their individualized education program (IEP).

Ironically, a similar national initiative focusing on the importance of work experiences for typical high school students (i.e., those without disabilities) was enacted after the special education law in the form of the School-to-Work Opportunities Act of 1994 (PL 103-239), which emphasized the need for all students to prepare for the world of work during their secondary school years. To support states' compliance with these legislative mandates, the federal government has funded millions of dollars of research, model demonstration, training, and systems change projects.

PRINCIPLES OF INCLUSIVE EDUCATION

At the same time that community-based curricula were being adopted across the United States, greater numbers of students with significant disabilities were being integrated into general education classes in their neighborhood schools (Certo, Haring, & York, 1984; Gartner & Lipsky, 1987; Stainback & Stainback, 1988). The inclusion movement was based partly on the normalization theories of Wolfensberger (1972), which stated that the degree to which people with disabilities reach their full potential is directly related to the normalcy of their lives. Parents of students with significant disabilities, aided by a core group of university faculty and researchers, began advocating for their children's inclusion in general education classes with supports and special services being provided within those environments as necessary.

Although the original inclusion efforts were based primarily on parents' wishes for enhanced social connections and friendships for their children, some research studies and volumes of anecdotal evidence have shown that students' academic learning was also related to the amount of time that they spent with classmates who did not have disabilities (Karagiannis, Stainback, & Stainback, 1996; Strully & Strully, 1989). Although most research focused on the benefits of full-time inclusion, one study approached the question from the opposite

perspective, documenting the negative effects of part-time mainstreaming (Schnorr, 1990). Schnorr found that a student who was integrated into a general education class for just part of the school day,
leaving for therapy and small-group instruction, was not viewed as a
real member of the class. Classmates referred to him as a special friend
or were simply puzzled about why he was there at all.

The adoption of inclusive practices has been uneven from state
to state (Danielson & Bellamy, 1989). In some states, it is unusual for
students with disabilities to be placed outside of the mainstream (e.g.,
Vermont, Massachusetts), whereas in others, more than 90% are in
separate classes (e.g., Mississippi). Even in states like New Hampshire,
where inclusion is strongly supported, almost twice as many elementary school–age students as high school students are in general classes
(Special Education Information System, 1996). This pattern of less inclusion being implemented as students get older is true in every state.

A CONFLICT BETWEEN RECOMMENDED PRACTICES

For parents and educators in the 1990s, two sets of conflicting recommended practices need to be reconciled (see Table 1). On the one

Table 1. Summary of arguments for and against separate, community-based
instruction

Arguments for	Arguments against
Students cannot benefit from being in general education classes.	Curriculum can be modified so that students can learn in general education classes.
Students with disabilities cannot make friends with students without disabilities.	Friendships and a wide variety of social relationships can develop when students share time, space, and experiences.
Opportunities to learn functional skills are available only in the community.	Opportunities to learn functional skills are available throughout a typical school day and through extracurricular activities.
The only place to learn a job is in a community business during the school day.	There are many in-school opportunities to learn general work habits and skills. Specific job experiences can be found after school, on weekends, and during the summer, when typical students are working.
Students stay in high school until the age of 21, so vocational and independent living skills training must be part of their school day.	Students should be out of the school building at age 18 and engaged in the same kinds of work and educational pursuits as their former classmates.

hand, it seems as though there are benefits to providing students with disabilities with specialized community and vocational learning experiences while they are still in high school. In fact, schools are required by law to do transition planning for students with disabilities. On the other hand, the academic and social benefits of inclusion rely on students' being full-time members of general education classes and their school communities. There is no reason to think that this is less true of older students than of younger ones. We suggest that, for many reasons, the time has come to end the practice of separate, community-based instruction for students with disabilities.

WHY NOT COMMUNITY-BASED INSTRUCTION?

There are at least five significant reasons why separate, community-based instruction is educationally unsound:

1. Opportunities for learning basic academic knowledge and skills are lost.
2. A typical academic schedule provides a well-rounded education.
3. Functional skills can be learned in general academic classes and typical school routines.
4. Social connections and friendships develop from shared experiences and familiarity.
5. Academic curriculum can be adapted to accommodate individualized learning needs.

Opportunities for Learning Basic Academic Knowledge and Skills Are Lost

The social inequality that results from students with disabilities leaving the school for part of the day is compounded by academic inequality as well. Although the traditional belief has been that students with significant cognitive disabilities could not benefit from academic curriculum, new research has disproved that view. Koppenhaver, Pierce, Steelman, and Yoder (1995) uncovered unexpected literacy abilities in individuals with mental retardation, and, as a result, parents and teachers are including reading and writing goals on more students' IEPs. Students can and should have access to the learning that occurs in typical high school classes. There does not seem to be a point at which students top out or stop learning. Limiting a student's time in the school building to engage in community-based instruction limits the number of classes that compose his or her school career, missing out on the last years of entitlement to basic education.

A Typical Academic
Schedule Provides a Well-Rounded Education

Education is not simply the acquisition of isolated academic skills. It is important for all students to have opportunities to participate in a wide variety of classes, cultural events, extracurricular activities, and incidental learning opportunities (York, Vandercook, Macdonald, & Wolff, 1989). Being included in general education classes exposes students to diverse ideas, teaching styles, personalities, and demands. When students with disabilities are fully included throughout their education careers, they have a more complete view of the choices available to them after high school than if they were in life skills classes and community-based instruction.

Functional Skills Can Be Learned in
General Academic Classes and Typical School Routines

General education classes not only provide students with the opportunity to acquire knowledge and learn skills but also are the context in which many social skills can be learned, such as communication, cooperation, problem solving, self-initiation, responsibility, and many others. These generalizable skills have been shown to be more related to job stability than to the ability to perform specific vocational tasks (Brown, Evans, Weed, & Owens, 1987). Not being on time for work, having trouble beginning and ending a job, returning late from coffee breaks, and lack of social and communication skills are related to job loss (Sowers, McAllister, & Cotton, 1996). For many workers, and perhaps for individuals with disabilities in particular, a new job means learning a new set of skills specifically related to that job. Therefore, it is a much better investment of time to find opportunities and environments in which students can learn habits and skills that are required for every job. Throughout a typical school day, students must be punctual, solve problems, work collaboratively with others, follow through on commitments, and demonstrate appropriate behavior.

Social Connections and Friendships
Develop from Shared Experiences and Familiarity

Reflect on the different stages of your life and think about the circumstances that brought you and your closest friends together at that time. Your best friends in elementary school were probably kids who were in your class year after year. Many adults are still friends with a kindergarten classmate! In high school, when you changed classes from period to period, your closest friends may have been other members of a sports team or other extracurricular activity that you participated in for several years. As an adult, people you consider your close friends may be co-workers, parents of your children's friends, or people with whom you work in a community service project or organization. The development of a wide variety of social relationships, including friendships, depends on sharing time, space, and interests. Fragmented schedules, less time spent with the same group of students, and lack of participation in sports or extracurricular activities stands in the way of the development of those networks. When students leave the school building for community-based instruction, they miss being part of the daily climate and culture of the school.

Academic Curriculum Can Be Adapted to Accommodate Individualized Learning Needs

Community-based instruction was important at a time when inclusion of students with significant disabilities into general education classes was unheard of. As more and more students have been included, teachers' skills at modifying curriculum for students with varying learning styles have improved. It is no longer a struggle to figure out how students can be active learners within the general education curriculum (Tashie et al., 1993).

ALTERNATIVES TO SEPARATE, COMMUNITY-BASED INSTRUCTION

Although we propose that students with disabilities be fully included in a typical array of general education classes, we do not discount the need for them to learn independent living and work skills. To accomplish these goals in an inclusive way requires that we change our way of thinking and the way in which we have organized curriculum and services. Four strategies are presented to respond to this challenge:

1. Identify and enhance opportunities for students to learn functional skills throughout a typical school day.
2. Utilize typical, inclusive opportunities for students to learn work habits and skills.
3. Redefine appropriate education and transition for students with disabilities who are 18–21 years old.
4. Create new, inclusive opportunities for students to learn work skills while in school.

Identify and Enhance Opportunities for Students to Learn Functional Skills Throughout a Typical School Day

In Table 2, many environments and activities are listed in which students can learn and practice functional skills. Because many of these

Table 2.   Environments and activities in which to learn functional skills

Functional skill	Environment or activity
Money and purchasing	Cafeteria, school store, marketing class, school dances and sporting events, clubs
Laundry	Home economics, art
Grooming/dressing	Between classes in the rest room, physical education, art, home economics, getting ready for school in the morning
Mobility	Between classes, physical education, on and off the bus, cafeteria, industrial arts, keyboarding, community service
Job habits and skills	In-school job, community service, in classes, doing homework
Socialization and communication	In school all day long and after school during extracurricular and social activities

opportunities are also times when students are socializing, it is important not to intrude on teens-only situations for the sake of instruction. After an initial teaching phase, natural support strategies should be used to maintain the skill. For example, a teacher may accompany a student with disabilities in the lunch line for the first few times he or she goes through, showing him or her where to get a tray and silverware, how to make selections from the Type A lunch or the à la carte menu, and guiding him or her through the checkout process. Other students in line and the cafeteria workers are invariably willing to provide cues and assistance to the student, perhaps after a brief conversation with a teacher about the need for the student to develop independence in the routine.

Utilize Typical, Inclusive Opportunities
for Students to Learn Work Habits and Skills
Within the high school curriculum, there are many inclusive opportunities for students to learn general and specific employment habits and skills. Most high schools have marketing and business courses that require work in the school store or in a community business. Many high schools recognize the value of community service learning for all of their students. For example, at Souhegan High School in Amherst, New Hampshire, all students must perform 40 hours of community service to fulfill their graduation requirements. A community service job fair is held every fall at the school so that students can choose a site that reflects their interests and talents. Students are

required to check in weekly at the school's community service office, which is in a corner of the student lounge, to log in the hours that they worked. A reflective paper about their experience becomes part of their senior portfolio. Through this program, students learn punctuality, responsibility, communication skills, and the value of volunteerism and service to their community.

In 1985, almost 62% of all 16- to 19-year-olds worked during some part of the school year. At least one third of all high school students hold part-time jobs in any given week, and three quarters of all seniors work an average of 16–20 hours per week (Greenberger & Steinberg, 1986). Students with disabilities also have these patterns of work when they are in high school (Lichtenstein, 1990). With such an unprecedented number of young adults working during their high school career, schools should capitalize on this phenomenon to address vocational training for students with disabilities.

A student with a disability can get an after-school or weekend job, and the work schedule of some school personnel could shift from 7 A.M. until 3 P.M. to 3 P.M. until 11 P.M.—those hours when students would need training and support on the job. Similarly, students with disabilities can work during the summer, just like their typical peers. The concept of extended-year programming should be age-appropriate and, for students nearing graduation, should focus on getting them ready for the world of work or postsecondary education.

Redefine Appropriate Education and Transition for Students with Disabilities Who Are 18–21 Years Old

In most states, schools are responsible for educating students with disabilities until they reach the age of 21. Unfortunately, students often spend the years following their senior year in the high school building, continuing to take classes with students who are no longer age-appropriate peers. Many become second- or third-year seniors as they await graduation. Some students may not even graduate—an important rite of passage for adolescents—because they are given certificates of completion. This practice denies them valuable career opportunities because they do not have a high school diploma (Lichtenstein, 1990).

A dramatically different picture emerges when students' education is designed to be inclusive and typical (see Table 3). These students enroll in a typical schedule of academic classes with the goal of obtaining a high school diploma. Accommodations to credit and course requirements can be incorporated into the student's IEP. While they are in school, they take advantage of the same work opportunities as their classmates without disabilities. At approximately age 18, after participating in the graduation ceremony with their classmates,

Table 3.   Comparison of students' schedules

The way it used to be	How it ought to be
Community-based instruction supplements instruction in self-contained classes. Paul was in a self-contained class for students with moderate and severe disabilities. In class, he participated in prevocational tasks, such as sorting, folding, and matching. Two times per week, Paul went into the community with a classroom assistant to shop for groceries and volunteer at the town library.	*Students with disabilities are enrolled in age-appropriate grades and participate in all general courses.* Matthew is a junior in his local high school. Out of a seven-period day, he participates in six content area classes: physical education, business math, French, chefs, environmental biology, and word processing. His seventh period is a study hall. His study hall period is spent working in the school media center as a library assistant. He also participates in managing the school store as part of his business math class.
Community-based instruction supplements a schedule of nonacademic mainstream classes. Barbara was enrolled in the life skills program while in high school. In the morning, she took three tenth-grade classes (home economics, physical education, and band) and lunch. Because few nonacademic subjects were offered in the afternoon, Barbara spent the rest of the day working on community skills and vocational instruction away from the school building.	*Students with disabilities graduate from high school at age 18 and receive ongoing support from the school district.* Suzanne is 18 years old and graduated with a diploma in June. It did not have an asterisk or other special designation, although modifications to the typical graduation requirements are documented on her IEP and in her cumulative school record. She works at a part-time job in the community, takes one class at the community college, and learns independent living skills in her home and the community. The school district will offer her support until the age of 21.

they will still have at least 3 more years of public education entitlement to learn vocational and independent living skills or to obtain additional education or training. It is during these years that they should be supported to focus on their career aspirations. Their education during these years should take place out of the high school building. They should go to work or take classes every day and should be supported to develop work and social connections in the local community. Their individualized transition plan should focus on the supports they need to move away from home, establish a social life, become a lifelong learner, and work a part- or full-time job. In short, they must learn to continue the typical life that they had in high school.

These shifts in practice would obviously necessitate a change in the job roles and responsibilities of the high school teaching staff supporting those students. Many high schools base one or more staff people at local community colleges. Others work with employers to configure worksite-based support systems for their employees who have disabilities.

Create New, Inclusive Opportunities
for Students to Learn Work Skills While in School

Another alternative to traditional community-based instruction for students with disabilities is the establishment of inclusive mentorship work programs that link students to community businesses. At Holt High School, located just outside Lansing, Michigan, such a mentorship program was developed by their community transition coalition. A comprehensive description of the program and its positive effects on students with and without disabilities is described through the personal stories of two Holt students.

Ben

Ben Wolf is an eleventh-grade student who is intellectually talented and experiences significant disabilities including attention-deficit/hyperactivity disorder (ADHD) and emotional disabilities in the form of anger and depression. He often behaves inappropriately with adults and peers, making it difficult for him to be successful in high school. Ben's academic challenges began in junior high school. Although he is very capable, he found it difficult to stay focused on school and to follow through on assignments. He finished ninth grade with only a few credits. Thus, he began tenth grade feeling depressed, angry, and anxious about his transition to the high school environment. The first semester of tenth grade was miserable for Ben, and he continued his downward spiral by skipping school, failing classes, and getting involved with alcohol and drugs. His depression became more serious, and he left school for treatment before the end of the semester.

Ben returned for the second semester with a very radical look compared with the majority of high school students. He had shaved one half of his head, leaving the remainder of his multicolored hair at shoulder length. Ben wore dark, unkempt clothes, and his jacket was emblazoned with a Pink Floyd logo and peace symbols. He had pierced an eyebrow, his lip, and his tongue and adorned them with silver rings and studs. Along with his new appearance, however, Ben also had new, positive goals for himself. He was committed to being successful in school and to connecting positively with people.

He developed a schedule with his counselor, selecting courses that he felt would sustain his interest. One that intrigued him was a class in self-determination (Wehmeyer, 1992). (See Chapter 8 for a complete description of Holt's self-determination curriculum.) In this course, Ben had the opportunity to identify what had made school such a frustrating experience for him, explore his individual strengths and challenges, and develop a self-advocacy plan to share with his teachers. He continued to struggle, however, with two major questions: How are my academic courses relevant to the world outside the school's walls? What talents and skills do I have to contribute to the world of work? Because these are the same questions that all high school students wrestle with, schools and communities must help students find meaningful answers to these questions so that they stay in school and make a commitment to learning.

In response to the growing number of students who seemed disinterested in learning and to provide an inclusive work experience for students with disabilities, members of the Holt High School community formed a transition coalition in 1994 that was composed of school personnel, parents, community alternative education agencies, adult services agencies, and businesses. The goal of the coalition was to develop a coordinated system of mentorship experiences, coursework, and transition planning that could meet the needs of typical students, those who are deemed at risk for school failure or dropping out, and those with identified disabilities who struggle with questions similar to Ben's. (Holt High School is a suburban school with 1,200 students in Grades 10–12, including approximately 100 with identified disabilities.) The Holt system is based on a taxonomy developed by Kohler (1994) that includes five major domains: student development, student-focused planning, interagency collaboration, family involvement, and program structure and attributes. The student development domain includes life skills instruction, employment skills instruction, career and vocational curricula, structured work experience, vocational assessment, and accommodations and support. The student-focused planning domain includes IEP development, student participation, and accommodations and planning strategies. The interagency collaboration domain includes an interorganizational framework and collaborative service delivery. The family involvement domain includes family training and family empowerment. The program structure and attributes domain includes program philosophy, strategic planning, program evaluation, and human resources development.

The anchor of the School-to-Work Mentorship Program is an elective course in self-determination (see page 190). Its goals are to provide opportunities for students to

• Explore their own vocational interests, abilities, and aptitudes

- Develop the skills necessary for future employment and explore career options
- Practice self-advocacy skills within the worksite
- Develop transition plans based on their unique needs and goals

The 1995–1996 pilot class enrolled a diverse population of students, including some traditionally viewed as honor and average, students with disabilities, and alternative education students, and offered them a comprehensive, community-based work and learning experience. Adults from Holt-area businesses shared information about their careers through class presentations and a career exploration fair. All students received an individualized vocational assessment to help them determine their career interests and preferences. School personnel helped students develop a career plan and taught them basic vocational skills such as writing a resume, keyboarding, and interviewing.

After students were matched to jobs and employers, support was provided cooperatively by their employers through new employee training and by co-workers, by school staff who visited the jobsites weekly, and, in some cases, by staff from a local rehabilitation services center. The students, employers, and high school teachers participated in weekly debriefing sessions to discuss issues and concerns that students were experiencing in the workplace. Students' progress and the development of their career plans were discussed at parent meetings.

Both students and their employers benefited from the program. In addition to learning valuable job skills, students learned to advocate for their own support needs. Employers learned that, with the right support, students whom they might not have considered as potential employees had much to offer their businesses. Cynthia Wright, a rehabilitation counselor at Michigan Rehabilitation Services who worked with students in the School-to-Work Mentorship Program, shared the following observation:

> Learning about the world of work in a real-life, hands-on situation, with real people is extremely valuable. Having a variety of experiences in different occupations could have a positive impact on their whole lives. I think the reason why the School-to-Work Mentorship Program has been so successful is the strong commitment of the team, the willingness of the team to collaborate with agencies and businesses, and the support of the school administration.

Impact of the School-to-Work Mentorship Program on Ben

Ben Wolf, discussed previously, enrolled in the first semester of the School-to-Work Mentorship Program as a way to resolve his questions about how academic courses related to life outside of school and what talents he had to contribute to society. During the semester, Ben identified journalism as an area of interest. After writing a résumé and practicing his interviewing skills, Ben was ready to apply for a position at a local newspaper. Although he had begun to let his hair grow out to an even length in its natural color, the acceptability of his appearance for the workplace was still an issue. Ben's teachers decided to let the influence of classmates and members of the business world address this situation. As all class members were preparing for their job interviews, class discussions were held with members of local businesses regarding interview strategies and appropriate attire. During the week of Ben's interview, Ben came to school with a new haircut and a more professional demeanor. He completed his interview successfully and scheduled his first day of work at the newspaper.

His duties at the newspaper consisted of answering the telephone, writing articles, and assisting his mentor to perform the weekly community survey. Everyone involved in the mentorship program gave it positive reviews. With honesty and critical self-reflection, Ben recognized his positive contributions to the newspaper and the areas in which he needed to improve. He related his experience:

> My duties as a temporary . . . staff member include relaying phone calls, taking messages, filing photographs, and writing occasional stories. Though my performance of these duties has been, admittedly, quite far from flawless, my learning of the ropes of a white-collar position of employment has been achieved to a quite satisfying degree. My mentor explained the *Writer's Market* and *Poet's Market* publications and lent me a copy of a letter describing the process of submitting material and all the ramifications thereof. I became interested in working as a freelancer and have considered exerting my efforts toward getting material published and earning my income by those means. Unquestionably, this program is the most valuable and practical academic course in which I have ever been allowed to set foot. The only difficulty I encountered was to keep up my job attendance. I hate taking phone messages and meeting deadlines. Truthfully speaking, my involvement with the School-to-Work Mentorship Program is really the only thing stopping me from switching from high school to alternative education. The School-to-Work Mentorship Program has been the most valuable part of my high school career. It's really made it for me, man!

Jeanne Tomlinson, a Holt teacher, member of the school-to-work team, and Ben's service coordinator, shared her reflections about the impact of the program on Ben's self-confidence:

> This experience has positively affected Ben in that, as the time approached for him to interview for a community placement, he made major changes in his physical appearance. He changed his radical hairstyle to one that was more conservative. He stopped wearing all of his facial jewelry and started dressing more neatly. He used his tremendous writing abilities to publish several articles. . . . He demonstrated more responsibility about following through on his responsibilities. He learned to be more appropriate in his

interactions with adults and students. Most important, he gained self-confidence.

The editor of the newspaper, who was Ben's mentor, believed that this experience showed Ben that he had the potential to make a contribution to the field of journalism. He said that Ben had the potential to be an excellent journalist or any other professional in the communications field. Although Ben's writing skills reflected maturity, the editor said, Ben needed to improve his punctuality and telephone-answering skills. The editor also believed that tangible rewards for the first few weeks in the mentorship program would be effective in motivating students, especially students at risk and with disabilities. Deb Wolf, Ben's mother, described the mentorship program as having had a profound impact on Ben's education and his life:

> He was very faithful about going to work. . . . He was proud to see his stories and name in print and to receive the recognition that went with it. This was a great boost for his ever-fragile self-esteem. The wonderful thing about this opportunity is that it is offered not only to academically successful students but also to troubled students like Ben who need to experience success outside the academic arena. This was a golden opportunity for Ben, and, with the help of his mentor, school staff, and employment support from Michigan Rehabilitation Services, he made the most out of it. He learned that school is not the only place where he needs to be punctual, be polite, and work. It helped him realize the need for developing patience, self-control, and personal responsibility. I consider the whole school-to-work experience a very positive and significant one for my son and earnestly hope that the school district will continue to offer it as an option to all students.

SCHOOL-TO-WORK MENTORSHIP PROGRAM ALSO BENEFITS TYPICAL STUDENTS

Although Ben Wolf was a student who experienced significant school and life adjustment challenges, mentorship experiences can also benefit typical students who are searching for direction after high school.

Stephanie

Stephanie Craft is an eleventh grader at Holt High School. She is a very mature and conscientious student with a solid academic record. She has a part-time job and plays softball. Stephanie enrolled in the school-to-work program to clarify her interest in law enforcement. She wanted to explore this career by working for the county sheriff's department and to find out what talents she could offer the field.

The Holt School-to-Work team approached the sheriff's department with her request. Their first response was that they had an internship program for college students majoring in criminal justice but had never involved high school students in this program. After a second contact, they were willing to consider mentoring a high school student, provided that the student successfully completed the same application process as the college interns. This process included a 20-page questionnaire, a drug screening, and a 2-hour interview with three deputies. Stephanie was willing to complete this demanding process with the understanding that she might not meet their criteria for participation in this program. The three deputies were very impressed with both her interview and her responses on the questionnaire. They offered her an opportunity to work with their department for 12 hours per week for 10 weeks as long as she understood that overtime might be necessary if she and her deputy partner were handling an emergency situation. She readily agreed to this condition, and her mentorship program began the next week.

During her mentorship experience, Stephanie rode in the patrol car for several hours each week, giving her the chance to learn about the daily routine of a law enforcement officer. She observed the deputies helping accident victims, ticketing speeders, and responding to a hostage situation. The second phase of her mentorship was working at the county jail summarizing and filing data on inmates. In addition, she assisted the deputies with supervising visitations and overseeing the activities of the prisoners. In this program, Stephanie was given a series of experiences that helped her get a feel for the work of a police officer. Deputy Tim Howery at the Ingham County Sheriff's Department had positive feelings about Stephanie's performance, offered to write her a recommendation for college, and even suggested that she apply to work for the department after graduation. He commented,

> Stephanie was the best candidate to test this system. She has continued to follow the rules and guidelines that were established. She has been enthusiastic about her position here. I believe the entire program has been a very positive experience for both of us. Because of her attitude and enthusiasm, she brought a lot to the program, and I feel she got a lot out of it.

Stephanie gave voice to her experience in the following letter of appreciation she wrote to the sheriff:

> I am very happy to say that I have completed 111 hours of an internship at the Ingham County Sheriff's Department. I had a wonderful time! I would like to take a couple of minutes to thank you and your staff for giving me the great opportunity I had. When I began the "School-to-Work" Program at Holt High School, I wasn't quite sure

where my future was headed. I have always had an interest in the law enforcement area, and I thought about making a career out of it. Now that I have experienced all that I have with your department, I am sure of my direct route to getting a job as a police officer. When I reach the age of 21, I will be applying at Ingham County. I would love to be an officer there. One of my many reasons for this is the excellent staff at the department. Everyone I rode along with was exceptionally nice and willing to answer any type of question I had. Even back in the jail was a neat experience. Everyone seemed to be in good spirits at all times, laughing and joking with one another but getting their job done at the same time. Once again, I would like to thank you and your staff for opening up my future for me and giving me the opportunity you did. I hope in the future I have some sort of contact with you.

P.S. The shirt fits and the mug is great to drink my hot chocolate in!

Stephanie plans to apply to the criminal justice program at the local community college during her senior year. Because of her experience in the School-to-Work Mentorship Program, she will be able to clearly articulate why she wants to be a candidate in their program and provide them with a description of her mentorship with the sheriff's department.

OUTCOMES OF MENTORSHIP EXPERIENCES

There is a significant relationship between community-based mentorship programs and students' obtaining meaningful, paid work in community environments following high school. Students who were most successful received ongoing opportunities for direct training in community employment sites throughout high school and obtained paid employment before graduation (Hasazi et al., 1985).

To investigate the impact of Holt's School-to-Work Mentorship Program, 16 students' journals and exams, employers' evaluations, and project teachers' reflective papers were analyzed through qualitative methods. Students completing the program exhibited the following outcomes: They clarified work adjustment issues, strengthened their career interests, established life goals and future plans, developed a stronger sense of their individual strengths, and developed a stronger sense of responsibility. Their employers reported that the students excelled in following age-appropriate directions, working with others cooperatively toward a common goal, demonstrating punctuality, notifying employer of tardiness or absence, completing job tasks on time and according to specifications, and learning new tasks or skills enthusiastically. Holt teachers noted that students participating in the mentorship program had clearer ideas about what they wanted to do after high school and enhanced self-confidence about the likelihood that they could reach their goals. They also found that students demonstrated an improved sense of control and responsibility.

FACTORS RELATED TO A SUCCESSFUL SCHOOL-TO-WORK MENTORSHIP PROGRAM

Although the outcomes of Holt's mentorship program were positive for students and employers, creating access to this opportunity for every high school student and maintaining the program's quality over time requires an investment in the structures and relationships that are related to its success. Holt Transition Coalition members surveyed for a program review (14 school personnel, 7 community and agency members, and 9 business representatives) stated that teamwork among participants, a common vision, core members' commitment, common planning time, and parent involvement were the major factors in forming collaborative relationships for an effective transition system (Taymans & deFur, 1994).

Factors such as negative attitudes, misconceptions, lack of knowledge of other fields, wrangling over delegation of authority, and lack of previous training or experience in interdisciplinary teaming often present barriers to collaborative work for an effective transition system (West, Taymans, Corbey, & Dodge, 1993). According to the Holt School-to-Work team, the barriers they experienced to the formation of collaborative relationships included lack of understanding of and unfamiliarity with the services that agencies and businesses can offer, liability issues, time required to develop worksites and to coordinate the program, rigid working schedules of school staff, resistance to changing systems, a negative perception of vocational education, and inflexibility in an academically oriented high school system.

The experiences of the Holt community offer valuable lessons for other schools committed to creating restructured, inclusive mentorship programs. First, the value of inclusion must be affirmed, not just for some students, but for all; not just for part of the day, but for the entire school day; and not just for young students, but for teenagers as well. Second, new coalitions representing students, parents, teachers, and business owners must align traditional academic curricula and community-based learning experiences. All students will eventually be workers, and, even for those going directly from high school to postsecondary education, work experiences during high school offer valuable learning opportunities. Third, community agencies that have traditionally served only people with disabilities (still too often in segregated environments) must also support the value of community inclusion and restructure their service options so that they are able to provide supports to high school students and new graduates in typical, integrated worksites.

Sean's Story Revisited

Recall that Sean's team recommended that, when he enters high school, he gradually decrease the amount of time he spends in typical classes and increase the time that he spends in community-based instruction. After considering the pros and cons of that recommendation from the perspective presented in this chapter, the team decided instead that Sean should maintain a typical high school schedule and enroll in four core academic courses, two elective classes, and one period of academic support each day. As a student in a marketing class, he will be required to work in the school store for 2 semesters ordering supplies, stocking shelves, using the cash register, studying customers' buying patterns, and maintaining good customer relations. The marketing teacher and a science teacher advise a school club that produces and markets maple syrup. Sean decided that he would like to join that club and, as a member, will be involved in all aspects of the maple sugaring business.

Sean's parents believe that it would be valuable for him to have a job for a few hours on Saturdays. They agreed to take responsibility for finding out where Sean's friends work and then contacting those employers to see if they have any additional openings for a part-time employee on the weekend. During summers, Sean's extended-year program will also involve work experiences, exposing him to a variety of jobs so that, as graduation nears, he will be better prepared to make a decision about his post–high school life. The decision to make Sean's high school schedule typical and inclusive instead of special and separate ensures that he will gain a wide variety of skills that are related to success in adulthood without removing him from the mainstream of school life, for it is here that he will learn not only academic and functional skills but also lifelong lessons of belonging and membership.

CONCLUSIONS

Many of the changes proposed in this chapter would necessitate a major restructuring of the special education and community service systems. Ironically, it is the inclusion of students with disabilities, who cannot wait to become part of the mainstream, that will move the system toward making those changes. If students with disabilities continue to participate in separate, community-based instructional experiences, then the notion that their education is the responsibility of a wholly separate system will be perpetuated. It is only when all students are full-time members of our school communities that the will to change will be matched by action.

In Chapter 10, the transition of students with disabilities from high school to the adult world is considered and ways in which a unified system of guidance and life planning can include and benefit all students is suggested.

Implementation Suggestions for Teachers

1. If you currently provide community-based instruction for students with severe disabilities, then pick one student for whom you will develop inclusive opportunities to learn functional skills.
2. On a copy of the student's IEP, highlight all of the functional skills that are identified as important for the student to learn. For each one, identify five in-school, inclusive environments, general education classes, or typical school routines in which the student might learn those same skills. Using the strategies described in *From Special to Regular, from Ordinary to Extraordinary* (Tashie et al., 1993), work with your general education colleagues to get that student included in a number of typical classes in which those functional skills can be learned.
3. Working with the student and his or her family, identify after-school extracurricular or work opportunities for the student in which lifelong functional and independent living skills can be learned. Using a combination of natural supports and facilitation from school personnel, involve the student in those activities or in a job.
4. Make a videotape of the student before you make the change in his or her schedule. Videotape periodically and analyze any changes in the student's behavior or skills.
5. Invite the student's parents to observe during the school day and in the after-school activity.
6. Ask the student to give feedback about the change in his or her schedule.
7. Make similar changes in program and schedule for other students for whom you provide support or case coordination.

Leadership Suggestions for Administrators

1. Identify a special education teacher who is willing to make the changes suggested and support him or her to attend workshops on inclusion and natural supports.

2. Start conversations with general and special education teachers in your building about the disadvantages of separate, community-based instruction for students with disabilities, and promote the inclusion of students with disabilities in existing school-to-work or mentorship programs. If these programs do not exist for any students, then take a leadership role in working with your business community to develop them.
3. Start small, with one or two students, for example. Evaluate your successes and shortcomings. Revise accordingly.
4. Involve parents fully in these conversations and changes. They are lifelong advocates for their children and must be actively involved in activities that relate to their children's ability to become part of their communities when they graduate.

REFERENCES

Brown, F., Evans, I., Weed, K., & Owens, V. (1987). Delineating functional competencies: A component model. *Journal of The Association for Persons with Severe Handicaps, 12*(2), 117–124.

Brown, L., Branston, M., Hamre-Nietupski, S., Pumpian, I., Certo, N., & Gruenewald, L. (1979). A strategy for developing chronological age-appropriate and functional curricular content for severely handicapped adolescents and young adults. *Journal of Special Education, 13*(1), 81–90.

Calculator, S., & Jorgensen, C.M. (1994). *Including students with severe disabilities in schools: Fostering communication, interaction, and participation.* San Diego: Singular Publishing Group.

Certo, N., Haring, N., & York, R. (Eds.). (1984). *Public school integration of severely handicapped students: Rational issues and progressive alternatives.* Baltimore: Paul H. Brookes Publishing Co.

Danielson, L., & Bellamy, G. (1989). State variation in placement of children with handicaps in segregated environments. *Exceptional Children, 55,* 448–455.

Donder, D.J., & York, R. (1984). Integration of students with severe handicaps. In N. Certo, N. Haring, & R. York (Eds.), *Public school integration of severely handicapped students: Rational issues and progressive alternatives* (pp. 1–14). Baltimore: Paul H. Brookes Publishing Co.

Gartner, A., & Lipsky, D. (1987). Beyond special education. *Harvard Educational Review, 57,* 367–395.

Greenberger, E., & Steinberg, L. (1986). *When teenagers work: The psychological and social costs of adolescent employment.* New York: Basic Books.

Hasazi, S., Gordon, L., & Roe, C. (1985). Factors associated with employment status of handicapped youth exiting high school from 1979 to 1983. *Exceptional Children, 51,* 455–469.

Individuals with Disabilities Education Act (IDEA) of 1990, PL 101-476, 20 U.S.C. §§ 1400 *et seq.*

Karagiannis, A., Stainback, W., & Stainback, S. (1996). Rationale for inclusive schooling. In S. Stainback & W. Stainback (Eds.), *Inclusion: A guide for educators* (pp. 3–15). Baltimore: Paul H. Brookes Publishing Co.

Kohler, P. (1994). *A taxonomy for transition programming.* Urbana: University of Illinois at Urbana-Champaign, Transition Research Institute.

Koppenhaver, D.A., Pierce, P.L., Steelman, J.D., & Yoder, D.E. (1995). Contexts of early literacy intervention for children with developmental disabilities. In M.E. Fey, J. Windsor, & S.F. Warren (Eds.), *Communication and language intervention series: Vol. 5. Language intervention: Preschool through the elementary years* (pp. 241–274). Baltimore: Paul H. Brookes Publishing Co.

Lichtenstein, S. (1990). *Fact sheet on young adults with disabilities.* Durham: University of New Hampshire, Institute on Disability.

Rehabilitation Act Amendments of 1992, PL 102-569, 29 U.S.C. §§ 701 *et seq.*

Schnorr, R. (1990). "Peter? He comes and goes . . .": First graders' perspectives on a part-time mainstream student. *Journal of The Association for Persons with Severe Handicaps, 15*(4), 231–240.

School-to-Work Opportunities Act of 1994, PL 103-239, 20 U.S.C. §§ 6101 *et seq.*

Sowers, J.-A., McAllister, R., & Cotton, P., (1996). Strategies to enhance control of the employment process by individuals with severe disabilities. In L.E. Powers, G.H.S. Singer, and J.-A. Sowers (Eds.), *On the road to autonomy: Promoting self-competence in children and youth with disabilities* (pp. 325–346). Baltimore: Paul H. Brookes Publishing Co.

Special Education Information System [Electronic database]. (1996). Concord: New Hampshire Department of Education.

Stainback, S., & Stainback, W. (1988). Educating students with severe disabilities in regular classes. *Teaching Exceptional Children, 21,* 16–19.

Strully, J.L., & Strully, C.F. (1989). Friendships as an educational goal. In S. Stainback, W. Stainback, & M. Forest (Eds.), *Educating all students in the mainstream of regular education* (pp. 59–68). Baltimore: Paul H. Brookes Publishing Co.

Tashie, C., Shapiro-Barnard, S., Schuh, M., Jorgensen, C., Dillon, A.D., Dixon, B., & Nisbet, J. (1993). *From special to regular, from ordinary to extraordinary.* Durham: University of New Hampshire, Institute on Disability.

Taymans, J., & deFur, S. (1994). Preservice and in-service professional development for school to adult life transition. *Career Development for Exceptional Individuals, 17*(2), 171–186.

Wehmeyer, M.L. (1992). Self-determination and the education of students with mental retardation. *Education and Training in Mental Retardation, 27,* 302–314.

West, L., Taymans, J., Corbey, S., & Dodge, L. (1993, October). *A national perspective of transition planning across states.* Paper presented at the Division on Career Development and Transition International Conference, Albuquerque, NM.

Wolfensberger, W. (1972). *The principle of normalization in human services.* Toronto, Ontario, Canada: National Institute on Mental Retardation.

York, J., Vandercook, T., Macdonald, C., & Wolff, S. (Eds.). (1989). *Strategies for full inclusion.* Minneapolis: University of Minnesota, Institute on Community Integration.

10

Transition or Graduation?

Supporting All
Students to Plan for the Future

Carol Tashie, Joanne M. Malloy, and Stephen J. Lichtenstein

Paul

Paul, who is 17 years old and has significant disabilities, entered his senior year in high school with a plan for the future. Like most of his classmates, he is both excited and apprehensive about the future but is confident that his plan will guide him through the next phase of his life. Paul's plan includes graduation with his classmates, rather than remaining in school as a second- or third-year senior and exiting at age 21; a balance of part-time employment and part-time college; a career path that involves computers; and a healthy and active social life with college peers, co-workers, and family. Paul is certain that his plan will help him navigate the next stage of his life and assist him in making decisions along the way.

In towns and cities all across the United States, high school students like Paul[1] are thinking, dreaming, and worrying about their futures. They are pondering their options regarding college, discussing their career choices, and hoping for futures of financial independence and personal satisfaction. Students are preparing for the future by choosing the necessary coursework, pursuing extracurricular interests, making connections with classmates, working at after-school jobs, and making contacts with school and community members. Every day, high school students are involved in situations and opportunities designed to prepare them for their future lives and careers.

Most high schools have recognized the need to develop systematic processes to help students plan and prepare for their lives after high school. They are beginning to realize that it is not enough simply to guide a student through the college application maze, suggest an interest inventory to facilitate career decision making, or recommend military service as a steppingstone to a future career. Schools are restructuring so that curricula, community partnerships, and guidance support systems help students more effectively plan and prepare for the future.

In many schools, however, there remains a distinct division in the ways in which students with and without disabilities are supported to dream about and plan their futures. Because high school students with disabilities are often separated from their classmates during the school day (e.g., taking special education classes; engaged in separate,

This chapter was supported in part by Grants H235S50043, H158A1003, and H086J50014 from the U.S. Department of Education. The opinions expressed by the authors are not necessarily those of the U.S. government.

[1]Although Paul is fictional, this story is typical of many students with disabilities in New Hampshire schools.

community-based instruction), they often miss out on typical school-wide future-planning activities. Although students with disabilities are required to be supported to develop individualized transition plans (ITPs) under the Individuals with Disabilities Education Act (IDEA) of 1990 (PL 101-476), these plans are often disconnected from the typical graduation-planning activities in the school.

This chapter discusses ways in which schools can and should support all students to plan for their futures through a unified system of career and future planning. Because much has been written about transition planning for students with disabilities, the danger of developing a segregated system of planning solely for students with disabilities is discussed first. *Transition* as a concept and practice is critiqued, and alternatives are proposed. Second, the recommended practices related to supporting students with disabilities to become valued members of the typical high school community are discussed. A Graduation Planning Checklist that reflects these recommended practices is included. Finally, ways in which schools can be restructured in order to truly support all students as they plan for the future are addressed. A career- and life-planning process is presented, and the systems changes necessary for the introduction of this process in a school are proposed. In order to provide readers with some practical applications of the proposed ideas, this chapter follows Paul's story because his story illustrates the practices that we believe can and should become commonplace for all students in all schools.

How Did Paul Develop His Plan?

Although many schools still view transition planning as a process only for students with disabilities, Paul's school is committed to supporting all students to develop plans for the future. Paul's weekly advisory class uses a student-directed futures-planning process to help students determine their interests, talents, and desires. This planning process includes individual and group activities designed to help students develop a better understanding of self, a greater knowledge of the world of work, and an ITP for further developing both. Paul began this process in his sophomore year and, like other students, developed a personal career- and life-planning portfolio that assisted him in making a variety of decisions.

During his junior year, with the help of his guidance counselor, Paul invited some of his friends and family members to a planning meeting. He wanted to get assistance in refining and implementing his personal futures plan. Paul felt comfortable with his goals but needed some help in furthering his opportunities. This small group of people met several times at Paul's house to brainstorm strategies for him to gain greater experience in his areas of interest. Because of Paul's interest in computers, it was suggested that the group be expanded to include Paul's computer teacher, a local computer programmer, and his uncle, who works for a large computer retail business.

Paul is currently a senior in high school. Through advisory classes, meetings with his guidance counselor, and planning meetings, a clear vision has emerged for what Paul wants to do now and once he finishes high school. This information has been useful in helping Paul choose classes and after-school activities (e.g., clubs, sports, a job), as well as make connections with people who can support his future goals.

TRANSITION OR GRADUATION?

It has been more than 20 years since the passage of the Education for All Handicapped Children Act of 1975 (PL 94-142), which guaranteed each student with disabilities access to a free and appropriate public education (FAPE). For most of those years, a FAPE translated into segregated education for a majority of students with significant disabilities (e.g., labels of mental retardation, autism, multiple disabilities) (U.S. Department of Education, 1987). However, in the 1990s, proponents of inclusive education have successfully promoted the benefits of and strategies for educating students with disabilities in general education classes in their neighborhood schools (Karagiannis, Stainback, & Stainback, 1996). Today in New Hampshire more than 65% of elementary school–age students labeled as having mental retardation, multiple disabilities, or deaf-blindness are educated full time in general education classes with their peers without disabilities; and that trend is reflected in national data as well (New Hampshire Department of Education, 1996; U.S. Department of Education, 1994).

Although the movement for full inclusion of students with disabilities has significantly changed the way they are educated, it appears to have had less of an impact on the ways in which students with disabilities are supported to plan for life after high school. With the passage of IDEA and its mandate for transition planning for all students with disabilities, many schools have once again begun to develop a new and separate system of supports for students with disabilities in high school.

Transition is generally thought of as the system of planning that supports the movement of a student with disabilities through and out of high school—the bridge between school and adulthood. The intent of such planning is to ensure that students leave school knowing who they are, what they want to do with their lives, and the supports they will need to accomplish their goals. Few can deny the spirit of such a system. However, at a time when schools are beginning to merge general and special education into a unified system, the creation of a separate transition system just for students with disabilities appears to be counterproductive. Students with disabilities are being encouraged to develop ITPs at the same time that schools are encouraging typical students to develop graduation plans—one with the support of special educators and the other with the support of guidance counselors and advisors.

If we are to view students with disabilities as fully included members of the whole community, then it becomes clear that transition must fit into our notion about quality inclusive education for all. Questions such as "How do students learn to make good decisions and good choices?" "How do they select the courses they will need to prepare them for life after graduation?" and "What are the opportunities and connections they take advantage of outside of school that will help them be successful after they graduate and move into adulthood?" must guide the process for supporting students with disabilities throughout their school careers and into adulthood. Efforts must be targeted not at developing a different, special system of high school education and transition for students with disabilities, but rather on making the typical educational experience and graduation-planning process open, meaningful, and effective for all students (Shapiro-Barnard et al., 1996).

WHAT'S WRONG WITH TRANSITION?

There are several major problems with the traditional view of transition for students with disabilities. First, many high school students with disabilities are not included in the typical school experience—general education classes, extracurricular activities, and graduation planning that can assist them in the development of their future goals. As discussed in Chapter 9, many students with disabilities progress through their school careers spending less time in the school building with their peers and more time in the community. This not only prevents students with disabilities from taking a full schedule of general education classes but also isolates them from the very peer group by which they need to be accepted in order to be successful in school and as they enter into the world of adulthood. It also serves to negate the valuable learning—academic, life skills, and social—that occurs for all students in these general education classes.

Second, the traditional transition process tends to perpetuate the notion that paid professionals are the only ones who can support students in school, at home, in the community, or on the job. Many professionals see transition as something that happens to students with disabilities to help them move from special education into the world of categorical adult services. Depending on the community, this can mean making the transition from school to work, from school to sheltered work, from school to day habilitation, or even from school to waiting list for services.

Third, only students with disabilities "transition"; all other students graduate. This system itself implies a separation between students with and without disabilities. With a strong emphasis on the merger of the separate systems of education (general and special), it seems counterproductive to maintain or develop a separate system of transition (Stainback, Stainback, & Forest, 1989).

IS THERE A BETTER WAY?

Although the intent of transition is a positive one, it is clear that the practices are often segregating. In order to move beyond separate planning processes for students with and without disabilities, the following changes must occur:

- Full inclusion of all students in the typical school community
- Changes in the roles of professionals and paraprofessionals
- Adoption of the typical educational timetable
- Graduation as an outcome for all students
- Flexibility in supports beyond graduation

Full Inclusion

There are numerous benefits of inclusion for students with and without disabilities (Karagiannis et al., 1996). When students with disabilities are educated in general education classes, they are able to gain skills and knowledge that will guide them in their present and future decisions. They are able to focus on literacy skills and academic learning. They have effective role models for learning and social interactions. They gain a vast array of information to guide future decision making. High school students who choose which courses to take, which areas of study to pursue, and which extracurricular activities to engage in are better able to make informed decisions about their future life choices.

The inclusion of students with disabilities in a high school can be an impetus for change in the way in which the school addresses the issues of career and future planning. For students with disabilities, the notion of school-supported career planning is not new. IDEA mandates such a process. However, schools truly committed to full inclusion reject the notion of separate planning strategies for students with disabilities. They recognize that systems must be developed that support all students to plan for their futures. Therefore, these schools have begun to develop schoolwide career- and life-planning processes for all students.

Changes in Job Roles

Changing the perspective about high school education and the transition or graduation process requires a change in some of the ways in which people have traditionally viewed their job roles and responsibilities. A shift is necessary from a model of direct professional or paraprofessional support to a model of encouraging and nurturing natural supports in the school and community (Nisbet, 1992). School and community members must provide support to students with disabilities in much the same ways that support is provided to others (e.g., by employers to new workers, by church and service organizations to new community residents). In addition, the hours that school personnel work may need to change in order to support students outside the typical school day (Tashie & Schuh, 1993).

A Typical Educational Timetable

The traditional way of educating students with disabilities was full time in the school building through elementary school, job shadowing and community-based instruction through middle and high schools, attaining employment by age 20, and, finally, transition compressed into the last few months of the last year of school (Horner, Meyer, & Fredericks, 1986).

To accompany and guide the new vision of graduation planning, a new timetable—a typical educational timetable—must be embraced. Typical students go through their high school experience—freshman, sophomore, junior, and senior years—and then graduate into the world of adulthood. For many students with disabilities, the timetable is quite different. A student with disabilities may repeat his or her senior year two or three times in order to exit school at age 21.

It is essential that students with disabilities, who may be eligible for educational services through the age of 21 years, progress through high school in the same way as typical students. Moving through the grades, taking required courses, choosing electives, participating in extracurricular activities, and celebrating the end of their high school career upon completion of their first and only senior year is important for all students.

Graduation

In most states, a student's eligibility for special education services and supports ends upon receipt of a standard high school diploma. For this and other reasons, many schools have presented students with disabilities with alternative diplomas or certificates of completion, or, in the words of one parent, a certificate of occupancy, in order to continue services through age 21 (Institute on Disability, 1995).

Today, schools and communities that embrace the typical time-table of education for students with disabilities are struggling to ad-here to legislation and regulations while delivering effective educa-tion. These schools have acknowledged the need for a compromise until policy catches up with practice. They believe that support must continue after the formal graduation ceremony at the end of senior year to young adults in jobs, colleges, or technical schools; adult ed-ucation classes; community activities; and so forth. In many of these schools, students with disabilities participate in all of the ceremonies and activities of senior year, including graduation, but do not receive their standard diploma until age 21. Although this compromise is not ideal, schools and communities recognize the need to move forward with practice as one way of changing policy and regulations.

Flexibility After Graduation

New high school graduates make a variety of choices. They go to college part time or full time; they work part time or full time; and they live on campus, at home, or in an apartment with a roommate. Students with disabilities need to have the same choices. School dis-tricts must work in close collaboration with young adults and their families and with employers, college officials, and community orga-nizations to determine which supports will be needed to assist stu-dents in achieving their goals and dreams.

How Does Paul Prepare for His Future During His High School Years?

Throughout his high school career, Paul has chosen to take gen-eral education classes based on the requirements and electives available to all students at his grade level. Because of his desire to pursue a career in computers, Paul's coursework has been focused in the areas of business and computers. As a senior, Paul is taking business math, an advanced communications course in the English department, a computer class, earth science, world history, and drama. As in the past, his teachers have clear expectations for his work in their classes, and grades are assigned based on how well he meets his individualized education program (IEP) goals.

In addition to school, Paul has a full life outside of school. His after-school job at a convenience store allows him opportunities to practice many of the skills he is learning in school as well as the skills necessary to be a successful employee. Although he does not see himself working in this job forever, he finds the hours, wages, and work experience valuable and enjoys the opportunity to use the store's new computerized cash register. He also likes meeting new people and talking with his high school classmates who frequent the store. His guidance counselor stops in once each week to discuss with Paul and his employer how this job can reinforce some of Paul's coursework and contribute to his career goals.

PLANNING FOR GRADUATION

High school is not simply a steppingstone to the future. Although many of the skills and much of the knowledge gained during high school can enhance an adult's life, high school is a valuable time in and of itself. Therefore, in order for high school students to adequately prepare for the future, they must make certain that they are engaged in meaningful activities. For high school students with disabilities, this means that they need to be supported to be active, full, valued members in all aspects of the typical high school community.

Through our work with schools throughout New Hampshire, we have identified a number of components of a student's high school education that are essential in promoting success in and out of school. These components, listed in the Graduation Planning Checklist (Figure 1) are practices that support students with disabilities to learn skills and knowledge, gain confidence and leadership abilities, develop relationships and connections, and experience a sense of belonging. The checklist is a useful tool for students, schools, and families to make certain that students with disabilities are supported to take advantage of valuable opportunities in their schools.

One note of explanation: Several of the practices indicated on the checklist will vary, depending on the school that the student is attending. Because one of the guiding principles of the checklist is what is typical, the specifics may depend on the particular school. For example, one school may require students to attend eight periods of

Graduation Planning Checklist

Each "yes" answer indicates a recommended practice. Each "no" answer should be followed with a plan of action.

	Yes	No
Does the student have a typical daily schedule—all age-appropriate, general education classes in the neighborhood school—and the supports provided so that he or she can be successful?	____	____
Does the student move through the grades in a typical fashion (ninth to twelfth grades) and participate in all grade-related activities (e.g., move-up day, graduation planning)?	____	____
Does the student use natural environments and people to gain supports (e.g., study halls, guidance, nurse, lockers)?	____	____
Is the student valued for his or her participation in school, and do grades, transcript, and diploma reflect this?	____	____
Is the student involved and supported in desired extra-curricular activities?	____	____
Is the student supported to have friends and meaningful relationships in and out of school?	____	____
Does the student have an after-school, weekend, and/or summer job, if desired?	____	____
Is the student supported to participate in community-based instruction only during times when other students are engaged in such activities (e.g., after school, weekends, summers, after senior year)?	____	____
Is the student supported to develop typical connections within the community?	____	____
Is the student supported to develop meaningful skills and knowledge through participation in typical classes?	____	____
Is the student regarded with respect for his or her gifts and abilities and supported with the highest of expectations?	____	____
Is the student involved in typical career- and futures-planning courses?	____	____
Does the student have regular contact with the guidance counselor?	____	____
Is the student the leader in planning present and future choices, as demonstrated by choosing classes, choosing extracurricular activities, choosing career paths, or leading the team?	____	____
Does the student graduate from high school after his or her senior year and continue to receive supports in the community via the school system?	____	____
Is the student supported to pursue career, continuing education, housing, and recreation choices after completion of senior year in high school?	____	____

Figure 1. Graduation Planning Checklist.

classes each day, whereas another may require only four extended classes each semester. Whatever is required by that school is what is typical. However, other practices on the checklist are the same, regardless of which school a student attends. For example, every student in every school must be supported to take control of his or her own life and be the leader in all futures-planning activities. This practice holds true whether a student is attending a traditional high school or a completely restructured one. A discussion follows on several of the themes of the Graduation Planning Checklist.

Typical Schedules
Many high schools are in the midst of restructuring their school day to meet the changing needs of students. The traditional eight-period day is giving way to block schedules, collaborative coursework, and flexible sessions (Canady & Rettig, 1995). Schools are recognizing that students and teachers may need more time together in order to engage in meaningful learning. Despite these changes, every school still determines its own set of required and elective courses, the credits necessary for graduation, and other educational requirements.

In order for students with disabilities to be viewed as members of the school community, it is essential that those requirements be met for them as well. No longer is it appropriate for students with disabilities or their special education teachers to pick and choose the courses that a student will take. If all students are required 3 years of high school English, then it is imperative that students with disabilities be required—and supported—to take those classes. All classes should be chosen based on the requirement of the school, the interests of the particular student, and the requirements of each student's post–high school destination (e.g., college, employment). Students with disabilities must be expected to maintain a daily schedule in keeping with the general expectations of the school, moving through both the school day and their school careers in a typical fashion.

Beyond the knowledge gained, the literacy enhanced, and the skills developed, the present and future benefits of maintaining a typical high school schedule are clear. By participating in the complex and highly charged world of high school, students learn to manage time, appreciate diversity, connect with peers, handle adversity, and maintain control in ever-changing situations. These skills serve all students well while in school and serve adults well beyond graduation.

What Does Paul Do After School?

Throughout Paul's elementary and secondary schooling, he was entitled to school district support in order to be successful during the school day. During his freshman year, the question of supporting Paul to participate in extracurricular activities arose. The school had always supported Paul during the school day, but no one was quite certain about how to support him after school. Paul's family and school team discussed ways in which he could be involved in extracurricular activities without the support of additional paid staff. Initially, Paul and his family were skeptical. Paul had always had a paid assistant to accompany him to classes and other school-sponsored events. They wondered how he could participate in extracurricular activities without someone to support him. Once again, Paul's classmates were enlisted to help solve this problem. The students suggested that because a teacher, advisor, or coach was a part of all school-sponsored extracurricular events, it would make sense to rely on this person for adult support. Any additional assistance could be provided by peers.

Paul was interested in joining the drama club; therefore, the drama advisor and students were asked to meet with Paul, his mother, and one of his teachers to discuss how this could work. Although nervous at first, Paul's peers soon began supplying the supports Paul needed, and Paul became a full and valued member of the drama club. Because Paul uses a wheelchair, a classmate volunteered to be Paul's partner in all choreographed acts. The teacher asked peers to help program Paul's speaking role into his augmentative communication device. In order to get to evening rehearsals, the students figured out who lived near Paul and who would be able to carpool with him.

After School

Ask high school students to tell you about their favorite part of the day, and many speak enthusiastically about sports, clubs, hanging out with friends, and even an after-school job. Although this does not mean that the school day is not valuable and interesting to students, it does indicate just how important an after-school life is for high school students.

In order for students with disabilities to be full-fledged members of the high school community, they must be supported to have an active after-school life. School-sponsored extracurricular activities, "hang time" with friends, after-school jobs, and community volunteer and recreation opportunities are all examples of activities in which high school students typically engage after school. Students with disabilities need support and possibly encouragement to participate in these events.

As Chapter 9 fully described, many students with disabilities spend a portion of their school day engaged in activities that most other students do after school. Shopping in a grocery store, eating at a fast-food restaurant, and part-time employment are common events in a teenager's life. Unfortunately, teenagers with disabilities are often doing these things when their peers are involved with English or math or history. Because community-based instruction removes students with disabilities from their peers, it serves to accentuate the differences rather than the similarities among students. Even in schools that are working toward inclusion, it negates many of the positive effects of being a high school student.

A special mention should be made about supporting students with disabilities to develop and maintain relationships with classmates and friends. For most typical students, this is a common and easily attainable component of their lives. For many students with disabilities, this aspect of their lives may be challenging. Several reasons for this situation exist. Many students with disabilities have spent some period of their lives segregated from their peers and may not be as well connected to or familiar with the expectations of their peer group. Other students may have difficulty with communication skills, may not yet have an adequate augmentative communication system, and may not be able to talk effectively with their classmates. Still other students may find themselves experiencing the new-kid-on-the-block syndrome when they enter into a new school or community. Whatever the reason for the challenge, it is essential that all students be supported to be well connected with their peers as described fully in Chapter 7.

What About Supports?

Once Paul, his parents, and his classmates saw how well Paul was supported in the drama club, they asked the school to reconsider the need for a full-time assistant in all of his classes. Although it took most of his sophomore year, Paul's teachers and peers gradually became comfortable with providing most of the support he needed during classes. The assistant continued to be available as needed to support Paul for personal care needs and to support classroom teachers.

Outside of school, Paul was also successful in developing natural systems of support. During his junior year, he got a paying job in a local convenience store. Because of the great success with natural supports in school and extracurricular activities, his team enlisted the help of an employment consultant to work with the store's manager. The manager decided that a co-worker could provide Paul with on-the-job training for 2 weeks and would continue to be available on an as-needed basis.

Natural Supports

Within every high school, there is a system of supports that students use to navigate their way through the maze of classes, grades, and graduation requirements. In some schools, this system is highly developed; in others, it is less so. Students rely on course-of-study catalogs, guidance counselors, their parents, and friends to decide in which classes to enroll. They rely on grades and class standing to indicate how their teachers feel they are progressing. They rely on coaches and advisors to give advice on everything from classwork to relationships. They rely on friends and classmates for just about everything.

Students with disabilities must also be encouraged to utilize the natural supports that are available within their own school. It is no longer acceptable for students with disabilities to receive IEP progress reports when all others receive grades and transcripts. It is not acceptable for special educators to choose classes for students with disabilities without regard to school and class requirements. It is no longer wise to encourage students with disabilities to rely on special adults (e.g., special educators, paraprofessionals, transition counselors) for all aspects of their schooling, when guidance counselors, advisors, and classmates are readily available.

The utilization of special supports in high school can lead to a dependence on special supports into adulthood (Powers, Singer, & Sowers, 1996). Far too many young adults and their families assume that they will require specially trained people all their lives in order to be successful. This assumption can make the transition to adult life quite difficult. Although supports and services are an entitlement for school-age students, they are not so for adults. Adults who are able to garner support in the most typical fashion—via co-workers, family members, roommates, neighbors, and friends—are more likely to live full and satisfactory lives.

What About Friends?

Friends have always been an important part of Paul's life. Because Paul had been in a school for students with disabilities prior to high school, he entered high school as an outsider. For this reason, great efforts were made to introduce Paul to his new classmates and to support the development of meaningful and reciprocal relationships. Paul's mother met with his ninth-grade advisor and asked for an opportunity to speak with some of Paul's classmates. At this meeting, Paul's mother enlisted the help of the students to plan how Paul could get involved with other students in the school. The students were not asked to become Paul's friends; instead, they were asked to brainstorm solutions to the question "How can Paul make new friends?" This group of students made numerous suggestions—many of which the adults involved had never considered. Within a few months, Paul began to know his classmates and a few friendships started to develop. As the years went on, there were occasionally issues that arose regarding how best to support Paul in other aspects of high school life, and this group of students continued to be available to brainstorm ideas.

Meaningful Participation

Simply being in general education classes does not guarantee that a student's participation will be meaningful or respected. For far too many students with disabilities, the doors to the general education classroom have opened, but the expectations for learning and behavior have stayed as they were in the special education classroom. We have observed several high schools in which students with disabilities are encouraged to take general high school classes but are not given clear goals and expectations for these classes. In these schools, teachers often express frustration at having a student with disabilities in their class but no clear understanding of how that student will participate in lessons, demonstrate knowledge and understanding of content, and contribute to the overall sum and substance of the class.

Good education demands that every student have clear goals and expectations for each of his or her classes in regard to skills and knowledge, academics, participation, and belonging. Good education also requires that each student have an effective means for demonstrating progress in all of these areas. When students with disabilities are members of general education classes, it is essential that these educational requirements be met. Grades should reflect the content, skill, and participation goals that a student has for a particular class. Transcripts should reflect grades. Of course, high school diplomas should reflect the student's achievements in all classes.

Youth Leadership and Self-Determination

Imagine being asked simply to participate in your own major life decisions. How would you feel if you were asked only to attend a meeting to plan your future? What if you were not even told that the meeting was taking place? How could you truly be in control of your own life when others around you are plotting the course?

For far too long, decisions about which classes to choose, which interests to pursue, and which career path to follow were made by people other than the student with disabilities (Powers et al., 1996). Well-intentioned special educators, transition counselors, and even family members often made decisions about a student's present and future life without his or her knowledge, input, or consent. It is now clear that no one except the student should take the lead in planning his or her life. Only he or she truly understands his or her dreams, hopes, and aspirations.

There are countless opportunities in every high school for students to learn leadership and decision-making skills. When students decide which classes they will take, which extracurricular activities they will join, and even which topic they will research, they are learning the fundamentals of personal responsibility and decision making. When they are guided to take an active role in determining which supports they need and which adaptations may be necessary, they are practicing self-determination skills. When students are encouraged to take active roles in schoolwide governance activities such as student councils, peer outreach, and advocacy organizations, they are engaged in the principles of community leadership. All of these opportunities teach students how to be leaders in their own lives and in their communities.

Graduation

Although high school is a complex, exciting, and sometimes challenging time in a student's life, it is, in fact, finite. In most high schools and for most students, high school ends—with a bang—4 years after it began. Few other times in a person's life rival the fanfare of completing high school: Senior week, yearbook signings, parties, and, of course, graduation. Graduation is truly the culmination of high school and the beginning of the rest of your life.

Although some schools are changing their practices and extenuating circumstances have always existed, most students do in fact get their high school diplomas after 4 years of high school. For many students with disabilities, however, high school ends in a less than momentous way. Because most state regulations allow students to receive educational services through their 21st or 22nd birthdays, many students with disabilities find themselves attending high school for not 4 but 6 or even 7 years. Many schools have interpreted state regulations to mean that students stay in high school up to the day their entitlement is over (i.e., their birthday). Students return to school year after year, becoming second- or third-year seniors and then finally exiting school, sometimes with no ceremony at all. It is common for students to complain that their high school career ended not with a bang but with a whimper.

There is a better way. Graduation is a rite of passage that all students should enjoy. Students with disabilities should graduate with their classmates, following their school's typical time line. For students entitled to educational supports beyond their senior year, those supports must be provided in places that are typical to new high school graduates—a college campus, a job, or a new apartment or home.

Will Paul Graduate?

One of the biggest decisions that Paul, his parents, and his school team faced was determining whether he would receive a standard high school diploma upon completion of his senior year. In addition, there was a great deal of discussion regarding the appropriateness of a standard diploma versus a certificate of completion (i.e., the IEP diploma). In many schools, certificates are still used instead of diplomas for students with significant disabilities. According to state regulations, the certificate would enable Paul to receive supports from the school district until age 21, whereas the receipt of a standard diploma could result in a curtailment of school services. Paul has been adamant that he deserves a standard diploma to recognize the hard work he has done. He considers the certificate a liability for the future because most colleges and employers, as well as the military and the civil service, do not recognize it. However, he does feel that continued support from the school district is necessary in order for him to successfully pursue his goals.

Although Paul and his family feel that neither option is perfect, they have recognized that school and state policy have not yet caught up to recommended practices. For this reason, they have agreed to a compromise. Paul will postpone receiving his diploma in favor of continued supports. He will fully participate in all graduation activities, including the ceremony, and will receive a standard diploma on his 21st birthday, along with his transcript reflecting the supports and accommodations that he received. Until that time, Paul will receive school district support, which will occur outside of the high school environment—in college and on the job.

POST–HIGH SCHOOL PLANS

Thus far, the discussion here has been about how to support students to plan for a successful school experience. However, students must also be given assistance to specifically plan for their lives beyond high school and to determine which path they would like to follow after graduation.

For most people, graduation from high school signifies an end to childhood and an entrance into the world of young adulthood. Correspondingly, young adulthood is typically a time of expanding options and possibilities. Most young adults make decisions regarding continued education, jobs and careers, family, relationships, volunteerism, and the like. For young adults with disabilities, however, these decisions have always been severely limited. Most students with significant disabilities have been expected to make the transition from school to a low-paying, perhaps sheltered, job; live in a group home or an institution; and participate in recreational activities designed for people with disabilities (e.g., Special Olympics, bowling leagues for people with disabilities). Continuing education is never considered necessary or even possible. Relationships are with paid staff members, family, and special friends (Perske & Perske, 1988). Involvement with volunteerism is always as a recipient and not as a contributor.

Students with disabilities, including students with the most significant disabilities, must be encouraged to have dreams and plans for the future (Brown & Lehr, 1989). Dreams of continuing education (e.g., college, technical school, adult education), movement up the career ladder, home ownership, a family of one's own, and a meaningful role in the community are all possible and must be supported. School districts can play an important role in supporting students beyond their senior year of high school to begin to achieve some of their dreams.

Traditionally, schools have supported students to remain in high school until such time as they aged out or were able to complete requirements to achieve a diploma. This left many students stuck in the school building simply waiting for their time to end. We have worked with many schools in New Hampshire to assist them in viewing a student's school career in a different light.

As stated previously, students with disabilities should follow the typical time line of high school education. Prior to their senior year, students should be given ample opportunities to think about and make decisions about their future paths. (The next section of this chapter describes a process that many New Hampshire schools are using to help students with these decisions.) Students should be engaged in experiences that support their aspirations and give them additional information about their choices. At the close of their senior year, students should be preparing for graduation and the end of high school.

For students with disabilities who would traditionally receive school district supports beyond their senior year, decisions should be made as to how, where, and by whom those supports should be given. Because at that point it is no longer appropriate for the student to remain within the confines of the high school, supports should be provided to assist the student in beginning his or her future path. For many students, this has meant that support is provided to help a student attend college, get a full- or part-time job, move into an apartment, and make connections within the community.

Many school districts opt to provide the support to new graduates themselves. They use school district employees to assist a student with developing a job, gaining access to continued education, or any of the other opportunities in which the young adult is interested. Other schools are offering a buyout option to students in order to allow them to choose not only the where but the who in terms of supports (Johnson et al., 1997). Many students choose to have family, friends, co-workers, or classmates provide support, with compensation being paid to them as appropriate.

How Will Paul Get into College?

Acceptance into college can be an arduous process for any student. Students must carefully choose to which colleges to apply and then engage in a variety of visits, meetings, and interviews. Paul and his family met with his guidance counselor several times to help Paul decide in which colleges he was interested and how best to initiate that process with the school. Because Paul is a trendsetter—not many students with significant disabilities have entered college to date—his guidance counselor, parents, and he are taking extra care in choosing and applying to a college. Although it has been suggested that Paul apply only to schools that have specially designed programs for students with disabilities, Paul and his family have discounted this idea. They believe that Paul should choose a college based on the same criteria that students without disabilities use (e.g., location, cost, courses offered) and then negotiate the provision of supports with that school.

With help from his guidance counselor, a favorite teacher, and some friends, Paul has narrowed his choices to three colleges in New Hampshire. After visiting all three, the choices were narrowed to two—based on the high degree of inaccessibility of one.

Paul's counselor guided him through the application process and has called the admissions officers on Paul's behalf. Paul had interviews at these schools and was accepted at both. He chose one based on the warm welcome he and his parents received and on the wide variety of courses and student services the school offered. Although the admissions officer was somewhat nervous, she agreed to assist Paul in selecting his classes, meeting his professors, and working with student services to negotiate supports and modifications.

Who Will Pay for College?

College poses a financial challenge for many students, and Paul is no exception. Although Paul will continue to receive support from the school district, neither he nor his parents believe that the school district should be expected to pay college tuition. Because tuition is an expense common to all students, financing for tuition will occur through a combination of scholarships, school loans, and family help. With the assistance of his guidance counselor, Paul learned that he is eligible for a Pell grant. In addition, Paul has applied for support from Vocational Rehabilitation to offset college and career supports. Supplemental Security Income (SSI) benefits will be used to pay for personal care support. The remaining typical college expenses will be paid through Paul's personal savings (accrued through his part-time employment), his part-time job, and support from his family. The school district will pay for only those additional supports that he requires to be successful in college—the same expenses that they would incur if Paul were still in high school or at a job in the community.

Money to pay for Paul's education is coming from a number of sources. Paul has made it clear that he and his family will decide how and where any money is spent. Funds will go directly to Paul (with the help of a personal broker when appropriate), and he will determine which supports are necessary and from whom they will be purchased.

Paul has been well supported by teachers and classmates throughout high school. There is reason to believe that these same kinds of supports will be equally successful in college. Paul and his family are meeting with both school district and college personnel to determine how Paul can receive the supports he requires. Paul has decided to use the support from the school district to pay for an employment consultant and to pay two college students to provide tutoring and note taking for the classes he is taking. In addition, because Paul would like to someday live in the dorms, an occupational therapist will be hired to coach him as he learns a variety of independent living skills. The college will provide supports around curriculum modification, social connections, and career counseling.

SCHOOLWIDE FUTURES PLANNING FOR ALL STUDENTS

Educators, policy makers, students, and families are struggling with ways to restructure high school curricula to ensure that students receive preparation and planning for life and career goals. Reform efforts are under way in many high schools to address the issue of integrating goal-setting and career-planning activities into their daily curriculum. Traditionally, much attention has been paid to helping students plan for college—guidance counselors and faculty have long given advice and help to students to take college preparation courses, choose appropriate extracurricular activities, and apply for admission and financial aid at the most prestigious colleges and universities. For many, acceptance to college was seen as a successful completion of high school rather than as a continuation of a path of career planning. Students who were uninterested in college or discouraged from even applying to college were often steered in the direction of employment. Students who were unsure about their future paths were given very little support to help them determine their goals. Standardized interest inventories were often used as an alternative to personalized career counseling.

The final section of this chapter discusses alternatives to separate futures planning solely for students with disabilities. Advisories, career-planning courses, school and community partnerships, and community service requirements are briefly described. A career-planning process that can be used individually with students or as a part of advisories or career-planning courses was developed by the Institute on Disability (Malloy, Freije, Tashie, & Nisbet, 1996) with consultation from faculty and students from several New Hampshire schools. Although schools that have implemented such systems have found that they serve as an effective base of planning for all students, they also recognize that individual students may require supplemental planning in order to effectively plan for their futures. Support must be given to students as needed to further develop and explore their future goals.

REFORM EFFORTS THAT SUPPORT FUTURES PLANNING

Greater attention is being given to helping all students make good decisions about their lives. Many schools are addressing the needs of students to carefully look at themselves and their interests to determine a career- and life-planning path of their own.

One of the strategies that schools have used to help students examine their goals is the development of advisory periods (R. Mackin, personal communication, February 1995). Advisory periods have been developed in many high schools as a way of helping students connect with one faculty member and a small group of students. Although the practice of advisories varies widely within individual schools, many schools view it as an opportunity for students to gain information, explore issues, and solve individual and common problems. Advisories have been used as a time for students to discuss and plan individual and schoolwide events, examine problems, receive academic help, and make course selections. Advisory schedules vary across schools, with some meeting daily and others one or more times per week.

Although advisories have become a common reform strategy in many high schools, ensuring that they are more than just study periods or extended homerooms is still a challenge to many teachers. Consequently, many schools in New Hampshire have begun to use advisories as a time to engage students in career- and life-planning activities.

Similarly, many schools engaged in restructuring have begun to offer or require career- and life-planning courses for students. These courses serve the purpose of providing students with a set time and curriculum designed to support future planning and preparation.

Although some schools are developing courses or curricula to support life and career planning, other schools are supporting students to be engaged in partnerships with community businesses. Efforts such as apprenticeships, mentorships, community service options, and business partnerships are ways in which students can learn more about the career options in their communities.

PLANNING FOR THE FUTURE:
A MANUAL OF CAREER AND LIFE PLANNING

During the 1995–1996 school year, staff from the Institute on Disability worked with several New Hampshire high schools to develop, pilot test, and refine a student-directed planning process. Several times during that school year, faculty and heterogeneous groups of students from the demonstration sites met for a facilitated work retreat. Students were encouraged to share their thoughts and ideas on what they would need in order to more effectively plan for their futures. Faculty were encouraged to provide input on what teachers would need in order to support students in these efforts.

Planning for the Future: A Manual for Career and Life Planning (Malloy et al., 1996) was developed as a result of these efforts. It is an open-ended curriculum that can be used by schools interested in helping students plan and prepare for their futures. Incorporating the values of diversity, individuality, and inclusion, the manual includes 26 sessions organized in a sequence that encourages careful self-discovery, planning, analysis, and communication of what has been learned. Through this process, students are encouraged to relate their individual experiences—in and out of school—to the career-planning theme. As the process continues, students gain a greater awareness of the world around them, learn how to identify goals, and develop realistic plans. Each activity is designed to have two purposes: First, students identify goals and gain self-awareness in order to connect their school and after-school activities with a life and career direction; and, second, students learn to work together and begin to take ownership and control of their lives.

Although many schools have used this process through advisory periods, this is not the only place in which the exercises in this manual can be used. A student can use this process through a one-to-one relationship with a guidance counselor or other faculty member. The exercises can be used in a semester-long career-planning class or during an intensive multiday retreat. For some students, the exercises in the manual may not be enough to develop a plan for the future; for these students, the manual can be supplemented with other planning processes that include family, friends, and other significant people in the student's life.

The manual is designed to be a guide for supporting all students as they plan and prepare for their futures. It is designed to be used with heterogeneous groups of students with supports provided so that each student can fully participate in all exercises. The exercises are intended to be used in a fully inclusive environment, one that appreciates and celebrates the diversity of the student population.

Many of the exercises in the manual rely heavily on verbal and written communication. Teachers and advisors are urged to plan carefully for the participation of students who use alternative forms of communication or who have difficulty in reading or writing. For some students, the process of self-discovery may require input from a variety of sources. Students who have difficulty communicating and answering questions may need additional time and resources to complete some of the activities and worksheets. Teachers and advisors can support students by identifying the people who could help them communicate the necessary information. Prior to a session, students, friends, and a favorite teacher can review the worksheet or exercise with them in order to provide relevant information and opinions.

However, because this process must be directed by the students' interests, goals, and dreams, it is important that they have the last word. During the sessions, students must be supported to synthesize all of the information to arrive at their own conclusions. Sample exercises are offered in Figures 2 through 4.

WHERE WILL PAUL GO FROM HERE?

For most students, college is a steppingstone to a career and an adult life filled with opportunity, challenge, family, and friends. Paul views

---

Session #5: Would You Rather . . . ? Questionnaire

Choose the option that you would most want to do or the statement that most fits your personality, likes, or dislikes. If there is more than one option you like, then pick the one that you like the most. If you do not like any of the options listed, then pick the one that you dislike the least.

1. I would rather
    a.   Write about the soccer game
    b.   Be a radio announcer for the soccer game
    c.   Play professional soccer
    d.   Teach soccer to young kids
    e.   Develop a soccer video game

2. I would rather
    a.   Design and build fine reproduction cabinets using antique tools
    b.   Help a young person who has a drug problem
    c.   Be a neurosurgeon
    d.   Be a radio talk show host
    e.   Prepare taxes for people

3. I would rather
    a.   Sell cars
    b.   Repair cars
    c.   Use a computer to design a new car
    d.   Clean the inside of cars
    e.   Start up a new car company

4. I would rather
    a.   Drive a travel bus
    b.   Be a travel agent
    c.   Write travel books
    d.   Fix airplanes
    e.   Be an air traffic controller

5. I would rather
    a.   Supervise a team of swimming instructors
    b.   Be a member of a team of swimming instructors
    c.   Be a student in a swimming class
    d.   Sell pool equipment
    e.   Maintain the pool

Figure 2.   Sample career-planning worksheet.

Session #11: My Typical Day Now and in My Dreams

Complete the chart indicating your typical day now and in the ideal situation. Indicate with a check mark one change that you would like to make. Identify how
you will make this change by indicating to whom you need to talk, your time line,
and your projected outcomes. Be prepared to share your plan and results with your
group or your advisor.

My Typical Weekday

Now   My ideal

My day begins: My day begins:
-
-
-
-
-
-

My day ends.   My day ends.

My Typical Weekend Day

Now   My ideal

My day beings: My day begins:
-
-
-
-
-
-

My day ends.   My day ends.

Figure 3.   My typical day.

his college years as an opportunity to gain knowledge and skills, make
new friends, and further develop his career goals. One of the first
services that Paul will use in college is the career counseling center, a
place where all students are assisted in selecting courses and activities.
He will also continue to meet on an as-needed basis with his planning
committee and with friends he makes at college. Although there are
no guarantees in life for anyone, Paul and his family know that Paul
is headed in the right direction—a direction that he is controlling and
others are helping him map. Where will Paul's life eventually lead?
No one can say for sure; but with the supports and plans that are in
place, it is certain that Paul's life will be led by his dreams.

CONCLUSIONS

As the turn of the 21st century approaches, it is clear that schools and
communities must respond to the ever-growing needs of a diverse

---

Session #16: Interview with a Worker

Interview a person who has a job that interests you. Use the following questions as a guide for your interview, and be prepared to share your results with your small group and/or advisor.

1. Which company, business, or firm do you work for?
2. What is your position or title? What do you actually do?
3. How did you get into this job?
4. Do you hold a college degree or occupational license?
5. Which skills are necessary for you to do your job?
6. How are you involved with other people on the job?
7. Do you use any special tools, equipment, or machinery on your job?
8. What do you like about your job? What do you dislike?

Figure 4. Sample interview worksheet.

student population. The old way of doing business—the school schedule based on an agrarian calendar, the tracking of students, the segregation of students with disabilities—is being questioned every day in schools throughout the United States. High schools in particular have led the quest to determine how best to educate students so that they can become productive, caring, and effective members of society. The movement toward career and life planning for all students is just one part of this quest.

Schools must be certain to involve all students in their quest for better education. It is no longer acceptable to develop systems for one group of students to the exclusion of another. We must recognize, in principle as well as in practice, that the best way to teach students to be effective members of their communities is to provide them with a fully inclusive education that respects and celebrates the diversity of American society.

Implementation Suggestions for Teachers

1. Use the Graduation Planning Checklist to evaluate whether students are on the right path to a typical high school graduation.
2. Do *not* keep students in the school building after the typical age of graduation. Even if your school is responsible for students' education until age 21, students should be in age-appropriate settings such as businesses, community colleges, technical schools, or 4-year colleges.
3. For each student, work together with guidance counselors to develop a post–high school plan.

Leadership Suggestions for Administrators

1. Visit local community colleges or vocational technical schools and develop a collaborative relationship so that students with disabilities can enroll with support. If there is an academic support center on campus, provide training to them so that they can work with your staff to provide academic assistance to students with disabilities.
2. Develop a community coalition of business owners and adult services agencies to create supportive worksites for students who are 18–21 years old.
3. Merge the transition-planning and graduation-planning functions of your high school's special education and guidance departments.
4. Establish a comprehensive, developmental, schoolwide futures-planning process that includes all students. Consider the use of a career-planning manual such as the one described in this chapter (Malloy et al., 1996). It is designed to be used with heterogeneous groups of students, some of whom plan to go on to college and some of whom plan to go into the work world right after high school.
5. Reconfigure the job descriptions and responsibilities of some high school staff so that supports are available to students ages 18–21 who are still part of the school system but do not take classes at the high school.

REFERENCES

Brown, F., & Lehr, D.H. (Eds.). (1989). *Persons with profound disabilities: Issues and practices.* Baltimore: Paul H. Brookes Publishing Co.

Canady, R., & Rettig, M. (1995). The power of innovative scheduling. *Educational Leadership, 53*(3), 4–10.

Education for All Handicapped Children Act of 1975, PL 94-142, 20 U.S.C. §§ 1400 *et seq.*

Horner, R.H., Meyer, L.H., & Fredericks, H.D.B. (Eds.). (1986). *Education of learners with severe handicaps: Exemplary service strategies.* Baltimore: Paul H. Brookes Publishing Co.

Individuals with Disabilities Education Act (IDEA) of 1990, PL 101-476, 20 U.S.C. §§ 1400 *et seq.*

Institute on Disability, University of New Hampshire. (1995). *Turning points: State of the state report.* Durham, NH: Author.

Johnson, L., Brown, L., Temple, J., McKeown, B., Sontag, E., Solner, A., & Ross, C. (1997). The buyout option for students with significant disabilities during the transition years. In W. Sailor & E. Sontag (Eds.), *School restructuring and inclusive education.* Manuscript in preparation.

Karagiannis, A., Stainback, W., & Stainback, S. (1996). Rationale for inclusive schooling. In S. Stainback & W. Stainback (Eds.), *Inclusion: A guide for educators* (pp. 3–15). Baltimore: Paul H. Brookes Publishing Co.

Malloy, J., Freije, G., Tashie, C., & Nisbet, J.A. (1996). *Planning for the future: A manual for career and life planning.* Durham: University of New Hampshire, Institute on Disability.

New Hampshire Department of Education. (1996). *Special education information system.* Concord: Author.

Nisbet, J. (Ed.). (1992). *Natural supports in school, at work, and in the community for people with severe disabilities.* Baltimore: Paul H. Brookes Publishing Co.

Perske, R., & Perske, M. (1988). *Circles of friends: People with disabilities and their friends enrich the lives of one another.* Nashville, TN: Abingdon Press.

Powers, L.E., Singer, G.H.S., & Sowers, J.-A. (Eds.). (1996). *On the road to autonomy: Promoting self-competence in children and youth with disabilities.* Baltimore: Paul H. Brookes Publishing Co.

Shapiro-Barnard, S., Tashie, C., Martin, J., Schuh, M., Malloy, J., Piet, J., Lichtenstein, S., & Nisbet, J. (1996). *Petroglyphs: The writing on the wall.* Durham: University of New Hampshire, Institute on Disability.

Stainback, S., Stainback, W., & Forest, M. (Eds.). (1989). *Educating all students in the mainstream of regular education.* Baltimore: Paul H. Brookes Publishing Co.

Tashie, C., & Schuh, M. (1993). Why not community-based instruction? In C.M. Jorgensen (Ed.), *Equity and excellence* (pp. 15–17). Durham: University of New Hampshire, Institute on Disability.

U.S. Department of Education. (1987). *Ninth annual report to Congress on the implementation of the Education of the Handicapped Act.* Washington, DC: U.S. Government Printing Office.

U.S. Department of Education. (1994). *To assure the free appropriate public education of all children with disabilities: Sixteenth annual report to Congress on the implementation of the Individuals with Disabilities Education Act.* Washington, DC: Author.

Index

Page numbers followed by "t," "f," or "n" indicate tables, figures, or footnotes, respectively.